WILLOWER

Rewriting Life After Unimaginable Loss

DEANNA KASSENOFF

Sidewise
PRESS

Willower: Rewriting Life After Unimaginable Loss
© 2023, Deanna Kassenoff. All rights reserved.
Published by Sidewise Press, Jacksonville, Florida

ISBN 979-8-9890081-0-0 (paperback)
ISBN 979-8-9890081-1-7 (eBook)
Library of Congress Control Number: 2023917096

HOLIDAY
Words by BILLIE JOE Music by GREEN DAY
© 2004 W.B.M. MUSIC CORP. and GREEN DAZE MUSIC All Rights Administered by W.B.M. MUSIC CORP.
All Rights Reserved
Used By Permission of ALFRED MUSIC

GOOD RIDDANCE (TIME OF YOUR LIFE)
Words by BILLIE JOE Music by GREEN DAY
© 1997 WC MUSIC CORP. and GREEN DAZE MUSIC All Rights Administered by WC MUSIC CORP.
All Rights Reserved
Used By Permission of ALFRED MUSIC

BOULEVARD OF BROKEN DREAMS
Words by BILLIE JOE Music by GREEN DAY
© 2004 WC MUSIC CORP. and GREEN DAZE MUSIC All Rights Administered by WC MUSIC CORP.
All Rights Reserved
Used By Permission of ALFRED MUSIC

Book Cover Design by Deanna Kassenoff
Publication managed by AuthorImprints.com.

For David, my tough, honest, and faithful ox;
Joey, my intelligent, powerful, and lucky dragon;
and Sam, my courageous, magnetic, and unpredictable tiger.

"Imagination is more important than knowledge. Knowledge is limited. Imagination encircles the world."
— Albert Einstein

CONTENTS

about survival

Over the last winter break, one night at bedtime, the boys—Joey, six, and Sam, eight—wanted me to read an "action story" to them.

I sat on the edge of Joey's bed with *The Mammoth Hunters*, from Jean Auel's Earth's Children series, and flipped to the page I'd bookmarked. Wrapped in his colorful blanket, Joey climbed into bed, snuggled beside me, and blinked at the mammoth-sized book. "How many pages is *that?*"

"A *whole* lot." I grinned. "Did you go pee?"

"He did," Sam confirmed as he curled up with his pillow and blanket on the floor. Sam was "too old" for "bedtime stories" and usually read on his own, but this night, since I was reading an action story about mammoth hunters, he joined Joey and me.

While Reggie the Chihuahua nuzzled into the bend of Sam's knees, I picked an age-appropriate but action-packed hunting scene and got right into it.

It was the character Ayla's first mammoth hunt. With only spears, how would she and her clan, so small and weak, take down the largest creature that walked the land? They'd use their strengths: intelligence, experience, and cunning. The hunters dashed toward the tusked beasts. They waved their smoky, movable flames, and shouted at the huge, shaggy, reddish-brown giants. The mammoth matriarch trumpeted warning cries. The herd was careening toward danger, stampeding into a gorge. Their screams blared and echoed off the icy rock walls.

Gripping their colorful blankets, the boys peered at me over their fingers.

"Too scary?" I asked. They shook their heads. "You want me to go on?" They nodded.

A young man threw a spear piercing the old she-mammoth's tough hide. A second spear was thrown, lodging deep in her belly.

Joey never made it through even minutes of story time. His eyes were heavy and fluttering within sentences. Sam and I giggled and held up our fingers, referees counting down a semiconscious boxer: "... four, three, two, one." Joey's eyes closed, and Sam and I signaled to each other that the match was over, whispering, "He's out!"

Sam settled back into his pillow and smiled. "I love you, Mommy."

"And I love *you*. Tired?"

He shook his head.

Reggie gave an old man's sigh, and Sam giggled. "Mommy, did you hear him? My little dude. That's my boy. Yes, you are! Yes, you are!"

Reggie reciprocated, tapping his tail, smiling. *Yes, I am. Yes, I am.*

Sam's eyes drifted back to the book, so I continued reading over Joey's, and Reggie's, deep breathing.

The old matriarch sank to her knees slowly, gracefully, valiantly. Praising her courage, a clan member touched the gallant old cow with his spear and thanked the Great Earth Mother for this sacrifice that would help Earth's Children to survive.

I closed the book. "That's enough for tonight. Let's get you to bed."

"Mommy, those hunters really cared about that mammoth, didn't they?"

"They sure did." I guided him to his room.

"And they cared about the Earth, too, didn't they?"

"Definitely." I tucked him in and kissed him good night. "Your lips are chapped, baby. Use your ChapStick." I touched his warm cheek. "Go to sleep now."

He reached for his cherry balm. On the nightstand, leaning against the lamp, his G. I. Joe action figure, Duke, was standing guard. Eyes open, alert, he never slept.

"Good night, Mommy. I'll see you in the morning."

"See you in the morning, brave hunter." I went to the door and turned back to look at him. Nestled in, he kissed the air with waxy, rose lips and blew from his hand out toward me. I told him again, "I love you."

"I'll see you in the morning," he assured me.

"See you in the morning," I said once more before turning to leave.

Through the night, when we were apart, it was the silence I feared most.

I finished devouring Jean Auel's Earth's Children series—the story of an orphaned girl, Ayla, and her life's journey during the time when Cro-Magnons and Neanderthals coexisted—three weeks before Sam's funeral. It had taken exactly forty-five weeks, according to my library records, to read those five mammoth-sized books. Those novels became my real-life survival guides.

For almost a year, I walked beside Ayla, my mentor. I hunted with her, raised a wolf cub, and ingrained in my mind her lessons on survival, perseverance, and aloneness.

I watched her care for Rydag, the boy she knew, with her trained medicine woman's eye, had a problem with the strong muscle in his chest that pulsed and pushed blood through the body. Like my Sam, Rydag was slight and fair with soft, curly hair, a gentle sense of humor, and wise eyes. Also, like Sam, he couldn't run as fast as the other children or play rough-and-tumble games.

And I committed to memory Ayla's gestures, the way she performed at Rydag's funeral ceremony as fine, volcanic ash rained down on us.

I tried to embody her strength and courage and wisdom—even her wardrobe. I wore a corduroy jacket the color of deerskin. Its faux-fur collar resembled an ermine's winter coat. I toted a cross-body messenger-style bag, a rough, textured thing with leather cords hanging from its sides, so my hands were free to hunt and gather. This prehistoric costume made me feel stronger. It kept me in character: a strong leader, mother, hunter, and healer. Plus, I had modern medicine on my side, and health insurance, and less stress than Ayla had thirty thousand years ago. There were no animals hunting my children while they slept ... or were there?

I tried to be vigilant, always ready, a predator and not prey.

But despite my vigilance and perseverance and modern medicine, death, as swift and cunning as a cave lion, snatched my beautiful boy and took him away. Today, I no longer wear the costume with the cross-body messenger bag. I'm not as strong as I was then, when I was in Cro-Magnon character. But I'm here, still, wandering between worlds, carving what I have seen (or imagined) on the wall of my cave. Like Ayla, I'm a survivor, one of Earth's Children, hunting and gathering and soldiering on through the silence.

This is what I know now: Readjusting to *living* without our deceased children (though we are never detached from them) is an ongoing, unpredictable, and lifelong relearning process. There is no final goodbye, no recovery or end, only *rewriting* our stories, the ones we tell ourselves so that we can keep going, so that we can try to make the silence mean something.

When people say, "I can't imagine," about the death of a child, living with such loss, I want to say, "I can *only* imagine. It's *how* I live with the unimaginable."

Don't get me wrong. Some days, still, the sadness swallows me up and I don't want to pretend any longer, or write, or go on without my beautiful boy. And that's when his voice comes through the loudest.

Mommy, I'm here ... Don't give up!

1

SAM'S HEART

a murmur

Before he could even walk, he imagined. Whatever Sam wanted to be, he'd imagine being. Buzz Lightyear. A fireman. A soldier. Chef. Doctor. Baseball player.

"Whatcha doing, Sammy?"

"I'm playing imaginary."

He played restaurant and cooked for us, played doctor and made us all-better, played baseball and yelled, "It's a hit!"

We kept a large plastic bin full of costumes, some homemade, some store-bought, in the living room which was now a makeshift playroom. There were polyester uniforms, coats, plastic hats, helmets, wigs, and silly pairs of oversize eyeglass frames. Somewhere in the bucket of disguises was a tiny parrot, the one we clipped to his shoulder the Halloween that he was two and pretending to be a pirate.

He had an imaginary friend, Jonathan, who seemed so real he'd become part of our lives. One night at bedtime when Sammy was four, I got an update.

"Mommy, Jonathan lost everything, even his family, in a house fire. That's why he's all alone."

"That's awfully sad, Sammy." I kissed him and tucked him in. "When you talk to Jonathan again, let him know he can stay with us for as long as he wants."

He also had imaginary pets: a horse named Gallop and two dogs, Booty and Missy. One time, we even "saw" a jellyfish while visiting new (real) friends for a playdate.

"We've never been to *this* house before," three-year-old Sam said. Then he noticed something on the side table in the foyer: an antique lamp with a ruddy, bell-shaped head. The milky bubble was the size of a basketball, and trailing beneath it were the tentacles, garnet-colored beads dangling on thin, brass strings. "Look, Mommy. It's a jellyfish!" he said, gaping at the floating sea creature.

"It's not a jellyfish; it's a lamp," our five-year-old host insisted.

Sam looked confused, injured, but didn't argue with his new friend.

There *was* a massive sea monster hovering nearby, so I *had* to speak up. "I see it, Sammy. It *is* a jellyfish."

He beamed up at me. "Mommy, we have the same eyes!"

We did. We saw the same things, and this filled me with joy, but also sadness. This world can be a lonely place for those who imagine things that aren't *really* there. For as long as I could, I would try and protect him—and his sensitive heart.

On this particular day, December 24, 2002, he was going to be an "office-man" and wear his clip-on tie and go to work with his daddy for a few hours, but he'd woken up feverish, lethargic, and glassy-eyed.

Dr. Grier, who was new to the pediatric group where we took the boys, was the doctor on call that morning. He examined Sam's throat, then looked inside his red-hot ears and confirmed an ear infection. But he kept listening with his stethoscope to Sam's heart.

I stayed quiet and smiled at my little boy's flushed face, noting how fiery it looked; even the faded birthmark, that reddish V between his eyes, had reappeared.

"I hear an unusual sound," the doctor said. "A murmur—a very *unusual* murmur."

That's odd, I thought. For over four years, since Sam was born, none of the other doctors in the practice had ever heard or mentioned a murmur.

"His fever *may* be amplifying it," he added, "but he'll need to see a cardiologist. We'll get that set up for you."

I remember standing in the doorway of Sam's preschool classroom, holding back tears. It was *only* one day a week, I assured myself. He was only eighteen months old when he toddled away from me. He didn't look back or wave goodbye. There were so many new people he wanted to meet and talk to, so many things he wanted to learn. I wanted to tell his teacher how different he was, tell her about his sensitive heart, but she saw it. In progress reports, she noted that Sam was always smiling and sweet, and comforted others when they were upset. He loved everything about school: making friends, learning new songs, playing games, creating art, going on field trips, and, most of all, story time.

But he constantly caught colds, stomach bugs, and mystery viruses. When he was two, he came down with Coxsackievirus, and I worried it might worsen and spread to other organs like his brain or muscles like his heart. I wanted to take him out of preschool because he kept getting sick, and baby Joey caught the bugs too.

Dr. Katz, Sam's pediatrician, insisted, "He's building his immune system. Better he gets this stuff now than later when he's in elementary school."

But every time he came down with another bug or hurt himself, I feared the worst. I wanted to keep him home, safe, but knew that wasn't foolproof either. Once, I panicked when he slipped and hit his head on the brick wall on the patio. Another day, playing in the backyard on what Sam called his "Slip-n-Slide Super Ride," he hurt himself sliding over something hard. A rock? When he showed me the swollen lump in his groin, I felt sick. It looked just like the lump Grandpa Don, my father, had in his groin, which turned out to be lymphoma. Another time, when he was three, we were flying his stunt kite outside on the sidewalk. I was piloting and he was laughing and running when it turned and dove as if it had radar-locked on him. I yanked the string, trying to slow the kite, change its direction, but it stayed on course. Full speed, wings fluttering, nose down, it struck him on the top of his head, and he crumpled to the ground. I was already running toward him, horrified at what had happened—and *I* had been the one pulling the string, responsible for this injury.

And then, there were the monsters that lived in Sam's closet. Every night at bedtime, we'd tuck him in, and David would spray the closet door with monster repellent and kill those monsters—all gone. Still, though, something *was* lurking in the shadows, something only Sam could see in his sleep. His heart-pounding screams came in the middle of the night.

Dr. Katz said these were night terrors. "When he has them, turn on the lights and try to wake him," he instructed.

We did this—turned on the lights, tried to wake him, calm him, tell him everything was okay, that he was safe, that we were *there* with him—but he would just stare through us, his wide eyes fixed on something too horrible to see while he was awake. All we could do was wait for the nightmare to pass and the screaming to stop. And it would. As suddenly as it started, the nightmare would end. His eyes would close, his breathing would soften, and he would sleep, remembering nothing in the morning.

By age three, the night terrors had stopped, and I wanted to forget them. Only *now*, a new kind of terror woke me in the night. Was there a monster lurking not in Sam's closet, but in his heart?

I knew it wasn't normal being so overprotective and hypochondriacal, panicking, worrying that every minor illness, fever, fall, or bruise might turn into something life-threatening. My overreacting, I noticed, had made Sam afraid and overcautious too. After all, what ten-month-old worries when his father stands on a ladder to change a light bulb?

"Careful, Daadee," Sam had said as he scrambled beneath David to support him with his little hand.

Amused at first, I took the picture, imagining its caption: *Super Baby Holds Dad Overhead!* But later, when I studied the photo, I recognized the look on Sam's face as my own. I didn't want either of us to be this way. I hated those adrenaline surges, flooding every fiber in my body with alarm—and not even knowing *why* the alarm was blaring. Would he have another accident? Another lump? Or something else? No matter how brightly the sun was shining, or how much fun we were having, it was *always* there, that ominous cloud that we couldn't seem to outrun.

For those two unsettling months between Christmas Eve 2002 and our cardiology appointment, I tried to tamp down my concern. Convince myself everything was going to be *fine*. Pretend that the amplified murmur was just another cloud in the sky, a puffy creature that would blow over like the ones we watched while lying on a blanket in the backyard, our heads together like puzzle pieces.

"Look, Mommy, that one's a T. rex." Sam pointed.

"Look, right behind it." I outlined the dog—or the dinosaur? "Do you see the poodle . . . or maybe it's a Poo-Rex?"

This was where I needed to stay for just a little while longer: in the clouds, pretending there was *nothing* to worry about. Instead of going to that dark place deep inside, where the new doctor had rooted out the most dreadful thing I could imagine.

spells

Sam was only two months old the first time it happened. His eyes looked different, I noticed. Distant, dull, darker than usual. Then his tiny body began contracting, his spine bowed, and his head tilted sideways, pulling his ear to his shoulder. He cried out, went quiet, and then his eyes started to flutter. I panicked. David and I gathered him up and sped away. The three-minute drive to the pediatrician's office took too long.

Dr. Katz lifted Sam up, then lowered him. Up again, then down; up, then down, trying to induce another episode, he explained. He said something about Sam's muscle tone—limp, or maybe stiff? I was paying more attention to Sam than to what the doctor was saying. I didn't like the way he was holding my baby by his armpits, supporting his tiny, drooping body with only his thumbs. I wanted to tell him *not* to hold him like that. Sam looked like he wanted to tell him not to hold him like that. I remember the exhausted look on his infant face. It wasn't a normal sleepy look, but an old-soul kind of tired.

"Waiting for an ambulance will take too long," Dr. Katz said. "Take him to the emergency room. I'll call ahead and tell them you're on your way."

At the hospital, a slew of tests were done. Blood work, an eye exam, X-rays, a scan of his upper GI tract, an EEG, and an MRI.

For the EEG, in which his brain waves would be traced, he needed to be awake. Sam and I were left alone in a small, dark room. I'd been instructed to give him his bottle *and* keep him awake. It made no sense. Feeding him would make him sleepy. If they wanted him to stay awake, withholding his bottle would've been the thing to do. He was so tired, yet I kept teasing him with the bottle, offering it, then taking it away when his eyes closed. I held back tears, harassing him, then nudging him, talking to him.

"I'm here, baby. I'm right here. Sammy, stay awake. It's gonna be okay. Keep your eyes open. I'm sorry—I'm sorry. I have to do this. Stay awake. We're almost done."

All the while, a dizzying house-of-horror strobe light was flashing, I think to induce another seizure. His eyes were swimming. He was trying desperately to close them and sleep.

"I'm sorry, Sammy. Just a little longer. We're almost done, baby. Stay awake . . ."

For the MRI, in which pictures would be taken of his brain, Sam needed to be asleep. Before the MRI, we sat in a room where at least fifteen other mothers in recliner chairs were sitting with their children or holding babies. In this scene out of a horror movie, drugs were being given to induce anesthesia, and glassy-eyed children and babies were falling asleep at different times in different recliners or in their mother's arms.

"Be ready to catch her when she goes to sleep. Don't let her fall," I heard a nurse tell one of the mothers.

Wide-eyed children who were still awake looked horrified, staring at the unconscious bodies around them. It all felt wrong. Holding my tiny infant, I was glad he didn't know what was happening around him, unable yet to focus on anything beyond my face.

A few weeks later, we followed up with a neurologist. All of Sam's test results had come back normal. His brain, his eyes, his growth and development, his gastrointestinal tract, his blood work, all *fine*.

"These episodes he experienced were likely *not* seizures, so we're going to call them *spells* for now," the doctor explained. "It would be *very* helpful if I could see videotape of a spell as it happens—*if* one happens again."

Not only would more spells, which were excruciating to watch, be burned into my memory, but some would be labeled, dated, and recorded on video as lasting reminders.

Even after a team of pediatric neurologists studied the recorded images of Sam's spells, no one had a definitive diagnosis. I would have to find one on my own.

A few months after that first spell, at his four-month checkup, Sam's bright eyes followed the pediatrician's finger as it swayed back and forth like a metronome. Dr. Katz lowered and lifted him again, but this time in a lighthearted, grandfatherly way, kissing Sam's cheek, holding him close to his face. "Sometimes, things like this just happen when a baby's nervous system is a bit immature."

Sam's whole face smiled as he gazed like a lip-reader at the doctor's mouth. I smiled, too, seeing the big picture. *Nervous system* and *immature* sounded benign, favorable, not too scary. Sam's big brain *was* pretty perfect. He'd even taught himself to roll over. He'd concentrate, tongue out; use his head; rock back and forth; gather momentum; raise an arm; and flop onto his other side. Then he'd flash me a big, gummy smile—mission accomplished.

I continued to record Sam's daily progress and track his spells. On average, the aftereffects of the spells, his taut neck muscles, and tilted head, lasted six to eight weeks. I learned to recognize when a spell was coming by the way Sam's eyes looked. When his usual happy and bright eyes looked weary and sad and dark, as if the light behind them had been snuffed out, I knew what would happen next.

Sometimes, things like this just happen wasn't an answer. No one seemed to be looking deeper. So I started digging through medical journals and studying medical jargon that pushed *my* brain to its limit.

One day, I found an article about infants with "seizure-like" symptoms and saw this word: *arrhythmia*. No one had said it to me before. When I asked Dr. Katz about it, he suggested I leave the medical research to the doctors. I did lack medical experience, and it *was* only one article, so I let the idea of an arrhythmia, an abnormal heart rhythm, sink into the mud in the back of my mind, a key tossed into the mire. No further reading required. I didn't want to see it or find it ever again. But I realize now, it was there in the mud all along, hidden in my subconscious, a sticky note between the pages of a closed book. That dormant word, like a tiny seed that contained within it all it needed to germinate, was growing, mutating into something dreadful.

Despite all that had happened, our first year together was magical, joyful. Sam grew like a weed, worked himself up into a sitting tripod, then learned to crawl. He couldn't walk but sped around on wheels in his baby walker and crashed into walls and doorjambs with shrieks of laughter. And that belly laugh. There's *nothing* better than a baby's belly laugh. It just seemed to others that he couldn't hold up his head yet. Leaning to one side, sometimes right, sometimes left, his face cocked slightly, he appeared to be an engaged listener. And he was—always listening, curious, smiling, and happy. I knew there might come a time when having a bent neck for weeks on end would affect the way he would walk or the things other children might say. But we'd deal with that then.

As time passed, I continued my research and learned about an infant condition called *benign paroxysmal torticollis*, or BPT. BPT causes neck spasms and "spells" that mimic seizures.

"Very insightful," Dr. Katz said, skimming the pages I'd brought him, seeming to agree with my possible diagnosis. He knew me better now. It was clear I was *never* going to leave the medical research to the doctors. Then, perhaps to remind me that *he* was still the doctor, he gave me a short lecture.

"This word, *tor–ti–col–lis*," he emphasized each syllable, "comes from the Latin, meaning 'twisted neck.' *Tortus* for twisted. *Collum* for neck. Torticollis. Wonderful word, isn't it?"

No, I thought, *it isn't wonderful.* Then again, I did prefer the word *torticollis* to the word *arrhythmia*.

At Sam's twelve-month wellness checkup, Dr. Katz wore a stethoscope with a finger-sized koala bear wrapped around the tubing above the chest piece.

"Sam the Man! Look at you!" The doctor scooped up Sam and examined his ears with a small, black cone. While he listened to his heart, Sam studied the koala. "He looks great. His height and weight are right on track." Smiling, Dr. Katz set Sam on the carpeted floor beside a box of blocks. "We look for certain milestones at this point," he said in a serious tone. "Can he stack three blocks yet?"

Sam was already examining the blocks, balancing, and stacking them into a tower of eleven cubes, curling his pudgy hands around the structure, holding it up without touching it, a magic trick. He smiled up at us, his audience, waiting for a reaction, so I had to ask.

"Sammy, what do you *see* on those blocks?"

Using the same magic finger that regularly pointed out airplanes to me in the sky, he pointed slowly, methodically, from the bottom to the top of his tower: "A, apple. B, bird. C, car. D, dog. K, key . . ."

Beaming, Dr. Katz told me what to expect in the future: genius. "Don't move him ahead in grades," he said. "You'll be told to move him ahead, but don't. Keep him with kids his own age. I'm thrilled to see his progress. We were *so* worried, weren't we, about his brain—and *now* look at him."

I looked at Sam, the mischief in his eyes, that windup. With one swift hand swipe, he knocked down the tower and grinned up at us.

"Oh, I see . . . you're smart *and* funny!" Dr. Katz was chuckling when the nurse interrupted.

"Knock, knock. Vaccines today! Measles, mumps, rubella, and chicken pox." As quickly as Sam had noticed that koala, he spied what the nurse was holding in her hands—syringes, needles, and tiny glass vials—and the screaming began.

His crying shook me. When Sam was born, he had a vascular mark on his fleshy forehead, a reddish V between his eyebrows. I'd read somewhere that this mark was the sign of a highly evolved soul. Whenever he cried or got upset, that down arrow between his eyes would darken. I knew his heart was different, the way he absorbed every detail. A gift *and* a curse, being so sensitive, so tuned-in. Whenever he heard another child crying, he'd stare at me with a pleading expression, tears welling up in his eyes, and I'd reassure him. "They're okay, Sammy. Don't cry. It's okay. You're okay."

I wasn't sure why I lost my balance so easily or what exactly I was afraid of, why I felt so anxious. Something about him seemed fragile.

We'd dodged a bullet this time, but what about the next? The spells *were* waning. Sam *was* perfectly fine. Still, I felt uneasy, nervous, crouched in anticipation. I was always scanning the horizon, hearing that persistent voice deep inside that kept insisting, *Trust yourself, your intuition. Stay alert. Be vigilant. Keep watch!*

a mass

Around 3 p.m., the day after Sam's fifth birthday, Monday, March 3, 2003, twenty-four hours after eating hot dogs and cake, celebrating, laughing, and bowling at his party, loading gifts into our minivan, and making plans to see our best friends again soon, the boys and I checked in at the pediatric cardiology office. As it turned out, Sam's younger brother, Joey, who was almost three, also had a murmur, so both boys would have their hearts checked.

To not set off any unnecessary alarms, David and I had decided beforehand that I would bring the boys to this checkup since I was the one who normally took them to doctor appointments. Sam was too clever and would've questioned why Daddy was at the appointment with us. The plan was to get these murmurs checked out, take care of what needed to be taken care of, and be on our way.

Blue vinyl chairs lined the white walls of the waiting room. I noticed how the primary-colored specks in the white, laminate-tiled floor, matched the toddler-sized tables and chairs in the center of the room. There were stacks of cardboard books on the tables, large wooden puzzles, and on a TV in the corner, a Disney movie, *Monsters, Inc.*, was playing. Sam and I sat against the wall staring at the TV while Joey stood at a table pounding wooden puzzle pieces to make them fit.

I nudged Sam and winked. "This is just a checkup. No needles, no shots, no big deal."

The cardiologist, Dr. Angstrom, examined Joey first. "A benign murmur," he explained. No further testing was needed. Sam's exam was taking longer. The medical assistant, Kandi, poked her head in the room and offered to take Joey to the playroom to show him the train set.

Joey slid off his chair. "Come on, Sammy. Let's go play."

Sam stayed quiet.

"Go on," I urged Joey. "You can help Miss Kandi set up the trains. Sammy will be out soon—just a few more minutes."

While Dr. Angstrom was listening, inching his stethoscope across Sam's chest, Sam was studying the doctor's face.

At my first sonogram, when I was four months pregnant with Sam (though we hadn't chosen his name yet), we found out we were having a boy.

"There." The nurse pointed to the monitor, to the tiny, fluttering heart. "Do you see it beating?"

David and I gaped at the tiny, convulsing blob on the black-and-white screen.

"Aw . . . he's stretching. How cute . . . he's got hiccups," the nurse said. "Do you want to know the sex? The baby is positioned perfectly for us to see it."

It was too late; we saw *it*. And David made a wisecrack about the baby definitely being *his boy*.

A few weeks later, routine blood work indicated something might be wrong. My ob-gyn suggested performing an amniocentesis, a test that detects certain genetic conditions from a sample of amniotic fluid.

During the amnio, nobody talked or commented on hiccups or made any wisecracks.

I lay on my back, head turned, staring at the TV monitor.

Sam looked like a little porpoise confined to a small, dark tank.

The doctor slid the ultrasound wand across my belly and into position. Holding an oversize needle in his hand, he told me to remain absolutely still. I tried to control my shivering and hold my breath and keep my eyes on the monitor, where the needle now resembled a dark speargun. As it vacuumed a stream of sparkling liquid, my little porpoise appeared to gasp. With his tiny, finlike hand, he swatted and waved at it, and a rush of bubbles whirled around him. And I heard what no one else appeared to hear: *Mommy, I'm scared! What is that?*

The speargun had come *too* close. Remaining absolutely still, as instructed, tears sliding down my face, I dove into that dark water and tried to calm him with my newfound mother-son telepathy. *Hold still, baby. It's going to be okay. You're okay. I see you. I'm here. I'm with you. I'm right here. We're almost done.*

The thing about being pregnant: If anything went wrong, we were tethered together. I would be right there with him.

A week after the amnio, David and I met with a genetic counselor who explained the results and showed us the pictures of Sam's twenty-three threadlike pairs, his forty-six chromosomes, and confirmed: "Nothing missing and nothing extra."

"If I were a betting man," the obstetrician said at our follow-up appointment, "I'd bet on the odds this baby will be just fine. This kind of test only gives us odds—the probability of something that may or may not happen. All of us are gonna get something one day. Colon cancer, for example."

I thought of how my stepfather Roger had withered away with colon cancer and died only three years ago. I pictured him, his gaunt face, over the doctor's shoulder, shaking his head. He couldn't believe what he was hearing either.

"Any other questions?" the doctor said, already opening the exam room door to leave.

"Yes. That brochure you gave me . . . about storing umbilical cord blood. Do you recommend doing this?" *In case, you know, one day . . . colon cancer, for example?*

The doctor shook his head and smirked. "My younger patients never read that stuff. You older moms worry too much."

He was right. I did worry too much, read too much, obsess over ridiculous stuff. *Fine* was good. Sam was going to be a fine baby with fine, downy hair. He'd grow up to be a fine man. Maybe, when he was *very* old, he'd develop colon cancer. But there'd be a cure for that then—or, maybe, he'd be the one to find the curative potion.

I'd bet on the odds this baby will be just fine.

When I was nineteen, my father Don was diagnosed with lymphoma. Grief-stricken, I saw a therapist to cope with the uncertainty of my dad's prognosis. We also talked about my part-time job at the ER, my plans to become an RN, and the things I had seen, the not-supposed-to-happen deaths of toddlers or teens. Small, broken bodies, auto accidents; blood-covered gurneys, gunshot wounds; or no blood at all, sudden cardiac deaths.

"You've seen an abnormal number of deaths," the therapist pointed out. "You realize this, don't you? Maybe we should talk about *that* next time." She confirmed what I already knew: I was sad. Not depressed, but extremely sad. "Try not to grieve a loss *before* it happens," she suggested.

I liked that therapist—I think her name was Susan—but I never went back to talk about the abnormal number of deaths I'd seen. On my own, I would just work on trying not to grieve a loss before it happened.

Life is doggedly unpredictable. My dad, who had to take an early "medical" retirement, went on to battle cancer for another twenty-three years while my stepfather, who'd just begun to enjoy his retirement, died a year after his diagnosis. Just before he passed, he reminded me: "Don't grieve before I'm gone. Don't cry. I'm still here. Afterward, you can cry a little, but then go on and live. You and David will have your own family one day. And you'll have a wonderful life. You'll see."

After Sam's EKG, we met Ruby, the ultrasound tech, who maneuvered a wand over Sam's bare chest while entering data in brief spurts on a keyboard. The overhead fluorescent light had been turned off, and Sam lay still watching *Shrek,* his favorite movie, on one screen while I watched his heart pumping in bursts of bright blues and reds on another. Sitting in that dark room—the wand, the TV monitor, the click of the keys—reminded me of another ultrasound. How happy, how excited we were then to hear that seventeen-week-old heart beating, *seeing* it, and then hanging that glossy black-and-white picture on the refrigerator.

I heard whispering out in the hallway. Then a handful of white coats entered the room and crowded around the TV screen and continued whispering. My mind was already running ahead, already thinking the worst, shouting at me over its shoulder, *It's an ambush! Run!*

I didn't want Sam to read my face or see my tears, so I slipped out and sat alone in the empty room next door. A nurse peeked in and asked why I was crying. He told me Sam was doing great. "He's going to be fine," he said, handing me a box of tissues. But I knew better. How many times had I heard those words before?

A few minutes later, Dr. Angstrom joined me in that empty room, placed a stool in front of me, and sat down.

He had a gentle voice; neat, gray hair; and a kind bedside manner. He wore glasses and a bow tie, which I would come to know as his trademark. I also came to know that when he spoke, he chose his words *very* carefully.

Maybe he was composing them. Or maybe he was giving me time to compose *myself,* to warm up and stop shivering. I stared at his mouth, waiting for something to come out of it. But nothing did, as if his words were blocked or lost. My body tightened. I knew something was very, *very* wrong.

When he finally spoke, I heard the word "mass." There it was; that menacing cloud we'd been trying to outrun had formed itself into a lion. It was crouching in the grass, stalking closer, inhaling my fear, eyeing my neck. Sometimes you can see it, the millisecond your life changes. Time stops, gravity crushes you, and the only thing you can hear is your heart pounding. You remain frozen in between the moments *before*—when you were alive—and the moments *after*—when you will die.

"A mass? How large? Do you mean . . . a tumor?" My thoughts were frantic, scratching, trying to dig under or climb over an impossible wall. *How? Yesterday, he was fine, laughing, bowling, blowing out birthday candles, opening gifts . . . And now? How can this be? How can the sun be shining, the sky so blue? What do you mean, it's large? How large? Can you take it out? Can it be taken out?* "Where is it?" I tried to breathe, focus.

"The interventricular septum," Dr. Angstrom said. On a sheet of paper, he sketched the shape of a heart, then the shape of the mass in the center. The mass was a football that filled most of Sam's heart. "I've never seen anything like it before."

"Could it go away? Could he—?" *No, no, no . . .* The lion attacked, clamped its jaws around my neck. My voice sounded hollow, weak. "What do we do?"

"Well, first I'd like to schedule a few tests."

I could hear the boys nearby playing Choo-Choo and laughing and talking to Kandi. I felt nauseous. David, I knew, was waiting to hear how the appointment went. I don't remember the phone call, what I said, only that I ducked into the bathroom afterward to be sick, unable to hold it in any longer.

"Daddy! Daddy! What are you doing here?"

It was late afternoon, after hours, and the cardiology office was empty when David arrived. While Kandi and the boys played roller coaster with the beads on an abacus puzzle out in the waiting room, David and I sat in a small examining room where Dr. Angstrom explained the rare mass again. I remember staring at the blank wall in front of me, listening to the boys laughing and talking on the other side of it. When there was nothing more to say, no more questions to ask, we gathered ourselves to leave, both of us in shock.

Sam noticed my pink and swollen eyes. "Mommy, have you been crying?"

I assured him I was just tired, then changed the subject. "Guess what? I've got a surprise for you."

"What, Mommy? What surprise? What is it?" the boys clamored.

"Tonight is SpongeBob night at Golden Corral! I think we should go straight there for dinner, don't you?"

That night, after the boys were asleep, I called my father. "They've already scheduled a cardiac catheterization for next week, on Friday. They want to biopsy the mass."

Each time I uttered the word *mass*, or thought it, was another punch in the gut. Such a small word, yet every time, it took my breath away.

time to act

On the mornings following that Monday, with that sketch of Sam's heart and that football-shaped mass burned into my eyes, I dropped the boys at school and drove around, feeling lost. I couldn't go home. I had to do something.

Desperate for direction, spiritual guidance, or encouraging words, I stopped at a Catholic church and met with a priest who had an accent and an Irish name I don't recall. He stayed behind his desk and seemed distracted, so I made it quick. He took my name and number and assured me he'd forward my concerns and contact information to a mothers' prayer group, then pressed a button and summoned an assistant who showed me to the door.

He'd subcontracted out my spiritual crisis. I left feeling emptier and even more lost than before. Though what did I expect? How could a *father* who has never *been* a father understand a mother's worst nightmare?

I drove to another church. Presbyterian, but this time I'd go it alone.

I slipped inside the empty sanctuary. The walls were a calming green, and the rows and rows of pews felt like a forest of trees. I found a shady spot and sat and gazed past the pulpit at the massive, stained glass mosaic of Jesus, his hands and feet nailed to a cross. His head hung down to the side. He looked sad, weary. I lay down on the purple, cushioned pew, closed my eyes, and imagined a gentle god stroking my head the way I stroked my boys' heads to soothe them to sleep, the way my father had stroked my head decades ago. Each stroke that passed over my ear was an ocean wave, calming and reassuring. This was all I wanted—to be calmed and reassured, heard, and understood.

Lying there I noticed the wooden pockets on the backs of the pews and the books inside them. I pulled out a Bible. Unfamiliar with its numbered verses, I thumbed through the pages the way I read magazines, back to front, right to left. *The way Hebrew is read*, I thought. I looked for numbers that meant something to me. A '3' for the month of Sam's birth, a '2' for the day, and an '8' because I'd read that patients with malignant cardiac tumors didn't live longer than two years. He was five, so if he lived to be eight, then . . . he might live. These were the tricks I played on my mind to control the chaos.

I found Psalm 32, chose verse 8, and read: "I will instruct you and teach you in the way you should go; I will counsel you and watch over you." I found Samuel, which in Hebrew, I recalled from a book of baby names, means "God has heard." Had He or She heard? I skimmed Job. Nope, not for me. I went back to the Psalms. *I will counsel you and watch over you.*

"Are you watching?" I asked. "Sam's heart? Are you listening? What do I do?"

I heard nothing.

"Please. I need help. I don't know what to do."

Nothing.

I was sleep-deprived, hungry, scared, and collapsing under the weight of what I knew: a time bomb was ticking inside my son's heart. I could only read and pray and hope for so long. I needed to talk to a living spiritual guide, not the Guide that I *hoped* was there. I needed to hear someone else's voice instead of the noise in my head. I needed help.

The next day, on Friday, instead of sitting in the sanctuary, I walked into the main office, where a woman with a whispery voice welcomed me.

My own voice sounded weak. "Is there someone here that I could talk to?"

She didn't question my business or even know my name. "Have a seat. One moment. I'll be right back." She disappeared down a hallway, and I was grateful for her pace, how she seemed to sense the urgency of my situation. Within seconds, she returned and motioned to the open door down the hallway. "Go on in. Reverend Penn will see you now."

The pastor was tall with salt-and-pepper hair and jet-black eyes. He wore slacks and a button-down shirt, business casual. His office was a combination of a study and a living room. When he invited me to sit down, I sank into the corner of the sofa, and he sat in the adjacent chair and placed a box of tissues on the coffee table in front of me.

I couldn't speak. He waited. I broke down and cried, and he handed me tissues. Finally, I told him about Sam's heart, the mass, and the looming heart catheterization.

He listened and lowered his eyes, shook his head, and distilled every critical point, repeating the details in clipped questions: "This past Monday? A mass? In his heart?" I nodded. "He's only five?" He shook his head again, and we sat in silence for a few minutes. Then he told me about his brother who had died very young from a brain tumor. "The person you are, right now, is not the person you are going to be, whatever the outcome."

I tried to block the thought that Sam might die. I needed him to live, *whatever the outcome.*

When Reverend Penn suggested I read the book of Job, I nodded, acting familiar with the title I'd learned only yesterday. He put his hands over mine and prayed. I thanked him for his time, and for listening.

After I left, I headed straight to the bookstore and picked up a Bible with a pretty purple cover—*Mom's Devotional Bible.* I checked to see that it had Psalms in it. It did.

As a way of coping with Sam's diagnosis, and my fear, knowing about the mass but not knowing what it was, I would continue searching for meaningful messages—something that might tell me what to do, which way to go—in the pages of my new purple book.

The following Sunday, I attended Reverend Penn's service with my close friend Suzanne.

I wanted to be lost in a crowd, to *be* like the crowd. I wanted to smile and say, *Good morning . . . May the Lord be with you . . . And also with you.* To act, if only for an hour, like I believed. I wanted to listen, cherry-pick a word or two, a nugget of wisdom, a sliver of hope from the pastor's sermon.

So Suzanne and I were caught off guard when, during his sermon, Reverend Penn began walking down the aisle toward us and telling his congregation about Sam's heart. There was a collective gasp, as if the entire room had choked on the word *mass.* My stomach tightened. My eyes burned, my heart pounded, and, as I held back tears, my nose began to run. Hearing Sam's name, followed by that awful word, travel from the tiny microphone clipped to the pastor's collar to those large, surround-sound speakers mounted throughout the sanctuary, I wanted to run too. Suzanne pushed a tissue into my hand.

Standing beside us now, telling his flock about Sam's upcoming procedure, the pastor raised his arms. The flowing sleeves of his robe were black curtains obscuring us from all those faces turned in our direction. I wanted to be at home where my boys were eating Pop-Tarts and laughing at cartoons, not in a church hoping, *wishing*, for some kind of miracle. I wanted everyone around me to disappear, so I could be alone again in that sanctuary. I wanted to lie down, close my eyes, and have a one-on-one interaction with my own imaginary god. I wanted to go back to the way things were just seven days ago. Or wake up in the future to find this was all a bad dream—no murmur, no *mass*.

"Let us all pray for this little boy and for his family," the pastor said. Then he left Suzanne and me and made his way back to the pulpit to continue his sermon.

The following week, I tried a different venue: the temple around the corner from the JCA, the Jewish Community Alliance, where the boys went to school. Sam's preschool class had come here, to Congregation Ahavath Chesed, on a field trip. Parade-style, in the shade of the majestic oak trees that lined the street, they'd marched down the sidewalk waving their blue-starred flags. That day, after school, I remember how thrilled he was, the way he pronounced *adventure* when he told me about his *ah-venture,* and how he wanted to go back to that temple again one day.

"Mommy, today I learned how to make stars. You draw two triangles, one pointing up, like this, and one pointing down, like that." His tongue poked out to the side as he added eyes and a smile inside each of his stars.

Again, I sat alone in the middle of the empty sanctuary. Through the tall windows behind the pulpit, I watched birds flitting about the shimmering oak trees. The lights were off except for one sconce flickering on the wall near the front of the synagogue. The cushioned chairs, I noted, were more comfortable than church pews. I flipped through a different book this time, a prayer book, and found this line: "Pray as if everything depended on G-d. Act as if everything depended on you."

That was it. Everything depended on me. I sat up then and listened to that voice coming from somewhere deep inside of me: *You've been grieving, languishing, praying for answers, guidance, seeking something, Someone, outside yourself to fix this. For days, you've been inhaling religion like a chain-smoker. Enough! It's time to act as if everything depended on you. Because everything does depend on you. Get to work. You've done this before, and you'll do it again—now go!*

blind hope

I started researching, scouring medical journals for information.

I read about cardiac anomalies, cycled through stories, and memorized cases. The ones in which patients lived, you could count on your hands. I read about a boy who'd been shot. The bullet had left a hole in his heart that was repaired using fast-growing supercells. I read about a girl who'd had an *autotransplant*, a pediatric first. Her heart was removed, repaired, and put back. Her own heart—repaired and re-transplanted! I skipped the reports which were written after autopsy, the same way I had skipped Job in the Bible. What was the point? I *had* to keep believing in medical miracles.

I kept a list of the doctors at top research hospitals who'd written about cardiac anomalies, specifically tumors or masses. I emailed or called them to ask impossible questions, the kind no parent should ever have to ask. Reading, questioning, working on finding the solution, gave me a sense of control. But control is a funny notion. It clouds your judgment so you think you have it when you really never do. Under its influence, I felt tireless, stronger, smarter, more determined. No matter how dark or dire the odds were, that cocktail of control mixed with blind hope kept me going. While the experts were asleep in their beds, *I* was going to find the answer, the *one* case study that would lay out how we were going to save my boy.

"You can't stay up all night reading. You've got to stop this obsession. You need to get some sleep," David insisted.

This was my way, not his. He trusted the experts and thought it was best to leave the research to them. I knew he was only looking out for me. We were overstressed, and lack of sleep would only weaken us more. It wasn't until a few months later, after we'd left an appointment with a genetic doctor, that David encouraged me to continue searching. He'd realized during the conversation about possible—and *treatable*—underlying genetic causes for Sam's heart condition that he was unfamiliar with the medical terms and wasn't sure what questions to ask.

"Keep obsessing," he encouraged me. "You may be on to something."

Though it seemed I was heading down a dead end road, I had to do something. I needed to know which of the rarest cardiac tumors could be treated, resected, or ablated. Which masses might or might not regress, or disappear. I needed to know what to do in case Sam ever needed surgery or a transplant, or if some new procedure in restorative medicine would let his heart repair itself with supercells.

As long as I believed he'd survive this, I could keep going, but the reality was, most of the reports I'd found were written postmortem, *after* the little boy or little girl had died. When there's a mass in your heart, the first symptom is usually sudden death. These were the two most unspeakable words of all. And the possibility of the unimaginable happening is what pumped more adrenaline through me, strangled me, scared me more than *anything* else.

a dot

How do you tell a happy and healthy five-year-old his world is about to turn upside down? That everything's still fine, but now, there's a football-shaped cloud that will shadow every minute of every day. A few days after learning about the mass, David and I met with a therapist who specialized in helping families with terminally ill children. Not that Sam was terminally ill—he wasn't even *ill*—but we wanted advice on how to talk to him about his heart and about his upcoming tests.

"Tell him the truth in an age-appropriate way," the therapist advised. Never having met Sam, she didn't know he was older than his age, so we'd have to wing it on the "age-appropriate" part.

"It's called a Holter monitor," I said, explaining the first test he would have only a week after his fifth birthday. "You wear it for only a day, and it records your heartbeat while you're playing," I said.

"But *why* do I have to do this?" Sam asked.

"Dr. Angstrom wants to record your heartbeat." I came up with an age-appropriate story. "Astronauts need their heartbeats recorded too. When they're in outer space they wear monitors just like this under their spacesuits. How cool is that?"

He was self-conscious about wearing the Holter monitor to school. We hid the tape recorder in a fanny pack under his shirt, but he was so small, and the wires were too long, so the loop of cables hung out from under his shirt. After school, he told me it embarrassed him for a while, but then he explained to his classmates that astronauts wear the same wires, too, under their spacesuits.

The test seemed harmless, but the pain and the crying came afterward. Pulling off the extra-sticky tape from his chest, tummy, sides, and back left his baby-soft skin raw and inflamed. The adhesive was unrelenting even after Sam had soaked in a bubble bath until the water turned cold. I wrapped his shivering, water-logged body in a blanket and held him on my lap.

"Look at those yummy fingers. I'm going to eat every one of those sweet little raisins."

Sniffling in spasms, staring down at his pale, wrinkly fingertips, he tried to smile.

I hugged him, rocked him. "I'm sorry, Sammy. I'm so sorry. Shh, shh, you're okay now. I'm sorry." I *hated* that mass.

When the twenty-four-hour recording came back normal, with no arrhythmia, I breathed a sigh of relief.

I'd waited until a few days before the heart cath to tell him.

"Sammy, Dr. Angstrom wants to do another test. A *special* photographer—a doctor with a special camera—wants to take a picture of your heart." I tried to sound breezy.

"Oh ... you mean a picture taker?" He used a term I hadn't thought of before.

"That's right, a *picture taker*." I smiled but felt deceptive, withholding details.

"Why?" He wanted to know more.

I made the monster smaller. "Well ... because you have a *dot* on your heart. And it's *very* rare. So the doctor wants to take a picture of it. That's all." I tried to act even breezier.

"Is the dot *on* my heart or *in* it?" he asked.

Another punch in my gut. His brilliant imagination had already drawn the picture.

"In it," I told him the truth.

I was running out of age-appropriate ways to say things, so I was glad he didn't ask the biggest question of all: *Is the dot going to make my heart sick? Am I going to die?*

Maybe he was thinking it. I'd been avoiding eye contact, but when I met his gaze, we read each other's eyes.

I don't want to make you cry, Mommy, his eyes seemed to say, *so I won't ask any more questions.*

I held back tears and thought, *We've got to be brave, Sammy. Okay? We'll be brave together.*

At night, I would sit on the floor beside his bed and watch him sleep. I would cry and pray to whomever might be listening: *Please, let me keep him, please, please ...*

a snake

I remember standing in my driveway the day after finding out about the mass, crying, telling my small circle of friends about Sam's upcoming tests. This tight-knit group had sprouted five years ago when we were all new moms. We used to meet weekly until the babies, all boys, reached school age. Then we arranged playdates and saw each other at birthday parties, and on occasion, we'd pick a restaurant and have a moms' night out. They had coordinated meal deliveries in the days leading up to Sam's heart cath. Lisa had brought us taco casserole and Doritos; Joan, honey-mustard chicken and rice; Suzanne, lasagna and salad.

"Why are friends bringing us dinner every night?" Sam wanted to know.

"Well . . . our playgroup is experimenting with dinner recipes," I lied. It amazed me, barely having the stamina to put a casserole in the oven, how pliable I was, cooking up answers out of thin air.

On our way to the hospital the morning of Sam's heart cath, David was driving, Sam was awake but quiet in the back seat, and I was staring ahead at the back of a truck, worrying about what was really ahead of us: needles, anesthesia, a snakelike camera; that mass, those risks. *He'll wake up*, I tried reassuring myself. *Everything's going to be okay.*

In the center of the truck's rear door were three flashing lights— one red light flanked by two yellow ones. I wanted this to be a sign. That Friday morning I needed those flashing lights to mean something. So I focused on the red beating light and repeated to myself, like a prayer, *Sammy's heart is in good hands . . . Sammy's heart is in good hands . . . Sammy's heart . . .*

It was still dark out. A layer of mist covered the road and made haloes around the streetlights. Inside the car was quiet, except for the intermittent swoosh of the windshield wipers. Sam's voice startled me.

"Mommy, are they going to have needles? Am I going to get a needle? Can they take a picture of my heart without using needles?"

I turned to face him. "Maybe one needle, Shmu. But it'll be okay. It's gonna be okay."

It *wasn't* okay.

The nurses that prepped Sam for his procedure were callous and cruel—not what he deserved. They instructed David to hold him down while they attempted, again and again, to push an IV needle into his small hand, which began spurting blood.

"Mommy! Please! Daddy! Stop!" he cried and begged, the sight of blood scaring him even more.

He wasn't even sick, so I couldn't tell him any of this would make him all better. "It's okay, Sammy. It'll be okay, baby. Hold still. It'll be okay." I was holding back tears, holding myself because I couldn't hold him, grab him, take him away from this nightmare.

After the IV was finally taped in place, the unapologetic nurses disappeared, leaving my beautiful boy drained from the fighting and sleepy from the drug.

When he was wheeled to the room where the special camera was kept, David and I walked beside him, stopping in front of the double doors we wouldn't be allowed to go through. The picture taker, Dr. Piedad, and his assistant, Nurse Ellen, were waiting for us.

"Good morning, Sam. Did you bring your music today?" Dr. Piedad asked.

Sam smiled and held up his Fleetwood Mac cassette tape.

"Wow!" the team applauded. "We get to listen to Fleetwood Mac instead of Barney! This is going to be great!"

David and I kissed our drunk, smiling baby boy goodbye, trusting that he and his five-year-old heart, which was into Fleetwood Mac, would be in good hands.

I remember Suzanne appearing and sitting beside me during Sam's heart cath in the hospital waiting room. The fear in her eyes reminded me of that day, four years earlier, when I'd pulled into her driveway where I found her standing, tears running down her face. We'd just had our babies when she'd received the news: breast cancer. All I could do was hug her and sit with her. Sometimes you need a friend by your side. No words are necessary; just their presence can sustain you a little longer. We sat together in silence, her hand over mine on the armrest, while David paced.

Sometime later, I remember Pam, our next-door neighbor, sitting beside me, putting a stick of gum in my hand. I hadn't eaten that morning. That sliver of spearmint melted in my mouth and supplied me with a little more endurance and hope, and staved off my hunger and thirst a little while longer. Studies have shown chewing gum activates neural circuits that help form memories. Perhaps this is why such a seemingly insignificant gesture is so unforgettable.

While Sam slept, that thin snake with camera eyes traveled through his body and into his heart. It bit off a tiny piece of the mass, then slithered out and exited at his groin, leaving fang marks in his baby-soft skin, permanent reminders of the *picture taker*. I replayed Psalm 32:8 in my head—*I will instruct you and teach you in the way you should go; I will counsel you and watch over you . . . I will instruct you and teach you in the way you should go; I will counsel you and watch over you . . .*

In recovery, as he was waking up, Nurse Ellen told us how well things went and how much they had all enjoyed Sam's music. She told us the doctor would be out soon to talk to us, but the way she avoided our eyes bothered me.

Sam was drowsy but smiling. Jenny, his recovery room nurse, had just gone to get his apple juice.

"She's *very* pretty," he said, then wrote a note on the napkin she'd left on his bedside table. *"Jenny, call me. Love, Sam K."*

When he asked me what our phone number was, I assured him I would add it to the note and give it to Jenny. My little drunken sailor nodded off again, and I slipped the napkin into my purse. One day, this would be a funny story to tell.

When Dr. Piedad greeted us, he pulled the curtain around Sam's bed to separate him from the conversation we were about to have. His face was serious, and he also avoided our eyes, looking instead at our hearts as he spoke in a low voice.

I remember only fragments of what he said.

"I've never . . . nothing like this before . . . went well but . . . it's very large . . . needs to come out but . . . too large . . . I'm sorry . . . Sam . . . incredible . . . very special boy."

I felt sick, and my legs were trembling. I peeked behind the curtain at Sam. He was smiling, hugging his new, heart-shaped SpongeBob pillow, which had been signed by the entire cardiac team.

"I'll be right back, sweetie. I love you." I held my breath and my tears. Panic-stricken, I excused myself and left David and the doctor behind.

Walking like a zombie through the halls of the hospital, which were filled with other dead-looking faces, I needed to get away. I needed that mass to go away. I needed to hide. I found the hospital's chapel and went inside, hit the floor with my knees and pounded an ugly vinyl-cushioned chair with my fists. *No one is instructing or teaching or counseling us! No one is watching over us!* I sobbed and screamed until my throat was raw, but no one heard me because No One was there.

decisions

Medical decisions, I was learning, are made by weighing which is worse: the deadliness of the disease or the side effects caused by the treatment, the drugs.

Following the heart cath, Dr. Angstrom suggested starting Sam on a beta-blocker, propranolol, to ease the workload on his heart. But I had the final say. I'd done my homework, read about the risks versus the benefits of this drug, but I wasn't sure. Was the mass more deadly than the drug? Or was the drug, which in rare cases *may* cause cardiac arrest, more deadly? *Act as if everything depended on you.* Now, there were two things to be afraid of, but I feared the mass more, so I said yes to the beta-blocker.

"Sammy, this medicine is just like the pink stuff you took when you had an ear infection," I said, measuring out his first dose of propranolol.

"It tastes good, Mommy. I like it."

But the beta-blocker made him dizzy and dull—the exact opposite of the bright little boy I knew.

Cassy, my best friend since childhood, noticed it too.

Passing through Jacksonville on their drive home to Naples in South Florida, she and her family were staying for a few days at a hotel in nearby Saint Augustine. The boys and I couldn't wait to see—as we called them—Aunt Cassy, Uncle Jerry, and Cousin Nicholas.

Sitting on the edge of the hotel's swimming pool, our feet in the water, Cassy whispered to me. "Oh my god, Sammy looks so tired— he's so pale. Something is wrong. It *has* to be the drug," she said.

While Joey played, jumping in and out of the pool, Sam bobbed in the water, clinging with his fingertips to the edge. His eyes were murky, dozy, sleepy looking. We kept our eyes on him, afraid he might sink if we looked away. I was uncomfortable with the decision I'd made. Was he *really* better off taking a drug that made him so stoned and sluggish he could hardly laugh, play, or swim?

"It has to be." I nodded. "But what if it *is* his heart? Cassy, I'm so scared."

"I know you are. Damn it. I know."

We took a picture that day, but I put it away, never wanting to see it again. It's etched in my memory all the same. Sam is in front of me, leaning against me, his head on my chest, my chin on his wet hair. We're trying to smile, but we both look drained, extremely sad. That mass was oppressive, and now the drug was suffocating us.

Planning ahead, knowing we'd be getting pathology results from the local hospital and thinking two heads were better than one, I'd asked Dr. Angstrom to also send Sam's biopsy to Dr. Brooke for a second opinion. Dr. Brooke, the leading academic cardiovascular pathologist at the Armed Forces Institute of Pathology in Maryland, had written several studies on cardiac tumors. I'd kept his name on the top of my list.

And so, we got back two reports with slightly different findings. One pathologist saw only "muscle cells," and the other saw cells resembling a type of "benign tumor" seen before in a previous study. There were still no definitive answers, but I was relieved; *muscle cells* and *benign tumor* seemed better than *malignant cells*.

It was astonishing how the thinnest sliver of hope, like a stick of gum, kept me going.

What was next?

For his stress test, covered in tape and weighed down in wires again, like an astronaut, Sam jogged on a treadmill. He was winded, but his heart rate recovered quickly, which made all of us, doctors included, very happy.

And then we were back at the hospital for his cardiac MRI.

This kind of test doesn't seem invasive, but when you're five, it involves an IV, anesthesia, intubation, risks, and more sticky tape, so more pain, crying.

Capturing still photos of a beating heart is a challenge, so it took longer than usual, and Sam was anesthetized for longer than expected, which annoyed the impatient recovery room nurse, an angry dog who shook him and barked in his ear: "Wake up! Let's go! Wake up!" Then she snarled at us, "You'll need to keep trying to wake him every thirty minutes."

At home that evening, after waiting hours for him to wake up, holding my breath, nudging him, watching his chest to be sure it was rising, whispering in his ear, "Sammy, wake up, baby. Come on, wake up, sleepyhead," he finally opened his eyes, confused but smiling, glad the bad dream was all over.

I thought of writing a complaint letter to the hospital's administration about the harsh treatment we'd experienced—and on more than one occasion—but I didn't have the energy. I put the coldhearted nurse, the all-day anesthesia, the not waking up, behind me, and prepared for our next battle.

Days later, we were back at that hellish hospital for blood work that would test for certain genetic mutations, though I wasn't sure exactly which ones. I had to be brave—for him. I had to make him believe *he* was brave, tell him how strong he was. His life was going to be different now, unpredictable. I had to prepare him for whatever battle he might have to fight next.

The phlebotomist was a stone-faced woman who wore scrubs covered in rainbow-colored happy faces that appeared to be jeering at us more than smiling. As we followed her down a dim hallway to a small room, her rubber-soled shoes squished and popped like suction cups, and I made a funny face at Sam to lighten the mood.

Without a word, the stone-faced woman pointed to a chair, and Sam sat. She wrapped a rubber band around his arm and pushed in the needle, filling one . . . two . . . three . . . four . . . five . . . six . . . tubes with his blood, all the while remaining indifferent to his now pale five-year-old face.

"Mommy, I feel like I'm gonna pass out."

"Look at me, Sammy. Not at your arm. Look at me. You're almost done."

Leaving the hospital, he was shaky and weak, and I worried what effect this blood loss might have on his heart.

"Sammy, you were *so* brave in there—*so* strong."

Then, making suction cup sounds with my mouth, I told him ice cream would replace the blood that had been sucked out of him. How skilled at lying I was becoming, making up age-appropriate stories on a whim.

A few days later, I got a phone call from the hospital. "Someone left the blood out, and it was supposed to be refrigerated," the caller said. "So it's no good. You'll need to return with the patient for another blood draw."

The hospital staff's incompetence, their heartlessness, the insanity of going back there again—I was certain about *this* decision. *I* was the lion now, claws out. "No," I told the caller. "The patient will *not* be returning for another blood draw."

brave and strong

A few weeks later, we learned that Sam's MRI was a miss, or, I don't know, the images were not informative. Did that mean they were blurry, out of focus, inconclusive? Whatever. All I knew was that we had carried him out of that hospital that day with his tongue hanging out of his mouth like a dog. That he had been asleep for far too many hours. That we had put his life at risk—and for what? For nothing.

Dr. Angstrom admitted his team lacked experience with this, having never seen a heart like Sam's before, and we agreed then on our next step: Boston Children's Hospital. There, we'd see Dr. Simon, the top pick on my list. He had developed the cardiac MRI program at BCH and had actually seen a handful of cardiac tumors, more than anyone else in the world.

"We'll get to fly on an airplane, Sammy! Maybe see a Red Sox game. Did you know Grandpa Don was born there, in Boston?" I tried to sound excited. "There's an *expert* picture taker there—the *best* in the world. He has an *extra* special camera and wants to take another picture of your heart—a *better* picture this time . . . that's all." But my voice shook, and I broke down and cried, which made him cry.

David cried. We cried together.

"Another picture taker? I don't want to go, Mommy. Please. Please, I *don't* want to go. No more needles. They'll have needles. *Please.* Why do we have to go?"

David and I held him and told him we didn't want to go either.

"It's just for a picture, Shmu. It'll be okay. You'll bring your bunny, and Duke. We'll go sightseeing, ride on a train—you've never been on a subway before. We'll visit an aquarium and go to a children's museum. And then we'll eat lobster! It'll be *great.* You'll see."

If he were sick, I could've told him the doctors there were going to treat him and make him all better. But he *wasn't* sick, and all we had planned was more poking and prodding, more tests that would frighten and hurt him.

Whenever people asked Sam what he wanted to be when he grew up, he would say he wanted to be an "army man," like his G. I. Joe action figure, Duke. So before our big trip, we made up a song and sang it together whenever we felt afraid:

> *Sam, Sam, the army man, friend to you and me*
> *Sam, Sam, the army man, keeps us safe and free*
> *Sam, Sam, the army man, at times he is afraid*
> *Sam, Sam, the army man, blows fear up with grenades*
> *Sam, Sam, the army man, his heart knows right from wrong*
> *Sam, Sam, the army man, he's so brave and strong*

And then we soldiered on.

I felt the need to eliminate *anything* that seemed frivolous, required too much attention, or wasted my time, like dusting the furniture or styling my hair. I don't know why, maybe it was guilt—how could I spend time blow-drying my hair when my little boy has a mass in his heart? Military "induction" haircuts, or buzz cuts, serve a psychological purpose: to strip individuality from recruits and promote the desired team mentality in a platoon. If my little boy was going to be an army man, then I was going to be a soldier in his platoon. A few weeks before our trip to Boston, nervous about what would happen next, I felt the need to cut or eliminate my hair.

As the stylist pushed, combed, and clipped, I watched long, wet curves of hair tumble down the front of my cape. Afterward, studying my reflection in the mirror, I saw an older version of Sam. We had the same face, eyes, coloring, and now, the same short haircut. It wasn't a buzz cut, but it was as short as it could be, and I felt braver and stronger, like an army man.

a godsend

On Easter weekend, forty-seven days after Sam's fifth birthday, the four of us went to the spring festival and Easter egg hunt at the Presbyterian church. I introduced David and the boys to Reverend Penn. As they shook hands, I noticed how the pastor looked at Sam as if he were praying over him with his eyes. I thanked him for inviting us that day and thanked him, with *my* eyes, for praying over Sam.

The boys hunted for plastic eggs and filled their buckets with candy as if it were Halloween. They got to pet a goat and clip-clop around the parking lot in a buggy pulled by a small horse. It seemed sunny, and happy families were everywhere. We were and were *not* sunny and happy. Not in the same way we'd been before. We were pretending, playacting, as if nothing had changed.

As we were heading out, walking through the parking lot, a woman pulled up next to us in her car and asked why we were leaving so soon.

"I suggest you go back for the Easter basket drawing. You just might win!"

"Thanks," I told the nice lady, rolling my eyes at David. I'd forgotten about the tickets the boys had dropped in the drawing box earlier.

Sam begged and rallied us to go back. "We might win! Come on, guys! Let's go!"

Joey was too young to know what the fuss was about but echoed his big brother: "Let's go, guys!"

They were right. We might win. Sam *could* win and live and beat the odds, despite that mass. How could I say no?

We walked back to the courtyard, where two huge Easter baskets sat on a large folding table, pink and blue cellophane shimmering in the sun. One for a girl and one for a boy. The boy's basket, the size of a five-year-old, was filled with sports-themed prizes. The lady who'd been sitting at the folding table stood and reached into the box and pulled out a tiny ticket. She paused, and in that pause, I knew who the winner was.

"Sam Kassenoff!" she announced.

Sam's jaw dropped and he began jumping and clapping. "I won! I won!"

The ticket lady squinted at me, possibly thinking, *You're not members here. I don't recognize that name*, or this, *I recognize that name— the little boy with the mass in his heart.*

As we were leaving, carrying that bulky godsend back to the minivan, the parking lot woman was still there, idling in her car with the windows down.

"Aren't you glad you went back?" she said, then pointed to the sky. "I think *Someone* up there is trying to tell you something." With a satisfied smile, she drove away.

2
LIVING NORMALLY

a pinhole

After we boarded the 767 and before we took off, the captain invited us to the cockpit.

"Have a seat, boys. But don't push any buttons."

We laughed as Sam climbed into the captain's seat, Joey into the co-captain's.

"Seriously, though," I said, pointing to Joey, "keep your eye on that one. He likes pushing buttons."

Wide-eyed, clutching his stuffed toy rabbit, Sam turned around to look at us, and I snapped the picture.

This was after 9/11, and cockpits were usually off-limits to passengers. I wondered if the flight crew knew why we were traveling to Boston. Did they usually invite children into the cockpit?

It was mid-May, and the weather in Boston was crisp and cool; the sky was sunny and blue. David's father, Sandy, and his partner, Doris, joined us at the hotel. They would watch Joey over the coming days while David, Sam, and I were at the hospital.

On our first day, Monday, we met with Dr. Simon. He was soft-spoken, wore thin-rimmed glasses, and could've easily passed for Dr. Angstrom's younger brother. He'd scheduled a series of tests for Sam—a sonogram, EKG, chest X-ray, and another MRI—and would be our point man throughout the week, he told us.

Before the MRI, still dressed in his jeans and sneakers, Sam sat in a brightly lit room on the edge of the bed holding Duke, his action figure, while a team of nurses prepared paperwork and equipment around him.

I pulled a nurse aside and asked how they planned to go about starting Sam's IV. "He's really afraid of needles."

"Oh no, he'll *never* see a needle—and neither will you," she assured me. "We *never* do that. Only when he's *fast* asleep—and after you kiss him goodbye—then we'll start his IV. We'll take good care of him," she promised and returned to her patient for a chat.

"Hello, Sam. Do you like bubble gum?" He nodded with enthusiasm. "That's great! Do you know *how* to blow a bubble?"

He promptly explained how as the entire room listened and nodded with deep interest.

"Well, this mask I'm holding has bubble gum air in it." The nurse held up a clear mask. "Can you show me—with this mask—how you blow a bubble?"

"Of course." Sam smiled, leaned into the mask, took a big breath of the candy-flavored air, and showed his bubble-blowing technique. His eyes blinked, then closed, and he folded over and fell asleep—just like that.

The nurse cradled him and laid his head down on a pillow. I thanked her and thanked her, again and again, wanting to hug her. She had no idea how *different* this experience was, how relieved and how grateful we were.

In the waiting room, there were children and babies everywhere: sitting on laps, lying wrapped in blankets, being pushed in wheelchairs or pulled in little red wagons. I overheard a father telling another waiting parent that his son was having his third and final heart surgery to repair his defect. He sounded upbeat, unafraid.

On a table next to my chair, I found a large picture book. On its cover, in big, block letters printed across a background of mountains, was the title *Venezuela*. This was where my great-grandmother and grandmother were from and where my mother had lived as a child. It was where I had spent summers when I was a kid, visiting with relatives in Caracas. I missed home when I was there, then missed my aunts, uncles, and cousins when I was home again.

I thumbed through the pages from back to front, stopping at each photo, remembering those beaches, that cable car, those mountains. When I came to the inside cover, I found a handwritten message: *With all my heart. Thank you to the best doctors in the world ...*

What were the odds, out of all the books in the world—and all the countries, that I would come to sit beside this one? *This has to be a sign*, I thought. I *needed* it to be a sign, to mean something—that we were in the right place, with the right doctors, the best doctors in the world. I wanted to believe that maybe there was someone "up there" trying to tell me something, that maybe my ancestors (*mis abuelas*) were letting me know they were watching over us. I hoped it was them, and not just my imagination, whispering to me. *I will instruct you and teach you in the way you should go; I will counsel you and watch over you ...*

To my astonishment, Sam would tell me he remembered seeing "old people" standing around him. "They looked like grandparents, Mommy. They stayed with me when I was sleeping, so I wasn't scared."

In the recovery room, David and I joined the circle of women in turquoise scrubs surrounding Sam's bed. He was wide awake, sitting up, licking an orange Popsicle. He talked and laughed with his new friends, flirting with his orange lips, having a good ol' time dressed in his new yellow scrubs. They were the ones he'd wear again at home when he played surgeon and repaired his stuffed animals' hearts.

Dr. Simon peeked in and asked David and me to join him out in the hallway. He spoke in a soft tone. While Sam was laughing on the other side of the door, the doctor's words sounded serious, flat.

"Maybe benign . . . very vascular . . . this tumor . . . or maybe malignant . . ."

People were hurrying by, avoiding eye contact. I needed better news—anything, please, just something good. Not wanting to cry in public, I asked if we could talk somewhere else.

We followed him to a closet-sized office, where the doctor pulled up Sam's MRI images on a computer monitor. He explained and pointed out areas on the screen, and I asked questions: What kind of mass is this? Can he live with it? For how long? Are there any possible treatments? Might it go away? What happens next?

The doctor shook his head and answered with apologies. "Only time will tell," he said. "If the mass is malignant, we'll know fairly soon. Malignant tumors grow quickly. If the mass *doesn't* grow or change over the coming months, then it's more likely to be benign."

Perhaps we could cut off the blood supply to that mass, I thought. I'd read about a therapy called *angiogenesis*—the cutting off of a tumor's blood supply—which was created by Dr. Judah Folkman, director of the vascular biology program here at Boston Children's Hospital. He'd said in an interview with PBS's *Nova* program, "There's a fine line between persistence and obstinacy. You don't know whether if you're persistent a little longer, you'll make it or whether you're being obstinate, [and it] doesn't exist."

Teetering on that fine line between persistence and obstinacy, I stayed focused on that pinhole of light. "And some benign tumors regress. It could regress, right?" I kept probing for answers, for *certainty.* The doctor *had* shrugged, I'd noted, so there was still hope. Uncertainty was my pinhole of light. An uncertain future was still a future. This was the loophole I'd found.

white coats

On our last day, David and I met with a cardiologist who specialized in cardiomyopathy. Dr. Matthews had kind eyes and messy hair and looked serious but casual. We sat together in a small office adjacent to a large classroom.

"So, you think the mass is *not* a tumor, but HCM?" I asked.

"Well, statistically, it's less likely to be a tumor and more likely to be hypertrophic cardiomyopathy."

Statistically? Less or more likely? Maybe more time, more research, was needed, I thought. I was exhausted. I felt dizzy. Maybe from lack of oxygen—or food? If I didn't consciously think about breathing or eating these days, I didn't breathe, and I forgot to eat.

"Go home and live your lives normally. Eighty percent of cardio-myopathy patients lead fairly normal lives," the doctor said.

What happens to the twenty percent? How do they live? I wanted to ask but didn't. "What about a defibrillator? I've been looking into getting one."

"I don't think that's necessary. There's no need yet to alter your life like that. An implantable cardioverter-defibrillator may be an option down the road when he's older, bigger. Right now, he's very young. The risks and complications far outweigh the benefits."

"Speaking of risks . . . Sam is on the beta-blocker propranolol. Is this something you would prescribe?"

"Absolutely not. He's asymptomatic. There's no reason for it. Start weaning him off immediately."

I shuddered. What might've happened if we had kept giving him this drug?

In the adjacent classroom, I could hear murmuring, chairs scraping the floor, notebooks rustling, and Dr. Matthews asked if we'd mind staying a little longer. "A few more specialists would like to talk to you."

Several white coats were sitting or standing on the periphery of the conference room. I wondered if a covert email had gone out: *Attention: five-year-old boy, very rare heart—one-in-a-million case. If interested, please report to the secret conference room. Meeting in progress now.*

David and I sat at a table across from a geneticist holding a pen and clipboard. She introduced herself and began asking questions and taking notes about our family history.

"I'd like to draw Sam's blood, run some tests for genetic mutations."

"Does this help him—or change anything?" I asked, more familiar now with this game of odds and probabilities.

"No, but—"

"No more needles," David said. He was boiling over. "Sam's done. I told him we're leaving after this meeting, so we're done here."

The geneticist nodded, then advised us. "You know . . . you should not plan on having any more children."

The room went silent. Feeling trapped and combative and already certain about *this* decision, I fired back, "I wasn't planning on it. I just want to keep the ones I have."

Days later, I would receive a call from a genetic counselor who had accompanied the geneticist to that last meeting. She apologized for her colleague's comments and told me I could call her if I ever needed to talk or had any questions. This meant a lot, and I want to thank her here, again, for looking at us *not* as a test result or a statistic, but for seeing the terrified parents we were and then picking up the phone.

a tune

Before leaving Boston, we spent a few days sightseeing.

We took a ride on the subway, the T. We went to the Boston Children's Museum, then to the New England Aquarium. We ate lobster for dinner. And, on our last night there, David took Sammy to a Red Sox game, which was televised, so I got to see and hear him on the TV in our hotel room. It cost an arm and a leg for front row tickets behind home plate, but there he was, right behind the catcher, my little boy, all heart, jumping, cheering, and screaming for the Sox, having the time of his life.

At the airport, while waiting to board our flight, Sam begged us for money.

"Nine dollars for a magazine? No, Sam, it's too expensive."

"But I'm really, *really* interested in airplanes and jets. I *really* want it, Mommy. Please, *please*, can we buy it? I think I might be a pilot one day when I grow up. So I really, *really* need to read this magazine."

A couple sitting nearby smiled at the scene Sam was making. "How old is he? Sure is making a pretty convincing case. Maybe he'll be a lawyer one day," one of the onlookers said.

Living a fairly *normal* life—parenting, saying *no* despite the constant fear of his sudden death—and learning to balance restraint with indulgence began there in the airport gift shop. I didn't want to spoil him, buy him anything he wanted anytime he begged, but I did want him to grow up and be a pilot or whatever his heart desired. So I said yes and bought that nine-dollar magazine for my little jet airplane enthusiast.

Later, less than a year before his death, I would say no to an electric toothbrush called Tooth Tunes that he'd wanted. We were standing in a Walmart aisle, at a cardboard display that advertised: *While you brush, music plays in your head!*

"No, Sam. You can hum a song instead while you're brushing your teeth. It's junk you don't need. Sorry, but it's a *no*."

It, too, had cost nine bucks. I should've bought the stupid thing. I would've remembered his big, foamy grin every time he brushed. Now, instead, I have this tune playing in *my* head: *"It's junk ... it's a no,"* and then I see his sad eyes again, staring at that silly toothbrush display, heartbroken. Just one more thing to add to my heap of guilt and self-blame, one more thing that I wish I'd done differently.

hypervigilance

It was almost the end of May 2003, and the end of the school year. There was a banner hanging in Sam's classroom, with drawings and signatures from his classmates to welcome him back.

One morning, after walking the boys into school, a mother I'd seen before but didn't know approached me in the parking lot, an expression of pity on her face. I'd become accustomed to that look. Several parents had likely heard about the junior kindergartner who'd been in the hospital.

She touched my arm and, for some reason, couldn't take her eyes off my hair. "Hi, I just wanted to say how *sorry* I am. I heard you were going through something—some kind of treatment. I'm so sorry."

I teared up. "Thank you," I said, grateful for this outpouring of concern.

"It looks like it's growing back, though. It's only hair, right?"

I realized what she'd meant then and nodded in slow motion. "Right . . . Yes, it'll grow back."

The minute I got home, I called Cassy. "Can you believe that?"

"Sissy, you've got a chemo-cut!" she said, laughing so hard she was barely able to cough up the words.

Both of us were in stitches. It felt good to laugh; it felt good to breathe. I realized how anxious I'd been, holding my breath for long stretches of time—before, during, and after every test or appointment.

That summer, we made playdates with friends, took trips to the beach, and the boys took piano lessons. Joey picked it up fast and enjoyed practicing. His fingers were pudgy but nimble and moved with ease up and down the keys. He was *really* good. Sam's fingers, though, were awkward and not as coordinated.

One afternoon on the drive home after a lesson, Sam complained. "It's not fair. He's two years younger, and he can play the piano better than me."

"You'll just have to practice more." I shrugged, glancing at their funny faces—Joey, grinning; Sam, sulking—in the rearview mirror. If I wasn't driving, I would've pulled out my camera. I was the picture taker now, capturing images of everyday life. Filling boxes with thousands of photos organized in envelopes by date. I'd bought a digital camera, so I didn't have to wait days for film to develop. I photographed the boys snorkeling in the kiddie pool, picnicking in the driveway, riding their bikes, laughing on their swing set, building sandcastles, staring out at the ocean, at the sunset. I zoomed in close-up, eyelash-close, and watched them watching life.

Before the upcoming school year, at a well visit at the pediatrician's office, Dr. Katz and I had a quick conversation while Sam was out of the room having his vision and hearing checked.

"I spoke with Dr. Angstrom," he said. "He still suspects this thing in Sam's heart is a mass, but that it *could* be HCM. *Hypertrophic*: too much. *Cardio*: heart. *Myo*: muscle. *Pathy*: disease. *Hyper–trophic–cardio–myopathy*—and we *don't* want it to be that."

These eight words haunted me, like ghosts in an attic, and I couldn't get them out of my head. *And we don't want it to be that.* If it *was* HCM, and 80 percent of cardiomyopathy patients lead fairly normal lives, I thought, why didn't we want it to be that?

That fall, David was pitching to Sam in the backyard when I heard them hooting and shouting. "It's a home run!"

With his plastic bat, Sam had hit the Wiffle ball over the house and was running the imaginary bases when I stepped outside.

David looked excited. "He can really hit! Did you see how far that went?"

"Hi, Mommy!" Sam waved as he rounded the bases.

He wanted to play baseball for a real team, on a real field with real bases, and not just in the backyard. So I started reading again, this time about HCM: *Children with HCM should not participate in competitive*

or contact sports. Tragically, undiagnosed athletes have died on basket-
ball courts or football fields from sudden cardiac death caused by HCM.

It was not confirmed, though, in the reports I'd read, if it had been
overexertion, excessive adrenaline, or impact during play that caused
the electrical failure.

Also not recommended: vigorous recreational exercise.

The data was scant and confusing. What did *vigorous* mean?
What types of recreational exercise increased the risk of sudden death?
Low-dynamic sports like golf or bowling seemed acceptable. Were yoga
classes safe? What about a TV aerobics class with Gilad, former Israeli
soldier turned fitness personality? Giggling and flexing their muscles,
the boys counted their kicks and punches, copying this real live action
figure who stood on a beach, throwing punches at the camera. Was
this safe?

When we saw Dr. Angstrom for Sam's monthly EKG and echo to
measure the mass and note any changes, I brought a list of questions.

"He can run and play and swim … and ride his bike, right?" I
asked.

Dr. Angstrom nodded. "That should be fine."

"What about Putt-Putt golf and bowling?"

"Yes. We just don't want him overexerting himself. At this age,
he'll self-regulate."

My mind raced. What if he doesn't self-regulate? What if he plays
too long, runs too fast, pedals too hard, or falls and hits the ground?
How will I know when too much is too much?

Was it too much on that sweltering afternoon earlier that summer,
when Sam was alone in the middle of the pool, struggling to keep his
face above the surface? It had been the word *survival* on the swimming
instructor's business card that caught my eye, but I didn't know he
was going to be pushed this hard. The instructor had handed out paperwork that said to come wearing layers of clothing on the last day of
class to simulate a real situation: falling into a pool fully dressed. Sam
was wearing jeans, a sweatshirt, a jacket, *and* sneakers. He was panting,

flapping his arms, kicking his legs. He flopped onto his back to float and rest like he'd been taught. His windbreaker puffed up and folded around his face like a pillow, smothering him.

I wanted to jump in and pull him out. "He has a heart condition," I reminded the leather-skinned instructor.

"He knows what he's doing. He's fine," she said.

Living *normally*, I realized, meant I wouldn't always be taken seriously. To say Sam had a heart condition, which was putting it mildly, lacked urgency. If I had, instead, used the more vivid *large, unremovable, football-shaped mass*, would that have helped? Since most people believe only what they see, and Sam was the picture of health, my vigilance seemed like neurotic overprotectiveness. But every second was about survival and, in this case, overexertion. *Act as if everything depended on you.* I should've stopped it. I should've told the instructor enough was enough. But I didn't. I wasn't sure. Was he just normal tired? Or overexertion-tired?

"How about Little League baseball?" I asked Dr. Angstrom. "It's not a contact sport and doesn't seem too strenuous, running in short spurts. He really wants to play. At this age, they hit the ball off a tee. Is that okay?"

He looked as disappointed as Sam did. "No. No baseball. We don't want him getting hit . . . with a ball."

It took me a second to realize what the doctor was implying. We didn't want Sam getting hit *in the chest* with a ball.

Living normally would never be normal again. The risk of sudden cardiac death was lurking around every corner, stalking us. So every day, and every night, David and I stayed hypervigilant. *Hyper: excessively. Vigilant: watchful.*

artists

I needed Sam to remain in the 80-percent group and *live*, so instead of playing baseball, we imagined we were artists and painted instead.

Outside on the back patio, I set cups of finger paint, water bowls, and chunky brushes into their plastic easel trays, and the boys circled me like hungry dogs. Draping the old oak trees in the backyard, the Spanish moss was filtering out the late afternoon sun.

"It's a perfect time for painting pictures," I said. "Red, blue, and yellow—you can make all colors from these."

"What do I paint?" Sam asked.

Joey echoed, "What I paint?"

I looked around, and they mimicked me, my miniature mirrors. "Paint one thing or everything you see. You have brushes and fingers and water for rinsing between colors." I positioned my lawn chair and sat.

"We can use our fingers?" Sam asked, and Joey held up his hands.

"Of course. Paint whatever you want: the sky, sunshine, clouds, trees, bugs, bees . . ."

They panicked. "Bees?! Where?"

I laughed at their faces, so reliant, so trusting. "Just paint. The bees won't bother you if you're busy because they're busy too."

They nodded and got to work. Joey attacked his canvas, mashing his brush, mixing colors into swirls of mud so thick the painting took on a three-dimensional quality.

Sam deliberated before he started. "Red and yellow make orange, right?"

"Right." I nodded.

Lightly brushing in careful strokes across the canvas, he formed a red bridge supported by curved pillars, and beneath it, he painted water, blue waves. Then an orange, stick-figure boy walked onto the bridge, his arms out for balance. Above him, a lemon sun shined, red birds flew, and above swirls of finger-made clouds, he painted the words "good day" on the white sky.

a puppy

It was early December 2003 when I circled the ad in the paper: *Puppies for sale*.

I didn't tell Sam exactly why we were going to this nice lady's house. "How about, just for fun, today we go and *see* some puppies?" I suggested. "We're definitely not *getting* a puppy. I just want to see what *these* puppies look like, so that one day, maybe, if we ever *do* get a puppy, we'll know . . ."

Sam was five, so he believed my made-up stories and didn't question the holes in this plot. He was just excited to see puppies. It was like a trip to the zoo, only better.

In the nice lady's kitchen, there was an assortment of colors: whites, grays, various shades of brown from dark to light gold. I stood on the other side of the baby gate, scanning the chaos that was barely contained there. The round-bellied whelps were waddling in circles, piddling on and off the newspapers that were scattered across the floor.

"Sammy, which one would *you* pick if you *could* choose one?"

"There are nine puppies to choose from," the nice lady pointed out.

Wide-eyed and tentative, Sam sat down in the middle of the kitchen. Eight little nippers instantly surrounded him, jumping and vying for his attention. Number 9 sat on the periphery, watching, waiting politely. When he saw an opening in the crowd, he inched forward and gently placed his paw on Sam's knee: *Pick me, please.*

"Him." Sam pointed to the quiet one. "*That's* the one I would pick."

I noted the puppy's color and markings, golden-brown, the only one with four white paws—*white socks,* I jotted down. He was timid and had a gentle nature and intelligent eyes.

The nice lady proceeded to tell me about *her* first dog—and her childhood illness. "I lived in and out of hospitals, and when my mother put that puppy in bed with me, it saved my life," she said in a sweet Southern drawl.

Maybe it *was* a pitch. But she didn't know us, didn't know about the mass we'd found in Sam's heart nine months earlier or about how desperate I was to save my child's life. This had to be a sign. And yes, I *wanted* to be sold; to believe this shy little dog might play a key role in the medical miracle I was praying for. Maybe one day, when Sam was much, much older, he would tell that same story: *And when my mother put that puppy in bed with me, it saved my life.*

A few weeks later, on Christmas Eve, the gold puppy with the white paws was caged in our kitchen, howling like a wolf. It was his first night alone and away from his littermates. Earlier, on a covert mission, I had slipped out after the boys were asleep to give that nice lady an envelope full of cash for one of her puppies.

"Every boy should have one." I had pitched the puppy idea to David. "Besides, pets are supposed to be medicinal. It'll be good for his heart. A dog will look out for him, comfort him, listen to him, love him, and make him laugh."

The tiny dog continued howling, and David continued cursing me for the gift I'd chosen. "He's gonna cry all night, every night—I know it. Then he'll start barking. This was a *huge* mistake."

Not knowing what to say or do about this regrettable purchase, we stopped talking and stared at the ceiling, exasperated by the unbelievably loud and agonizing cries coming from that four-pound werewolf. Startling us, Sam burst into our room in a panic, his eyes huge with fear, and jumped onto our bed. (So far, this puppy was *not* helping his heart.)

"Daddy! There's a wolf in the house! You hear it?"

We acted dumb and told him everything was okay. But the howling kept coming from the other end of the house.

"It's a wolf! Don't you hear it? *Listen.*"

The surprise was blown. Out of bed now, I held out my hand. "Come with us. We'll show you what the noise is. It's not a wolf, so don't be afraid. There's *nothing* to be afraid of."

We held hands and walked through the house toward the kitchen. The sounds grew louder but less scary, then stopped. Our voices had hushed the tiny beast.

"What is it?" Sam asked. He was on his knees, looking into the crate at the small, brown eyes staring back. "Is it a puppy?" He was unsure.

"Your puppy, Sammy. For you. He's your Christmas present."

Sam's fright turned into exhilaration in an instant. "Is he mine? He's mine? Really? I can keep him?"

"He's yours," David confirmed, defeated. "But you have to go back to bed and go to sleep or Santa won't come."

"You want the puppy to sleep in your bed?" I asked.

Sam's answer squealed out of him. "Yes! Right. He needs to sleep in my bed. With me. In my bed, okay? I'll take care of him!" He clapped his hands and hopped all the way down the hall back to his room.

I carried the puppy in what looked like a breadbox with holes. "I'll put him in bed with you, but he stays in his crate. Okay?"

Sam jumped into bed and held out his arms and beckoned with his hands. "Yes! Okay! Here! Put him right here next to my pillow."

Sniffing, the puppy, whom Sam would later name Reggie Jackson Little Dude, poked his nose through the cage door, and Sam laid his head an inch from it. The two slept nose-to-nose. There was no more howling from that day on. Both dog and boy were so completely satisfied, safe, together, comforted by each other's breath and warmth. Heart therapy.

stories

I started writing just after Sam was born. Scrapbooking was big at the time, but I preferred to scan photos into the computer and use a desktop publishing program to combine my pictures and short stories into columns, newspaper-style. I'd received, as a baby gift, a custom photo notebook with Sam's name hand-painted on the front cover, and this is where I kept the printed, dated, and numbered pages. A stay-at-home mom pretending to be a photojournalist, a correspondent for *Sam's Story* (and, two years later, *Joey's Journal*), I covered everyday things in an upbeat and humorous tone. One day, I would give each of the boys their own book as a gift, maybe after they graduated college or had children of their own.

I wrote about new words.

Like the one twenty-one-month-old Sam overheard "Krappa" Sandy use while he and his partner, Doris, were visiting. I reminded Sandy that Sam picked up *every* word he heard.

"Oh, he didn't hear me," Krappa said. "He's playing; he's not even paying attention."

Later that evening, I was cooking dinner. We were all gathered in the kitchen talking, and Sam was sitting on the kitchen floor playing with his trucks.

"Shit-Shit-Shit-Shit!" he cried out.

The grown-up conversation stopped. We all looked at each other, holding our laughter, then down at Sam, who didn't look up but continued cursing his trucks.

"Shit-Shit-Shit-Shit!"

"I can't believe it!" his grandfather said, overflowing with pride. "He used the word correctly! He's a genius!"

I wrote about brotherhood.

The way baby Joey, like a baby bird, had imprinted on his big brother, bonding with Sam more than with David or me—which was my plan all along.

From the moment he woke up in the morning, Joey wanted "Sammy."

And Sam relished his new role, taking charge, guiding, teaching, and molding his little brother into the playmate he'd been waiting for.

"Joey, come on. It's time to go pee and brush our teeth."

"Joey, look at me. Put your head down on your pillow like this. I'll read you a story now, but you have to stay in bed, okay?"

"I love you, Sammy."

"I love you, too, little bro."

I wanted my boys to be best friends. Maybe it was because I didn't experience this with my sibling. In fifty or sixty years, if all went as planned, after David and I were gone, the boys would still be close. They'd always have each other.

I wrote about funny things that happened.

Like the time David and I joked that Joey was going to be Sam's bodyguard.

Mainly because he was built thicker, stronger, and tougher than his big brother.

And then, one Saturday afternoon at the mall, while I was watching the boys romp around the indoor play area, it happened. When a bigger kid pushed Sam down, Joey lunged at the brute with his fists, ready to throw a punch. Just before he did, David grabbed him, and we made for the exit.

I wrote about unforgettable moments.

Like the time Sam, at four, proclaimed: "When baby Joey gets bigger, we're gonna get married. We're brothers and best friends."

My plan was working, sort of. I jotted down that zinger and envisioned reading it aloud at a wedding reception one day. Then, to clear my conscience, I explained to him that we *love* our siblings, but we don't *marry* them.

I hadn't written anything in a year, since we learned about Sam's murmur at the pediatrician's office on Christmas Eve 2002. The last things I wrote about:

Trick-or-treating and Halloween costumes.

The trip we'd taken to South Florida to visit family.

The Hanukkah candles we'd lit, and the toys Hanukkah Harry and Santa had brought.

The fevers, ear infections, and amoxicillin the boys had shared.

I didn't write about the murmurs or the mass.

I remembered what that therapist had said years ago: *Try not to grieve a loss before it happens.* I was *trying* not to grieve, not to be so anxious and afraid all the time. Except every month, every ultrasound, there it was, that *mass*, on that TV monitor. David and I had started going to talk therapy to learn to cope and live with our fear and anxiety. We went to the same place but saw different therapists; he saw Randi, and I saw Margery. I don't recall if the reason was due to scheduling, or if our insurance company had recommended it, but it worked out to be a good fit for both of us.

Everything seemed to be okay, but feeling weighed down with foreboding and fear, I couldn't write. And unless there was a reason for it, an upcoming appointment or test, we didn't talk about it, the mass in Sam's heart, either. Instead, we played with our new puppy, and read stories, and painted, and listened to healing music, and ate healthy foods, and went for walks and bike rides. Daily, we hugged and kissed and joked and laughed, which *had* to be medicinal, I told myself. What Sam knew was this: there was a dot in his heart, and that to be sure he stayed healthy we'd see Dr. Angstrom every month, and that everything was going to be okay.

3

COURAGE

a lifeline

In 1997, before Sam was born, we'd moved to Jacksonville from the Miami area. David had accepted an in-house counsel position for what used to be Barnett Bank. Thrilled to go from stucco and palm trees to brick and oak trees, we bought a ranch home with a fireplace and a big backyard.

I remember bringing newborn Sam home from the hospital, carrying him up the front walk, and smiling at the long-roped swing suspended from the old oak tree in our front yard. It looked like a pendulum keeping time, waiting for us. One day, my little boy, the prince of Beauclerc Oaks, would sit there and pump his legs and launch himself into space. Until then, I'd push him up and down our street in his stroller.

After he learned to walk, we went exploring up and down our sidewalk. I followed him, watched over him, shaded him from the sun, protected him while he searched for treasure, and filled his brown bag with acorns, roly-poly bugs, unusual leaves, smooth stones, snail shells, and his favorite, a feather, which he pronounced *theather*.

Before going back inside for a snack or a nap, I would hold out my arms and tell him, "I love you *this* much."

And he would make big circles with his tiny hands. "I love you more than the *world*."

And I would point up. "I love you more than the *sun*."

"I love you more than all the stars and *planets*."

"I love you more than the *universe*!"

And he would outdo me every time. "I love you more than *all* the sidewalks in the world!"

David and I were disappointed when we discovered the old oak with the long-roped swing—the thing that had sold us on buying *that* house—had become diseased and had to be cut down. Two-year-old Sam clapped and cheered at the big truck outside, as well as at the workmen who climbed, roped, and took down that tree section by section, then fed branches into a big, loud, chomping machine that shredded them into mulch. Every time it rained, mushrooms would sprout throughout our front yard in the ghostly shape of the tree's rotting root system.

Before I'd had a baby, a friend once told me, before cutting our call short because "the baby's going to wake up any minute now," that I was clueless. And that one day, when I was knee-deep in dirty diapers and couldn't remember the last time I'd showered, I would "get it."

Boy, did I get it. I had asked for it too! One baby was doable, but then with Joey, I'd doubled my workload. There were times I'd lock myself in the bathroom and cry. I'd hear Sam calling me, then knocking on the door, and I'd feel guilty for hiding, ignoring the jiggling doorknob, and not answering him. On the weekends, David and I tag-teamed, but on weekdays I was on my own with no relatives or close friends nearby to offer a hand. Everyone we knew lived a five to six-hour drive away. Between Joey's infant schedule and demands, Sam's terrible twos and toddler tantrums, the constant feedings, snacks, meals, endless laundry and diapers, combined with a heavy dose of sleep deprivation, I was exhausted—and losing my mind.

One day, needing a lifeline, I called my friend Ivone. Her two boys, also two years apart, were older than mine. She'd lived through this, hadn't she?

I hung on her every word: "Soon, they'll be sleeping through the night. It'll get easier, you'll see. In a few years, you'll be able to go out to dinner again—all four of you. No more bottles, no more diapers. And you'll realize you've made it. It'll get better, I promise. I remember how life changed for us once the boys were four and six. You'll make it. You're almost there," she assured me.

For his sixth birthday, Sam wore a top hat and a black cape with silver stars. A magician came to the house and put on a show. For the finale, as instructed, Sam tapped his wand and said the magic word, "Abracadabra," and from out of her hat, the magician produced a rabbit. For months, he raved about his magic party. "That was the best birthday ever!"

We were *there*. Sam had turned six, and Joey was almost four. Just like my friend Ivone had predicted, we were able to go out to dinner again—the four of us. And, I realized, we'd made it. Life *was* changing, getting better.

This was when I'd started trying to convince David it was time for us to go. Time to leave our old home on Beauclerc Oaks Drive South. I wanted to move away from the extreme sadness that seemed to be embedded in the walls of that old house. Away from that carpeting I had curled up on too many nights and cried. Away from those rooms I had tried to brighten with paint. I wanted to move away from that mass and start over in a new home where the flooring had no history, and the rooms smelled hopeful, and I could picture a brighter future.

Sam's heart hadn't changed in over a year since our first cardiology appointment, and he was doing great. I remember Dr. Angstrom nodding in agreement when I said, "It's possible that Sam might just grow up with this *thing* in his heart, right?" We wouldn't have even known about it if it wasn't for that ear infection. "Maybe he'll even outgrow it." Later that year, we signed a contract on a new home, which was under construction and would be ready by April 2005.

distance

For Sam's seventh birthday, we had a roller-skating party.

As the boys skated, I compared the two. Like Frankenstein on wheels, with his arms straight out, Joey clunked around the rink without breaking a sweat. Sam, I noticed, looked winded, sweaty, and flushed. He had learned to roller-skate at home on the patio, but here, I realized, the continuous effort, circling the rink, required way more endurance. I stayed vigilant, watching, questioning myself: *What if he doesn't self-regulate? Is he working too hard, overexerting himself?* He'd skated long enough, I decided. Acting nonchalant, I waved him in and made it all about hydration.

"Sam, come and drink some water. You look thirsty." He didn't complain about stopping but seemed relieved to sit and drink. "Guess what?" I said, still acting breezy, eyeing him to be sure he looked okay, "It's almost time for pizza, cake, and presents!"

The next month, on April Fool's Day 2005, we moved into our new home in Bartram Springs, a neighborhood named after the American botanist, ornithologist, and explorer William Bartram. In our new neighborhood, there were acres and acres of nature preserves, two playgrounds, basketball courts, a gym, two community pools, and sidewalks that stretched for miles, which meant miles of bike riding, exploring, and searching for treasure.

On our first night, the new house felt cavernous, dark, and empty, and the unfamiliar woods outside were black and spooky. We turned on the floodlight and stared out through the glass doors.

The boys gasped. "What are *those*?"

Meandering through our new backyard were four little armadillos, lost, zigzagging, seemingly confused by the sudden spotlight.

"*Those* are armadillos," I said.

"They're so creepy, Mommy!"

"They're a little creepy, but nothing to be afraid of."

"Can me and Joey camp out with you and Daddy tonight?"

Even though I didn't show it, I was a little spooked by the strange sounds the house made and the dark shapes of unpacked boxes in the corners. "Go grab your sleeping bags. We'll all camp out together," I said.

"Yay!" The boys ran off together, shouting and clapping. "We're going on an adventure!"

That fall, Joey began kindergarten, and Sam, second grade. We had enrolled the boys at the Bank of America Learning Academy, BOALA, a small public school for Bank of America employees, which was in the office park where David now worked. He drove the boys there every morning, and I picked them up every afternoon.

In the beginning of the school year Sam had been given a "special" aptitude test.

"I've never met a child like this before," the school psychologist said to David and me. "He's extremely gifted. Samuel could not have scored any higher."

"What does that mean?" I asked the psychologist.

"He's in the top percentile, Deanna. He's a genius!" David said, skimming the test results.

"You don't seem surprised," the psychologist said.

I shrugged. Sam was brilliant; I knew this. But I also knew this meant he'd be attending two schools: BOALA, Monday through Thursday, and Twin Lakes Elementary on Fridays for the gifted program. He'd ride on a school bus, driven by a stranger, to another, much larger, school farther away. I loved the idea of it, the learning opportunity, but I hated the added distance between us. I would have to get used to the idea, the way I had to get used to how far apart our bedrooms were now in our new house. BOALA was small; everyone there knew the boys. The other school was big, and no one besides his teacher would know Sam. I worried if something happened, if he fell ill and needed me or David, it would take us longer to get to him.

another murmur

It had been three years since I'd sat in a church thumbing through Bible pages, trying to calm the chaos in my mind. I'd connected numbers that seemed meaningful, a '3' for the month of Sam's birth, a '2' for the day, and an '8' because I'd read that patients with malignant cardiac tumors didn't live longer than two years. *If he lived to be eight, then he might live.* And there we were. It was March 2006. Sam had made it to eight: the age I'd been hoping and praying for, the number we'd needed him to get past. While he continued having monthly cardiology checkups, now we felt confident the mass was *not* malignant.

For his eighth birthday, we had Sam's party at Dave & Buster's. He loved playing video games. When he did, it meant he could ride a skateboard or a dirt bike or run or bowl or row a kayak or throw punches in a boxing match without tiring or overexerting himself. On the other hand, *I* never really liked playing video games, so when I put on those boxing gloves and began pummeling the degenerate lunkhead the arcade game's computer had assigned as my opponent, the boys' mouths were hanging open.

It felt good to get out some of my frustration, to swing at someone, to hit some*thing*.

That's for holding us hostage!

To release some pent-up anger.

That's for making us so afraid!

To jab and punch.

That's for torturing us every minute of every day!

I tried to kill that mass, beat it to death with my own fists. The match was over by the third round.

For sure, this was a side of me the boys hadn't seen before. They couldn't believe their eyes and ran to tell David about it.

"Daddy, Daddy! You should've seen what Mommy just did! Whoa, she can really fight! It was a TKO!"

"And you should've seen the other guy's face! She even knocked out his mouthpiece!"

At home, a few months later, the boys were laughing and playing video games one afternoon, and I was folding and putting away laundry when I found Reggie, the dog, lying on the floor in my bedroom. He was stiff, unblinking, staring but not seeing. He looked paralyzed; I thought he'd broken his back. Had he fallen off the bed? He'd taken a tumble once before, while chasing a tennis ball, and sprained his tail. This time he looked worse. I called to the boys and told them we were leaving, to go get their shoes.

"Reggie's *very* sick, and we have to go now!"

I scooped up the dog and hurried the boys out to the minivan.

Sam was on the verge of tears. "What's wrong with him, Mommy? He looks scared. Is he gonna die?"

The veterinarian, a gentle, young woman with a blonde ponytail and big, blue eyes, combed Reggie's body with her stethoscope while I described his contorted posture, distant stare, and stiffness, all of which had receded on the car ride over.

"He seems fine now, but he might've had a seizure," she said, listening for a while longer with her stethoscope. "I also hear a murmur in his heart. He'll need to see a cardiologist and have an echocardiogram to see what's causing that."

What? A murmur, a cardiologist, an echo? The present and the past rammed into each other. I was standing in both places at once: in *this* moment at the veterinarian's office with Reggie, and in *that* moment, that Christmas Eve at the pediatrician's office with Sam. *His fever may be amplifying it . . . but he'll need to see a cardiologist.*

"No," I told the doe-eyed vet. "Right now he's not symptomatic, so we'll just watch him. He's a dog. He's happy, and he has a *great* life. If he develops any symptoms, we'll address it then." *For now, we'll go home and live our lives normally.*

The vet looked puzzled but agreed with me that this could wait.

a pill

At Sam's monthly checkup, in December 2006, Dr. Angstrom said he thought Sam's heart was working too hard and suggested starting him on another beta-blocker, Toprol. This was unexpectedly bad news. He reassured me that a beta-blocker would help ease the workload on Sam's heart. He also suggested that, from now on, we could schedule our checkups every quarter instead of every month. I made a mental note that Sam's next checkup would therefore be in March. I felt nervous about the longer stretch of time between visits, but, to counter the beta-blocker prescription, the need to check his heart less often seemed like unexpectedly good news.

While waiting at the pharmacy, Sam seemed excited about the medication. "I'm old enough to take a pill now, and it'll make my heart better?"

Caught off guard, I had to think on my feet. I spun it the way the doctor had. "These pills are going to help your heart *work* better. And guess what? Instead of going for your echo every month, you only have to go every three months from now on."

He nodded, distracted by the shiny, silver medical alert bracelets displayed by the register. The heading on the order-by-mail cards said, *Keep yourself protected.*

"Should *I* get one of these?" he asked. "They engrave your name on it. That's cool."

"Is that something you'd want to wear?"

He shook his head and tinkered with a charm, studying the red star with the rod and snake on it. "Not really. But it is kinda cool-looking."

I was going to tell him if he really wanted one with his name engraved on it, we'd order it, but just then, the pharmacist returned with a bag and a few pages of warnings and side effects.

Raising his eyebrow, he motioned to Sam. "Is this for him?"

I nodded and brushed Sam's hair with my fingers.

"Do you have any questions about this drug?" the pharmacist asked.

I was concerned and did have questions. This beta-blocker hadn't been tested on the pediatric population. I remembered this from my research, but I also remembered Dr. Angstrom's face, *his* concern.

"Nope, we're good. Thank you," I said, plucking an order-by-mail card off the counter and slipping it into my purse in case Sam changed his mind about the medical alert bracelet later.

> 1/8/07
> I need to improve . . .
> • My science.
> Things I need to complete . . .
> • My 30 books
> Things I want to do . . .
> • Read more
> • Study more
>
> (from Sam's *Writer's Workshop Journal*)

Sam missed only one day of school that year. We'd managed to schedule all doctor, dentist, and orthodontist appointments after school or on "early release" Wednesdays.

At one of our afternoon appointments, Sam's orthodontist asked him how he liked school.

"I love school! I'm studying ancient Egypt this year," Sam said before opening his mouth wide.

"Really? Wow! *That* was unexpected," Dr. Mitchell said, snapping Sam's new retainers into place. "You're in high school now, right?"

"No." Sam laughed and rolled his eyes. "I'm in *third* grade."

He couldn't wait to show his retainers to his classmates. "Mom, aren't they cool? They look like watermelon." He smiled. "Do I look like a teenager now?"

It was the end of January, one morning before school, when Sam said he wasn't feeling well; that his head hurt, and he felt dizzy. He'd been taking Toprol for a little over a month. Was it the medication? Of course it was—it probably was. He hadn't complained of headaches and dizziness before.

"You're taking a sick day today, Sam."

"Mommy, I'm not really that sick."

"That's okay. We're gonna play hooky."

"What's that?"

"Hooky is when you're not really sick, but you stay home from school and rest, stay in bed, eat crackers and soup, work on a puzzle, read a good book . . ."

"Can we play hooky and watch a movie?"

I pinched my brow. "What movie?"

"Can we watch *Eragon*?"

"But you're reading the book. You sure you want to watch the movie before finishing the book?" I said, though I already knew what his answer would be.

Later that morning, we sat, spellbound, snuggled together under a blanket, Reggie nuzzled between us, and watched the movie *Eragon*.

"Mommy, the sapphire stone is really an egg. Inside is a baby dragon—a flying dragon!"

> 1/31/07
> Yesterday I was home sick. I missed school while I
> was gone. I hope I don't miss any more school this
> year.
>
> (from Sam's *Writer's Workshop Journal*)

We celebrated Sam's ninth birthday at Adventure Landing, a theme park in town. He'd made it to nine!

He wore his favorite dress shirt, with blue dragons battling on the front and back, their long tails whipping upward toward the collar, and his favorite jeans with a metal chain (a dollar store find that he'd picked up in the pet aisle) that hung from his pocket, exactly the way his idol Chris Daughtry wore his. I pretended not to notice that he'd cut a small section of hair above his forehead. It stuck out now, too short, stiff with hair gel. Already like a teenager, I thought, my little boy was developing his own style and showing me a possible future version of himself.

He and his friends played mini-golf, video games, and then laser tag. I hated the laser tag part. The room was dark; lights were flashing, and kids were running, shouting, screaming. Joey ran by, but I didn't see Sam.

"David, it's chaos in here! It's too dark. Do you see Sam?"

"I'll find him," David said, disappearing in the confusion.

> 3/26/07
> We just got off of spring break! It's 7:35 Monday. I had a great spring break. First my mom brought me to Target. I bought a new football and my mom bought a new picture frame. The next day, my friend came over and we worked on my music software. I like making songs and mixing. Then I started working on my Report. A couple days later we went shopping for a nice suit for my cousins barmitsva. Then we went to the mall. My dad said we could go to EB Games and pick something out. We bought Lego Start Wars. It is SO good!
>
> (from Sam's *Writer's Workshop Journal*)

At Sam's quarterly heart checkup, after the nurse weighed and measured him, I jotted down the numbers: *58 pounds, 51 ½ inches tall, 3/27/07.*

While Sam and I were alone, waiting in the exam room, he told me he'd written a poem in school that day and recited it for me.

"Some people say noise hurts their head . . . Some people say they wish they were dead . . . All because it's oh so loud . . . But I am absolutely wowed—"

I was jotting down the lines when he reached for the scratch paper I was holding.

"Mommy, I can write the rest."

For I cannot hear a thing
Not a single jingle or a ring
I cannot think of the cause of it
Maybe because I am deaf.

During his echocardiogram, while Sam was lying down, watching a movie, I stood outside that dark room, alone in the hallway. I tried to control my thoughts, curb my fear, and not hear a thing . . .

For four years, I'd listened to those *oh so loud* echoes: Sam's heart beating, swishing, pulsing, whooshing; those intermittent clicks on the keyboard as the ultrasound tech Ruby typed, measuring *that mass*. I'd watched that monitor, Sam's three-dimensional heart undulating, squeezing, pushing swooshes of colors, bright blues and reds. But this day, on what would turn out to be Sam's last checkup, I wanted to be *deaf*, unaffected by those sounds, those noises that had become lodged in my ears, instead of shaking with fear, always anticipating more bad news.

every minute

A few days later, while David and Joey waited in the van, Sam and I ran into Walgreens to pick up snacks for the long drive.

We were headed to South Florida for Jack's bar mitzvah. Four years ago, the boys had been too young to enjoy Shira's bat mitzvah. This time, though, they were excited to wear their new suits and ties and see their older cousins.

Always on task and on time, David would've been angry if he knew that while I was supposed to grab only snacks, I was planning to pick out a new lipstick to go with the new outfit I'd be wearing. When I told Sam my secret, he relished the idea of being part of my roguish plan.

"Don't tell Daddy that Mommy was wasting time picking out lipstick."

"Oh, I won't. It'll be *our* little secret."

I wanted to hug him, my partner in crime, for the way he'd jumped right on board, all-in. Though I knew he'd tell David, I also knew we'd be free and clear, hours later, halfway to our destination, and David would've already eaten the bag of pretzel sticks I grabbed as we passed by a shelf. And I, with the help of my little sidekick, would be packing the perfect shade of lip color. No harm, no foul.

Standing in the makeup aisle, examining colors, Sam held up a tube. "Mom, what about this one?"

"Oh, I like that! What do you think about this one?" He gave me a thumbs-up. "Perfect. We did it! I'll take both, they're BOGO, two-for-one."

We high-fived each other, pleased with ourselves, how agile and sly we were, and sauntered up to the checkout counter holding hands.

Every minute felt fragile. Every minute was weighed down with what *could* happen.

If I had *known* that in one month, in exactly thirty-one days, I would *never* see him again, *never* hold his hand again, *never* hear his laugh again, I would have hugged and kissed him *one* more time in that Walgreens. I would have told him *again* how much I loved him—*more than all the sidewalks in the world!* I would have told him that I would never *ever* forget this day, how happy he'd made me just by picking out a lipstick.

But I *didn't* say or do these things. I paid the cashier, and we hurried back to the idling minivan, where David was impatiently waiting.

"What took you guys so long?"

Sam winked at me, and I smiled at him and lied. "Sorry. Long line."

The next morning, to make better use of the time (and one bathroom), we split into two teams. While David and Joey got showered and dressed, Sam and I ate breakfast in the hotel restaurant.

In a blink, in those precious few minutes, time sped up. Changes that would've taken years I saw happen in seconds, like time-lapse photography. It was in the way he spoke, his voice, and in his eyes too. All of a sudden, they looked more knowing; more savvy, experienced; old before their time. Beneath our table, I felt the ground shifting, the earth falling away, a distance growing between us. A gap *was* widening. In leaps and bounds, Sam had gone from one side to the other, from child to adult. Somewhere along that invisible fault line, my no-longer-a-baby-but-nine-going-on-eighteen-year-old son had started calling me *Mom* instead of *Mommy*. He had a school life where he experienced things I didn't always know about. He cared about the way he looked, what he wore, and had started using hair gel. He had friends and crushes on girls. He rode on a school bus where he saw and heard things that he didn't tell me about. I was okay with the gap. Fine with the idea of growing older and having an adult child. This is what I wanted, more than anything: to envision a future that unfolded into something *even* better.

After breakfast, hurrying back to the room to get ready, we were walking at a brisk pace, but Sam seemed out of breath, as if we'd been running.

Was it a side effect of the medication? Or was it his heart—worsening? I slowed my pace. "We don't need to rush, do we? We've got plenty of time."

We were leaving for the bar mitzvah, all dressed up in our new outfits, when Sam complimented me on my pale linen suit and new shade of lip color. He didn't often see me dressed up, with my hair and makeup done.

"Mom, you look hot!"

I held back a giggle as I replied, "And you and Joey look *so* handsome."

The boys looked like little men in their suits, with crisp, white shirts and clip-on ties.

Just as we were heading out the door, the phone rang.

"Sorry to bother you on your vacation," the pet-sitter said, "but I lost your dog—well, actually, he ran away." She was unapologetic. "It's not my fault. He escaped through your fence."

My stomach flipped. "When? Today? This morning?" I asked, trying to remain calm.

She sounded bothered. "No, yesterday. I tried to find him last night, but . . . Just thought you'd want to know."

My mind raced, trying to figure out what to do when there was nothing I *could* do at that moment. She'd waited almost twenty-four hours to call! I'd interviewed this pet-sitter. She had a résumé. Years of experience. A glossy brochure had told me she was "a seasoned pet-professional."

She'd mentioned that her husband helped out sometimes, and I remembered being adamant about this: "My dog's extremely afraid of men, so you absolutely cannot bring your husband along on this job. Besides, Reggie requires minimal care—food, water, and a quick back-yard bathroom break twice a day."

"Did your husband come inside my house?" I asked her.

"Well . . . yes, but . . . I told you he helps me sometimes. He's the one who's been out searching for Reggie." She seemed to have no recollection of my explicit instructions.

"Great. He's afraid of men, remember? Now he'll run even farther away."

A small indoor dog like ours wouldn't make it out in the wild world of cars and nighttime predators. This was definitely not good for Sam's heart. Mine was already breaking over the loss of my tiny, four-legged son who was now all alone, vulnerable, scared, or possibly dead. Sam was crying as I explained the situation to David. We both knew we might never see Reggie again, but David acted hopeful. "It's going to be okay, Sammy. We'll find him. He's going to be okay."

I tried to sound upbeat. "Come on, guys. We're gonna have a great time today at Jack's bar mitzvah. You'll see. We're gonna have so much fun."

"As soon as it's over, we'll head straight home and find Reggie," David promised.

We cut our trip short, left right after the bar mitzvah, and returned home that night around midnight. David carried Joey to bed. Sam was still awake, upset. I tucked him in and promised we'd keep looking until we found his puppy. David and I took turns driving and walking around the neighborhood, searching and calling out Reggie's name. This was something I hadn't thought through on that Christmas Eve when I'd placed that breadbox in Sam's bed: heart therapy could also turn out to be heartbreak.

Almost three days after Reggie had gone missing, on Monday morning around three a.m., I was lying in bed, eyes open, when I thought I'd heard something. Was that the slap-click sound of the doggy door? It couldn't be. I got up and peered through the glass door. The moon was full and bright, and in the bluish light I spotted him zigzagging, low to the ground, staggering, stumbling, and ran outside and scooped him up.

He'd been eaten alive by mosquitoes or red ants, his eyes were swollen shut, and he was weak and severely dehydrated. After spending the next day at the animal hospital on IV fluids, steroids, and antibiotics, he returned home to cuddles and kisses. Reggie was on the mend, and Sam's heart was happy again.

fortune cookies

One Saturday evening in early April, we went out to our favorite Chinese restaurant for dinner. When the hostess held up four fingers, I smiled and nodded. *Four, yes.*

David, the boys, and I followed her to our usual booth, accompanied by a unit of tiny soldiers—G. I. Joe action figures with painted hair, serious eyes, and "supposable" joints for maximum motion and pose-ability. Joey's hero was Snake Eyes. Sam's favorite was Duke. We placed our usual order: chicken lettuce wraps, walnut shrimp, honey garlic chicken, one bowl of steamed rice, and one bowl of fried rice. Before the food arrived, Sam and Duke rallied their troops in a restaurant rescue mission. The soldiers scaled salt structures and pepper pillars. Joey's man, Snake Eyes, fired a whisper of bullets from behind blue sweetener sandbags: "*Baa-paa-paa-paa-paa.*"

Sam was the voice-over: "Danger! Danger! Surface-to-air missile—fire! Mission survival—repeat—mission survival."

With the same inflection as his big brother, Joey shot back: "He fired! Mission survival—repeat—mission survival."

Life-and-death themes recurred in Sam's play, stories, and artwork. He drew explosions, fires, police cars, rescue trucks, action heroes rushing to different scenes, and lone figures waving their arms from the tops of tall buildings as rescuers yelled from below, their words in speech bubbles: "Jump into the net!"

We never talked about it, the *d*-word, but I knew he thought about death, about his heart. He was too deep of a thinker to not think about it.

I remember the time we saw that *SpongeBob* episode, "All that Glitters," in which a spatula, whom we *think* is Spat, SpongeBob's spatula, has died. Hearing the electronic whine and seeing the flat, red line on the monitor beside his bed, and noticing the way eight-year-old Sam was staring at that red line and at SpongeBob who was crying at the spatula's bedside, I felt paralyzed, afraid to move or comment on what had just happened. But then, a cartoon doctor appeared and informed SpongeBob that *his* spatula was all patched up and ready to leave the infirmary. A happy ending! We laughed with relief. Survival *was* possible. It *had* to be.

Another time, when Sam was six, we'd been invited to the local news station to film a public service announcement for the upcoming Heart Walk. Pediatric heart patients surrounded the anchor as she touched up her makeup, then smiled at the camera and spoke. Off camera, she asked the children about their scars. "Lift up your shirts!" she said, almost like a cheer. Several smiling children began showing off what looked like tiny tire tracks on their chests. She applauded. "I bet you can all run faster now that your hearts are all better!"

In slow motion, it seemed, Sam was gaping, horrified, turning to look at all those scars jumping up and down around him. I moved quickly toward him, took him by the hand, and we left. We didn't belong there. I reprimanded myself. *Why did you take him there? What were you thinking?*

On the long drive home, he asked me if *his* heart could be fixed. I didn't think it was age-appropriate to tell him that a fix would mean a heart transplant, another child's heart. I imagined answering his next questions: *Yes, if another child dies, he or she wouldn't need it anymore . . . No, you'd have to be very sick, and since you're not sick . . .*

He wasn't sick, which was true, and his heart was strong, which is what I told him.

Sitting in our booth at the Chinese restaurant, waiting for our main course to arrive, I savored the dogged way the boys bit the crisp, oversize lettuce wraps and lapped up stray bits of meat. The excited way we all talked with our hands. The funny things we said or did and how much we all laughed. That was the most delicious part—the laughter.

After dinner, along with the check and four fortune cookies, the waiter gave each of the boys a Chinese calendar.

"I was born the Year of the Tiger!" Sam declared. "I'm courageous, magnetic, and unpredictable."

I checked Joey's calendar and pointed to his birth year. "You and I were born the Year of the Dragon," I showed him. "We're intelligent, powerful, and lucky. Oh, and look, Daddy's a tough, honest, and faithful ox."

We all cracked open our fortune cookies, and while we munched and chomped on them, we read our fortunes.

Still entertaining myself imagining David as an ox, I grinned and read my fortune aloud. "Mine says, 'A merry heart does good like a medicine.'"

Then Sam announced his: "Mine says, 'Courage is not the absence of fear; it is the conquest of it.'"

L.I.V.E.D.

On April 14, 2007, a Saturday afternoon, I found Sam in his room, sitting at his desk, hunting and pecking letters on his computer's keyboard, writing a story.

I remember feeling especially fatigued and wanting to lie down. I stretched and yawned, then flopped onto his bed and burrowed into his pillows. "Whatcha doing, Sammy?"

"I'm writing a thriller . . . but you *can't* read it."

"Well, now I *have* to."

He rolled his eyes and printed a copy for me.

L.I.V.E.D.

Living In a Vivid Ecological Demension

by Sam K., age 9

"Wow, Sam, I love the title, and the subtitle is great too!" I didn't mention the spelling error and continued reading.

This morning I woke up, or I was woken up by what sounded like shattering glass.

I looked at the clock on my bedside table: 2:34 am. "Wait a minute," I looked at the door and then back at my clock. "Ma? No what am I thinking? It's a Sunday, she won't be up for a good while."

I shivered and cautiosly got out of bed but the moment my foot touched the carpet, a seering pain shot through my body. A blinding red light filled my room. Next thing I knew, was that I was on the floor, holding my head screaming. The strange thing was, it only lasted about 5 seconds. I got up, still shaky, and looked out the window. It was raining quite hard outside. There was a flash of lightning, but in the flash of lightning, I could just make out a shadow, but the second time the lightning flashed, I noticed that the shadow had no owner, it had glowing red eyes, and was looking straight at me.

I'm Lex, I have a brother, Jio, my mom, Judy, and my dad, Soline'. I have alot of New York in me, but my dad is from Paraguay. It's tough being in New York High, but I get a great education. We live in New York City on 42nd Street. Anyway, that morning was probally the most freaky morning ever.

After I saw the figure out the window, I stood there thinking, that didn't just happen, I'm dreaming. But that morning at breakfast, I was proved wrong. I walked down the hallway still thinking of what I saw that night. I looked down at my oatmeal, but I noticed something strange. A paper was sticking out from underneath the bowl. I slipped it out and read,

This is the day you die,

Zalhasaxe

I looked at the name, Zalhasaxe, I had no idea who that was, and I didn't think I wanted to. I looked down at the paper, and right before my eyes, new letters spread across the paper.

Behind you.

I whipped around to see what was there, and then regreted it. A hidious, black, slimy looking creature was less then a foot away from me. It had a human shaped body and revolting red eyes with strangley small pupals that were rather freaky. "Hi." It said *with a grossdeque look.. I jumped and knocked my oatmeal off the table.*

"He,ee,hey," It sniggered crossing his arms, but apparently, he didn't cross them, instead, he reached behind it's back. there was a soft, swing, and there, in his hand, a bloody, rusted, five foot long, sword.

I sat there, stunned. "this is life, sucks eh?" It said raising the sword. "Really, sucks. . ." My brain worked harder than ever. "Well let's get it done with" It happened to quick. The tip of the sword slashed my arm leaving blood trickle all over the floor. It lifted the sword again, but this time it freezed right in the middle of swinging it, and in a blink of an eye, it vanished. I turned around examining the new wound on my right arm. I noticed that the letter on the table had vanished too. Now blood was more than trickling down, it was more like splattering everywhere. Then I heard footsteps above. No, I thought, No.

My mom would surely pass out if she saw blood splattering from my arm onto the hardwood floor!

"Sammy, it's good, so good, but hideous. So scary! What goes on in that big brain of yours?"

It was *only* an imaginative thriller, I told myself, and nothing more. Imagining a nightmare—*This is the day you die*—does *not* mean the nightmare will happen. I *had* to convince myself of this while masking my fear, acting amazed, and maintaining a smile. But we could read each other's thoughts; we always knew when the other was pretending to be brave.

Courage is not the absence of fear; it is the conquest of it.

The following weekend, on Sunday, April 22, 2007, with their allowance money burning a hole in their pockets, David took the boys to the bookstore where Sam was thrilled to find, instead of a book, an ancient Egyptian mummy kit. In his enrichment program at school, the theme for that year was ancient Egypt, and we'd recently gone on a field trip to the Cummer Museum on the Saint Johns River in Jacksonville, to stroll through its gardens and galleries, and explore an ancient Egyptian exhibit.

The kit included a plastic mummy, a full-color funerary mask, mummy-wrapping gauze, plastic canopic jars, protective amulet stickers, and, of course, the essential cardboard pet cat mummy. Looking back, I wonder if, besides writing stories, this was another way Sam might have been processing his emotions and fears—through the ritual and art of preparing his toy mummy for the afterlife.

smoke

There were wildfires burning nearby that day—Sunday, April 29, 2007. Morning news reports warned that the poor air quality posed health concerns. According to the American Heart Association, inhaling tiny particles in smoke from forest fires could increase the danger of acute heart problems.

Sam wanted to spend the day at a friend's house.

"Do you mind, Joey, if I go to Hannah's without you today?" he asked.

Joey saw his brother's friends as his friends, too, and usually went with Sam. Despite the two-year age difference, Joey kept up with the older kids' advanced humor and conversation. If a punch line went over his head, or someone sped through the rules of a game, he was expert at pretending to understand, then observing and mirroring what he saw. I listened and waited to see how things played out, expecting Joey to complain. He didn't, which was unusual.

"We'll do something special today, Joey," I offered as a consolation prize. "You, Daddy, and me, just us three."

Since the air outside was so hot, thick, and smoggy, we made plans to do something indoors.

After dropping Sam off at the Linden's house to play with Hannah, David, Joey, and I drove to the mall where we strolled, held hands, and visited our usual places: the Discovery Store, the pretzel stand, and the pet shop. We weren't used to being three, and it felt off-balance.

Later, leaving the mall, I noticed the darkening sky. Streaks of blackish powder were spreading like hideous fingers, reaching too close. Worrying about Sam's heart, I felt more anxious and alarmed than usual; I wanted us all home safe. On the drive back, with the windows closed, air-conditioning whispering, each of us lost in our own thoughts, I heard a siren blaring in the distance. I turned and looked at the back seat, at Sam's empty booster, then at Joey sitting beside it, and we smiled at each other. I can't explain why; it was just this way: David and Joey and I were the planets, and Sam was the sun we revolved around. He was the energy that kept us alive and on course. Facing forward again, I held back tears and prayed, pleaded, *Please keep us safe. Sam's heart, I need him to live; we need him. Keep us together, please, please...*

When we arrived at the Linden's house, Joey scrambled out of the car to join Sam and Hannah. While the kids played "just a few more minutes," David and I caught up with Hannah's parents, Kim and Dave. We had become good friends after the kids met in preschool. Our families had blended into two homes with four parents, two sons, and a daughter. We shared the same politics and beliefs, liked the same foods, and had the same sick sense of humor. One weekend, after dinner, the kids dared Dave to drink the "broccoli water" leftover from the steamed broccoli. They were retching with disgust as he guzzled down the green elixir, and then they erupted into laughter after he finished it. In moments like this, everything seemed like it would be okay. How could it not be? We were doing everything right: eating broccoli, living, laughing...

A merry heart does good like a medicine.

It was apocalyptic outside, but inside our air-conditioned world, sitting on our comfortable cushions, it was festive. Grown-ups talking, laughing; kids chattering and giggling at the google-eyed chameleon, Fifi, who was out of her terrarium, gripping and entertaining her audience . . . the living room was literally full of life. Pancake the Turtle was paddling and bobbing in the huge, green fish tank. The unnamed sucker fish was stuck to the glass, mouth wide open, vacuuming slime. Patch, the spotted dog, was standing on the periphery, tail wagging, and Lump, the lazy tabby cat, was curled on a chair, the tip of her tail twitching. On the desk across the room, a large computer monitor was playing a slideshow of photos—vacations; pets; Hannah's cousins; outdoor adventures; kids with gaping smiles, their arms hugging a gigantic boa constrictor at Hannah's recent reptile birthday party. Every few minutes, one of us would interrupt the conversation and point out a photo and laugh.

"Oh my gosh! Remember that day . . .?"

"Have you guys backed up all your photos?" I asked. "I finally did it yesterday; backed up *all* my photos. Everything."

They hadn't, they said. How could they be so nonchalant about their photos? I thought. Didn't they think it could happen to them—that *their* computer might crash? But then, most people didn't obsess over losing their photos the way I did.

I had to be vigilant. I was the picture taker, the memory keeper, family historian, photographing and cataloging our days. How satisfying it had felt tackling this long overdue project: saving copies of all my digital files, stories, and photos; clicking, dragging, and organizing them into those tiny, yellow folders. But while I was busy being vigilant, life flashing before my eyes, scanning thousands of images into my memory, my computer's memory, my external hard drive's memory, safeguarding them from loss, death was less than two days away.

It was a school night and getting late, so we gathered the boys and said our goodbyes.

"They had so much fun today—all day long," Kim told me. "The two of them talked and played and laughed nonstop."

Hannah stood in her driveway with her parents and waved good-bye, and the boys continued waving in the back window until we turned the corner.

Driving home together, our world was back in balance. We were four again: three planets orbiting their sun. And though I couldn't see it, I knew the almost full moon was above us, bright and beaming, somewhere beyond that dark blanket of smoke.

4
MONDAY

afraid

4/30/07
Last weekend I wrote a new song that I think is
really good! I need to work more on the lyrics but
otherwise it's perfect. I've been reading a lot of
Harry Potter and the Half-Blood Prince and I'm
almost done. I also went to my friend's house.
There's a contest where if you spell N-I-N-T-E-N-D-
O-D-S-L-I-T-E with the letters on the front of the
cheese stick wrappers you get a free Nintendo DS
and because my friend already has one, she was
going to give it to me. We only need 4 more letters
until we win!

(from Sam's *Writer's Workshop Journal*; his last entry)

I've replayed that last morning, that Monday, April 30, 2007, over and over.

How he had called me *Mama* instead of *Mommy* or *Mom.*

"Good morning, Mama."

In those private moments, at bedtime or just after waking up, Sam would soften his voice, regress to that younger, more innocent version of himself, and I would coddle him and play along, remembering those early mornings long ago when he used to call out from his crib.

"Mama. Mama?" And how we used to sit together on the back patio, he with his bottle, me with my cup of coffee, and watch the starry sky turn from blackish-blue to pinkish-turquoise.

He was up earlier than usual and ready for school, dressed in his favorite jeans and powder-blue polo shirt. He padded by me holding a book to his chest, and I smiled. "Good morning, baby." The fruity scent of his hair gel filled the air. The way he'd combed his curls, I wondered if there was a girl he wanted to impress.

It was quiet, still dark outside. From the kitchen, I admired him for a minute, his profile, his concentration, the way he was sitting in the recliner, his feet not yet reaching the ground, sneakers too bulky for his slight frame. He was reading *Harry Potter and the Half-Blood Prince,* and eager to finish it so he'd be ready for the seventh and final book in the series, *Harry Potter and the Deathly Hallows*, which would be out soon. I noticed on his forearm, just above his glowing green Timex, what looked like specks of dirt, the remnants of a fifty-cent vending machine tattoo. It had been over a month since we'd gone out for pizza, and I'd given the boys quarters to buy those tattoos. Trying to make it last longer, Sam had avoided washing that arm.

A few minutes later, Joey was up, and the morning sped up. The TV was blaring, SpongeBob was cackling, the boys were giggling, and David's electric razor was buzzing in the background. I made the boys waffles with peanut butter and sliced bananas for breakfast, then packed two peanut butter and jelly sandwiches, chips, cookies, and yogurts, and zipped up two lunchboxes. On Joey's, Scooby-Doo was grinning, silly and clueless. On Sam's lunchbox, a printed version of his G. I. Joe action figure Duke was serious, crouched and ready for battle.

No matter how many times I replay that morning, or the days leading up to that Monday, it always ends with this: David is backing out of the driveway, and I'm standing in my usual spot to wave goodbye. The boys always turned and waved; it was our thing. But this day, Sam didn't look back. He didn't wave goodbye. Joey did, but Sam didn't. He had PE on Mondays, and I worried that he was worried about that.

"I'm the slowest runner in the class," he'd shared with me a few weeks earlier.

"But you have the fastest mind," I told him. "Some kids are fast runners. Some are fast readers—like you. But very few are as smart as you. Maybe you're not the fastest runner, but you *are* the fastest learner."

"Yeah. I *am* the fastest learner, aren't I?"

"Yes, you are. When you were little, you used to say, 'Amn't I?' Do you remember that? I didn't even know *amn't* was a word. You're *my* teacher. I'm *always* learning from you!"

"I love you, Mommy."

"And I love *you*."

When David walked the boys into school, he stood in his usual spot to wave goodbye. Joey went to the right, to his first-grade classroom, and turned and waved. Sam went to the left, where the other third graders were filing in, but he didn't look back. David would tell me this later. "Sam didn't turn around. He didn't wave."

It was around nine thirty when I convinced myself it was a good day to renew my New Year's resolution and start exercising. The air smelled fresh compared to yesterday's thick and ominous smoke and ashes from the nearby forest fires. Gauging by the cloudless, blue sky, the wind had shifted.

In the gym, a man wearing a navy-blue Fire Rescue T-shirt was lifting weights.

"Hey." He smiled. "How's it going?"

He seemed calm, so I acted calm too. "Good." I smiled back.

Why didn't Sam wave goodbye? He's okay. No. Something's off. Stop it. He's okay. Everything's okay. I tried to think normal thoughts, but the weight-lifting paramedic had rattled me. Was he just a blip on my radar, or was he an omen, a premonition, an intuitive ping to pay attention to? My anxious and overactive imagination always got the better of me. If I had called the school that morning and told them, forewarned them, would this have changed the outcome? But what would I have said? *Sam is going to need medical attention. When? Not sure. I just saw a paramedic lifting weights. Please, just in case, call 911.* And how many times could I do this before becoming the insane mom who cried wolf?

I fussed with the metal pin stuck in a tower of weights, pretended to understand the directions and diagrams on the circuit training machine, and continued with my first and last workout of the year.

I was eating lunch when my friend Terri called to tell me that one of our high school classmates had died.

"She may have taken her own life," she said, sounding shocked, as if she couldn't believe her own words.

She *chose* death, I thought. "It happens. We die," I said.

My friend went silent. I should've apologized, but I was angry at the world, at that mass in Sam's heart. No one really understood my fear, my constant state of alert, my mission, my fight, my fatigue. I was irritable and snappish. *Death is all around us. Everywhere. Every minute. Why does everyone pretend it isn't?*

I was afraid when Sam got overheated or winded, rode his bike, his scooter, or got too sweaty. I worried that he might become dehydrated, and his heart . . .

I was afraid when he caught a cold or slept too soundly or said he felt funny but that he would be fine. All it took was one missed warning to go from *fine* to . . .

I was afraid when we were together that I might not know what to do if his heart . . .

I was afraid when we were apart that someone else might not know what to do . . .

I was afraid that morning because he didn't wave goodbye.

Why didn't he look back, like every other day, and wave goodbye to us? Was he feeling funny, unwell, afraid? Was something weighing on his mind?

At the beginning of the school year, I had reminded Sam's teacher, Ms. Winson, about Sam's "heart condition," and she had lovingly reassured me, "I'll be his mama when you're not here. Don't you worry."

It was different when I tried to remind his other teacher, Coach Paul, a formidable man, to *please* keep a close eye on Sam during phys ed. He didn't quite face me when I stopped him in the hallway, but stood half turned, a relay racer eager to run. So I kept it brief and repeated what Dr. Angstrom had advised. "Sam's cardiologist said he shouldn't push himself. As long as he self-regulates and rests when he feels tired or winded, he can take part in normal activities, but no competitive sports." I thought he might heed the warning if it came from a man, a doctor, and not just me, an anxious, overprotective mom.

"That boy looks just fine to me," he said, and then he was off.

This wasn't the first time I'd heard this. If he had at least used Sam's name, I might've taken some comfort in that. I was alone again on that desert island, sending out another SOS, trying to warn someone who thought *that boy looks just fine* that the possibility of the worst, most unpredictable kind of death was real. I wanted to scream: EVEN IF YOU CAN'T SEE IT OR BELIEVE IT, BELIEVE *ME!*

After this, I asked Sam if he liked his PE teacher. "Is he ever mean to you, or too strict?"

"No, he's *really* funny. He says things like, 'You kids use those juicy eyeballs and pay attention!'"

running

It was around one o'clock when the third graders lined up for PE along the wall in the hallway just outside their classroom.

"I'll never forget how he smiled up at me just before going out-side," Sam's teacher would tell me a few weeks later.

Outside on the playground, Coach Paul sent the class on their warm-up laps.

Sam was running beside his closest friend, Seth, when he stumbled and fell.

Nothing broke his fall. Not even his own hands. The earth, with its unforgiving gravity, struck my sweet boy's perfect face. The impact injured his perfect nose, his perfect lips. And I wasn't there to protect him, or save him, or shade him from the blazing afternoon sun.

"He just collapsed," the school administrator would tell me later. "I don't think he felt any pain."

How could she know? She'd said this to ease *my* pain. I wasn't there, but I still see these unerasable, unimaginable images. *Sam run-ning. Laughing, talking? Or not. Feeling pressure in his chest? Pain? Or nothing at all. A skipped beat, loss of power. Heart, stopping. Tumbling. Collapsing. Remnants of his fifty-cent vending machine tattoo, his Timex, the second hand still ticking, lying on the ground. His face. His eyes. The cloudless sky, the heat of the day. Children running, unaware. Then chaos. Someone shouting, "Call 911!"*

I was finishing my grocery list when the phone rang.

I checked the caller ID: *Bank of America*. It wasn't David's num-ber. Was it the school calling? My heart started pounding. I froze and stared at the phone, held my breath, and stood completely still as if I could wield some sort of influence over time by not moving. As if I could stop the world from turning and confuse Death so it would loosen its grip and leave empty-handed.

How many rings, how many wasted seconds did I stand there shak-ing my head until the rest of my body took over?

"Hello?" My voice sounded hollow.

"Deanna! Something happened to Sam! I don't know! David ran out!" a woman's voice (David's assistant, Valerie?) was shouting in my ear.

I knew. Every spinning particle of me knew.

My body lurched, dropped the phone, and ran. Bounding and panting like a frenetic dog, I ran outside into the sunlight, blind but focused. In this nightmare, I was the observer *and* the one falling. I saw myself from outside myself, flooring the gas pedal, wind hollering, engine roaring, driving, nearing 90 miles per hour, forcing my minivan through traffic, crying and yelling, "Please! No! No! No! No!" Drivers were on their cell phones, clueless, in my way. "Move! MOVE!" I pounded the steering wheel, willing Sam's heart to beat, honking the horn with my fist. "Sammy! No! No! No! No! No!"

From that stretch of US 1, speeding past marshland on one side of me, trees and train tracks on the other, it would take another ten minutes to get to the school. I was gauging the time when I saw a huddle of policemen up ahead, standing beside their cars and pointing radar guns in my direction—a speed trap. Through my open window, I started shouting, "Help! Help! Please! Help!" Did they hear me? Or was I the only one in this nightmare who could hear my screams?

I kept driving, honking my horn, trying to get around the cars and SUVs that seemed to purposely be blocking me, ignoring the incessant blaring of my horn and the approaching sirens.

I found out afterward that, while I was driving, a woman named Sandra, whom I've never met, was performing CPR on my little boy. David had sped to the school, which was only a minute away from his office. A fire engine and a fire rescue truck were arriving, and David, who was at Sam's side then, was waving and shouting at them from the playground, "Defibrillator! He needs a defibrillator!"

When I saw a police car and motorcycle in my rearview mirror, I pulled over and launched myself out of my minivan. Through the muffled sounds of tires skidding, motors revving, and traffic buzzing by, I heard my gravelly footsteps and saw myself running toward the police car, waving my hands, shouting, bawling in between gasps. "My son! His heart! His heart stopped! Help us!"

Through the cloud of dust kicked up from his tires, through his open car window, the officer squinted at me. "Get in!" he ordered.

I fumbled for the rear door handle.

"No! Here, in front!" He pushed the door open and held out a blue strap. "Seat belt!"

Tim Twisdale wore a midnight-blue uniform, and above his metal name tag was another metal pin, a silver ring with wings. I would come to learn that the winged wheel signified swift, precise motion—the wheel for motion, the wings for speed—and that to wear this pin, one must pass the most dangerous and difficult school of law enforcement. There was something more, though. It took only seconds for my racing mind to register and confirm the details: experienced posture, precise hair, straight face, and serious eyes. And then, in a flash, I knew who he was: Sam's action figure, Duke.

The cruiser's acceleration, siren, signals, clicks, and electronic noises lulled me as we sped through traffic. I felt disoriented but hyperaware of every sound, every vibration in the air. In between beeps and radio static, voices were murmuring in a language of numbers and codes I couldn't decipher. I tried to focus on Sam's heart. I tried to pray. I begged. I hoped and hoped—*Please, please be alive. Just live, please* ... I tried to message him through our telepathic mother-son connection. *Sammy, I'm almost there. I'm coming. Hold on, Sammy. Mommy's coming.* I tried to keep believing, hoping for a miracle, hoping that Sam was still alive.

I noticed Duke then, leaning forward, listening, straining to hear something. Could he hear it, too, vibrating in the air around us? Sam's energy, his voice?

Soldier down, Duke! Soldier down! Take care of my mom! I'll cover my dad!

Running the red light, siren blaring, we turned left toward the school. At the playground, I jumped out of the cruiser and ran toward the chaos: a fire truck, a rescue truck, David's car parked beside the playground, flashing lights, droning engines, voices, men in blue shouting, running. They were carrying Sam—his body bound to a stretcher, his face covered, tape and tubes—and pushing on his bare chest. David running alongside paramedics, red doors slamming shut. Stopping, lost, I didn't know what to do, where to go. I stood staring through the back window of the fire rescue truck at David inside staring back at me.

"One of the worst moments," he told me later, "was seeing you standing there crying, alone."

I heard someone shouting my name. *Sammy? Duke?* I followed the voice back to the police car and climbed in again.

Ms. Alder, the school's principal, was sitting in the back seat behind the metal mesh. "I'm here," she said. "I'm here."

As we hurtled through space, radio voices murmuring, engines bellowing, sirens wailing, I saw our convoy—a police motorcycle, a police car, a fire rescue truck—blaring and bleeding through traffic on I-95.

In the rescue truck, paramedics worked while David reassured Sam and made phone calls. He'd gone over this drill in his head countless times. He'd prepared a list. He'd kept phone numbers ready. He called Dave Linden, Hannah's dad, who was also a police officer, and arranged for him to pick up Joey after school. He called Sandy, his father, who was a five-hour drive away.

"Dad, we're going to need help taking care of Joey! We're going to need help while Sammy is in the hospital! Sammy, Daddy's here—I'm here, baby—I'm here, Daddy's right here."

The drive downtown to the children's emergency center seemed to take an hour, or was it fifteen minutes? Time was stretching, twisting, bending. In the car windows we passed, I saw warped reflections of flashing lights alternating with sky and drifting clouds, an occasional impassive face, and more drivers on cell phones, insulated in their intact and air-conditioned worlds. A child was dying, soldiers were fighting, and yet cars and SUVs continued blocking the battle.

I tried to focus on the red, flashing lights and imagine Sam's heart still beating. *Please, Sammy... Live. Wake up. Please, please, be awake. Please ... You'll wake up. Sammy, you'll wake up. And we'll be home again, eating Popsicles or Pop-Tarts—whatever you want. Please wake up, please...*

"Move! MOVE!" Duke yelled and swatted at the windshield, willing cars out of the way. He moved into the median with swift, precise motion and sped alongside the highway's cement divider, faster then, pressing on.

Mission survival, Duke ... Repeat ... Mission survival!

silence

When we pulled up outside the hospital's pediatric emergency room, I left the police cruiser and ran. I heard doors slamming, footsteps running, voices shouting, the gurney's clumsy metal wheels whirling, gnashing the pavement. I saw Sam's small, pale body and David running beside the paramedics. A cyclone of people wearing scrubs took over. Through the running and shouting, a woman climbed on top of Sam. She balanced on her knees, straddling him, arms straight, hands together, pushing, counting.

"WHAT MEDS DOES HE TAKE?" someone hollered.

"TOPROL!" I shouted back, thinking maybe, maybe, that was the *one* word, the key, that might save my boy.

Inside the ER, the running stopped, and the woman climbed down.

"No. Keep trying!" I begged. "Please, keep trying!"

Climbing up, another woman assumed the position, flat hands, pushing, pushing, counting, "One and two and three and ..."

David and I kept shouting, pleading, encouraging Sam, so he would hear our voices and know we were there. "Come on, Sammy, you can do it! Come on, baby! Come back! Come back! Come back, Sammy! Please come back! Sammy . . ."

I stood at his feet, my face touching his toes. I kept my eyes on his perfect toes. I kissed them and pressed my face against their softness. They were too cold. His naked, dovish body was passive but convulsing from the relentless pushing. I screamed in my head at the chaos, the tubes, the tape, the needles. Inside of me, a rabid animal was howling, biting, snapping at the chaos, then backing down, whimpering when the cyclone of people appeared to be giving up. *No! Please don't stop! Keep trying! Please! Please, Sammy, live. Live. Come on! Please, please come back! Sammy, come back!*

I skimmed the room, looking for any remote chance of a miracle. I saw a black monitor with glowing green numbers but no lines; it was blank. I looked behind me. The police officer I'd come with had stayed. He furrowed his brow, and his serious eyes mirrored mine. We wanted the same thing, to do *something*, but all we could do was stand there and stare, powerless.

And then, the pushing and counting and shouting, it all stopped. The silence was deafening. The monitor was black, with no glowing numbers. The chance of that one small but still possible miracle had been switched off.

"He never had a rhythm," I heard the ER doctor say.

But he had a rhythm. He has a rhythm. I wanted to argue but couldn't speak.

He turned and faced me. "You know he's not here anymore. That's not him. He's gone."

I looked back at the police officer. He lowered his head, turned away, and then he was gone too.

I didn't know what to do.

Someone covered Sam's body with a blanket.

No. No. No. No. Staring at his cherubic face, his sleeping eyes, caterpillar lashes, and bow-shaped lips, I was careening over a cliff into some dark, unknowable chasm in my mind, falling, flailing, searching, reaching out. *I'm here, Sammy. I'm over here! Where are you?*

There's a myth that says if you're falling in a dream and you hit the ground, you'll die in real life. I was waiting to hit the ground, waiting to die. My thoughts were already dying, colliding in midair, when a strange voice woke me.

"His curls are lovely," a woman said.

What? Who the hell are you? I glared at her.

"And that complexion," the presumptuous stranger continued. "Did he play soccer?"

In a blind rage, I stabbed her with my eyes, and David ordered her to leave. I didn't know who she was or what she wanted, but I continued stabbing her with my thoughts after she left.

Dr. Angstrom, Sam's cardiologist, appeared—or had he been there all along? I remember the pained expression on his face—his watery eyes, the way they held my boy, our boy. He loved him too. He *knew* Sam's heart.

"I don't know what to do!" I cried, reaching out from the chasm, still hoping there was something someone could do. But like the policeman, Dr. Angstrom was powerless. I could almost see his thoughts, like mine, colliding and dying. He held me. Or I went to him and held him. I don't recall, but I know we held each other.

"I don't know what to do!" I repeated.

"You don't have to do anything," he whispered.

I wandered back to Sam. Leaning over him, wanting to hold him, I nudged his cheek with my nose and pressed my chest, my heart, to his. When a froth of blood wept from his nose, I scanned the room. "Where is his nurse?" It was too bright. Everything was blurry. Dr. Angstrom came into focus and handed me a white towel. Gently, I cleaned my baby's face. Like a nearsighted newborn who needs to be within inches of its mother's face to see it, I needed to be closer to my beautiful boy's face. I needed his face. I needed to see it, breathe it, melt into it, memorize it, stay with it, with him.

Unable to stand any longer, someone, David, I think, helped me climb up onto the narrow gurney. Lying beside Sam, I pressed my forehead against his and smelled him the way I did after the nurse had laid him in my arms after his birth. I nuzzled my face against his neck, inhaled his scent, placed my arm over his chest, and molded my body against his.

I'm here, Sammy. I'm right here. Mommy's here.

Face to face, our souls held one another, and we stayed like this and slept. For how long, I don't know. Time wrung its hands and turned its face and waited while we slept.

Before he was born, we'd kept a running list of names. David liked Nolan, after Nolan Ryan. I like Gray, after Gray Grantham, a cool and handsome investigative reporter in a John Grisham novel. We considered Daniel, Reese, James, or Joseph, wanting a name that would fit a baby, a child, and a man. Something timeless.

"What about Sam?"

I don't recall who said it first, but as soon as we heard it, we knew.

His name would be Samuel. We'd call him Sammy, Baby Sam, Shmuel, Shmu, or Sam-I-Am. After all, he was born on the same day, March 2, as Theodor Seuss Geisel, Dr. Seuss. But mostly, we'd call him Sam.

Childbirth is usually depicted as a screaming, sweating, panting, and frantic experience. It wasn't that way for me. During my labor and delivery, there was no screaming, just nervous silence. I was cold and shivering, not sweating. Holding my breath, not puffing and panting. I never felt frantic, only afraid. During those minutes when the baby's heart rate dropped, something seemed wrong.

The nurse pressed a button and called for help. Like a ghost, fear crept into the room. If anyone was talking, I didn't hear voices, only those fast, high-pitched beeps, the baby's heartbeat, and then a fluttering sound of paper as the doctor put on a pale-yellow, parchment-like robe.

"You need to push now, or I'll have to pull him out," he said, holding up a medieval vacuum device.

I nodded and held my breath and pushed. I vomited, then continued pushing. My body tore. Blood vessels in my eyes burst. And my baby's cries broke the silence. His tiny hands, I noticed, seemed to be reaching out for something unseen in the air.

As the nurse weighed and wrapped our baby in a blanket, David counted his ten perfect fingers and ten perfect toes and announced over his shoulder, "He's perfect."

Before we left the hospital, the nurse had inked and pressed his tiny footprints onto paper. "A keepsake for his baby book," she suggested, handing me the page. At home, I removed the pastel baby-boy hospital bracelet from his delicate ankle and cleaned the traces of ink from his corn-niblet toes. I swaddled him in his Tiny Tunes blanket, covered his tiny hands with tiny tube socks to protect him from his tiny fingernails, and laid him in his crib. He looked like a dazed boxer defending himself, the way he pawed at his puffy cheeks and tapped on his swollen eyes.

I lay in the daybed beside his crib and listened to his breathing, his rhythm of delicate purrs, whimpers, and puppy sounds. When it was quiet, and there were no sounds, I'd check him, watching for the subtle rise and fall of his chest. It was the silence I feared most.

staying

"It's time to go." I heard David's voice.

Time to go? I needed to stay longer. Even animals stay longer before leaving their dead. A bereaved dolphin will swim with its deceased calf for days, pushing and keeping it above the surface. *Breathe.* Elephants will stand over their dead, rocking back and forth, gently touching the deceased. *I'm here.* Wolves will linger and wander in patterns, ears back, tails dropped, as if searching. *Where are you?* When your child is suddenly gone, how long is too long to keep pushing, touching, or lingering over him? I needed him to breathe. I needed him to know I would never leave him. I needed to keep searching. I needed more time. Maybe he wasn't really gone.

In survival mode, my brain was shutting down, splitting in two. I was sane *and* insane. Now, years later, I realize my inability to process what had happened, my *insanity*, was a normal and sane reaction to an abnormal and unimaginable event.

"I don't think I can walk," my sane voice said. *What if he wakes up and we're not here?* Then a wheelchair appeared. *No. I'm not leaving him.*

"It's time to go," David insisted.

No, I'm staying. Rocking back and forth, standing over my son, I watched as we, David and I, passed through that doorway and left. But then, inside my broken mind, I lay back down beside my little boy. With my hand on his chest, my face to his face, eyelash to eyelash, I stayed . . . and lingered . . . and wandered in patterns . . . and waited.

Sam, when you wake up, I'll be right here.

I'd left that hospital nine years before, holding a pink-and-blue-striped baby blanket filled with his life, to love, to protect. I clutched discharge papers, and his tiny footprints stamped in black ink.

Now, I was leaving again—leaving him?—this time holding a pocket folder, bereavement brochures, and a plastic bag containing his sneakers, his socks, and his watch. (It did not hold his favorite jeans or his powder-blue polo shirt. These were missing; they'd been cut away from his body.) Later, I'd be appalled to find in the plastic bag Sam's hand and footprint stamped on a page in green ink, and a small, heart-shaped box containing a lock of his hair. I suspected that same presumptuous stranger who'd commented on his curls was the one who had, without my consent, inked up my child's hands and feet and taken scissors to his hair. Yet another well-intended violation I would have to move past.

Somehow, our bodies moved from one place to the next. I recall this in fragments: A line of teachers filing out of a hospital waiting room . . . A caravan of cars heading back toward the school . . . Principal Alder sitting in a front seat . . . David and I, mute, sitting in a back seat . . . David's car haphazardly parked in front of the playground . . . Climbing in . . . Moving again, staring at a gray dashboard . . . Arriving at Kim and Dave's house, standing at a front door, stepping into a dark living room, hearing sniffling, weeping in the background, a faint voice somewhere: "Joey, your mom and dad are here." Seeing Joey's pale face, his small hand holding his Scooby-Doo lunchbox . . . Lumbering down a driveway, climbing in again . . . Staring at the gray dashboard . . . Moving, floating through space, three lost planets tumbling toward a dark and inescapable black hole.

David pulled over on US 1, and I climbed out and walked along the roadside back to my abandoned minivan, where I saw it happen again: the confusion, the tire tracks, the dust, my body screaming toward the police car. But then, I was alone, and there was only the sound of my slow-moving footsteps over gravel and weeds.

Driving home, feeling weightless, reckless, accelerating, coming close to the edge, I considered the sloping shoulder, that mire in the drainage ditch. Enraged, I stared down into that valley, no longer afraid of that shadow, no longer fearing death.

I was already dead.

shock

I sat there holding a blanket with smiling monkeys all over it, the one that had covered Sam's body in the ER. David and I sat on the living room sofa with Reverend Penn, who had arrived around six thirty that evening. Not knowing what else to do, I must have called him, though I only remember searching for his business card in my wallet, not the phone call. It had been four years since we'd last talked, since I'd sat on *his* couch, a complete stranger then, crying through tissues, telling him about the mass in Sam's heart and nodding when he told me, "In time you'll be a different person, whatever the outcome."

He seemed to be searching for the right thing to say, staring past me, scanning the photos of the boys smiling on the sofa table behind me. In a composed panic, he considered me, his eyes wide and desperate, as if I were holding a gun to my temple and my trembling finger might pull the trigger if he made a misstep. So I broke the silence and muttered something about the past and how I appreciated his kindness. He nodded and said something about how great my maternal need must be to hold my son. I realized then what I must've looked like, holding that monkey blanket as if it were a substitute baby. Stupid blanket! What was covering my son then, a zipper? I hated those smiling monkeys! Yes, I *needed* to hold my son. But since his body was dead, my greatest maternal need was to be dead too.

There wasn't much more to say—especially to a despondent mother holding a dead baby in her arms—and he knew this. With our permission, he bowed his head and prayed for us to his lord, Jesus. After he drove away, David and I stood on the front porch and watched in silence as the fiery, blood-orange sun disappeared from the sky.

When we closed the front door, the house was darker inside. I retrieved the monkey blanket and tossed it into the dog's crate. Reggie cautiously approached the fleece pile and smelled every inch of it. Watching him, I wondered what he saw with his nose. *Master Sammy?* He began to lick it. "Reggie, no!" I pushed him away from the blanket. There was blood on it. "No!" I picked up my baby again and sobbed. But when he turned back into a blanket, I threw it back into the dog's crate, turned away, and moved on.

Joey stood in front of the TV. Cartoons were playing, flickering around the edges of his small silhouette. "If Sam died, why aren't you crying?" he snapped.

David, being *in* shock, couldn't have explained the concept of it. And now Joey, not quite seven, was steeped in it too. I don't remember the rest of the conversation. I only recall my little boy's incredulous face, the twisting of the knife, and then a black wall.

Some memories have vanished, like chunks of glass swept from the road into the weeds, while others, the sharpest pieces, have become lodged in my ears.

A phone call: my father's chipper hello, my weak voice, "Dad? Daddy? My Sammy died today." Then gasping, choking sounds, my father's breathless crying, then my stepmother shrieking in the background.

Another call: my mother screaming, "No! No!"

And then another piercing memory: my high-pitched, wolflike howling rising and echoing off the bathroom walls above me as I lay on the tile floor dying. Terrifying, emptying, retching cries that twisted me into dry heaves until *nothing* was left.

After a while, I saw David floating in the distance on his own raft, and Joey, in his own lifeboat. We were paddling, drifting in the dark, lost at sea until we bumped into each other at Joey's bedtime.

"Joey, put on your pajamas. Brush your teeth. Go pee. It's time for bed," a robotic male voice said.

"Joey, come. Sleep in bed with us tonight. Please," another robot said.

He'd never slept in our bed before. Unlike Sam, Joey had never asked to sleep with us. He never seemed afraid, never came running into our room in the middle of the night. He'd slept in the dark and through the night since he was three months old. But he submitted to this change in routine and climbed onto our king-sized bed.

"Joey, honey, lift up your head. Here's your favorite pillow, your colorful blanket."

David and I lay on our sides facing Joey, who lay between us. He appeared to be sleeping, but his eyes were still open. We were corpses, not even breathing, staring at nothing. Mute, stiff, unable to touch or hold each other, but together on one life raft for the night.

I heard the clock ticking, a dog sniffing, his nose searching, his meandering, approaching footsteps. *Sammy?* I heard more sniffing, more footsteps in the distance. *Sammy?* The clock kept ticking, ticking . . .

Time was moving on without us.

I wrapped my arms and legs around my pillow, curled up in the frayed branches of my mind, and hid deep inside myself. There, I nuzzled my face against his neck, inhaled his scent, placed my arm over his chest, and molded my body against his.

I'm here, Sammy. I'm right here. Mommy's here. When you wake up, I'll be right here.

5
STILL HERE

choices

Tuesday morning came. Overnight, April turned into May, and the black sky was now gray. Ready or not, our migration, the forced shift from who we were to *Who are we now?* was beginning.

I was running through a dizzying mass of noise and chaos, flying through memories and overlapping voices, searching for anything to alter this outcome somehow and switch life back on again.

"Can I sleep in my own bed from now on?" Joey said, snuffing out the noise in my head. Not waiting for an answer, he climbed out of bed and relocated far away and into his cloud of morning cartoons.

There was nothing else we could do but disperse. If we had cried together, held on to one another, we all would've drowned, so we went our separate ways. Like the legs of a stool, we were supportive but independent, unable to touch one another. Joey's energy and obstinacy was, and still is, the tugboat that towed and pulled us forward. Early on, David and I decided—made a solemn vow—that no matter what we would get out of bed every morning. We would do this for Joey, who, as time went on, would push all his pain down deep, not *ever* wanting to cry or talk about his feelings, or about Sam. In the past, he'd cry over silly things, losing a card game, a sloppy Joe falling apart on his plate, a broken toy, and I'd try to comfort him. *It's okay. You'll win next time. It's good to cry. Here's a napkin. We'll fix this.* Now, no amount of comfort could ever fix *this*. Somehow, we'd remain supportive, tethered to one another.

I felt lifeless but hyperalert. I was unable to move, but hyperaware of activity around me—rolling suitcases coming through the front door; the dog barking; David's father, Sandy, and his partner, Doris, playing a card game with Joey; David doing, planning, making phone calls, arrangements, necessary appointments. I don't know how, but our bodies could walk and talk, even drive. Our first appointment was scheduled for later that morning.

At the funeral home, we were greeted by a woman who led us to a small room, where David and I sat in armchairs facing a large and neatly kept desk. There were no scattered notes, open files, stray paper clips, or other clues that business was conducted there. There was a floral love seat beneath a framed painting, a flowery landscape that smacked of heavenly peace. My eyes burned. The walls were too bright, a sunny, optimistic yellow. Nothing made sense. Sam was still in the hospital having open-heart surgery—a cardiac autopsy—that I had consented to ... was that yesterday?

When the funeral director joined us, he sat across the polished desk and introduced himself in a subdued manner and apologized for our loss in a soothing tone. He explained that we would have to decide, that day, whether to cremate or bury Sam. "Bodies are treated differently based on these choices," he said.

Choices? Freeze or embalm? Keep him or never hold him again? Burn his precious body to bits and ashes? Or leave him in a cemetery, in the dark, all alone? The choosing permanently injured my mind. *It's only a body*, I kept telling myself. *His essence, his soul, is no longer in it.* But it was *his* body. His sweet corn-niblet toes. His peaches-and-cream skin. His wavy, wheat-colored hair that smelled like apples. Some people, I know, disapproved of our decision, found it unacceptable, but they were incapable of understanding our reasons. To be clear, we wanted *him*, not ashes, not gravestones—him, our child, alive. We needed to keep him with us, not buried in a cemetery. What if we moved away one day? How could we leave him behind?

"Cremation," David said.

The funeral director nodded. Next, he explained, we'd need to choose a casket that was acceptable for cremation, nothing with brass or metal embellishments, handles and such. He laid out a few glossy catalogs, opened one that was filled with empty coffins, and slid it toward us. He pointed to a few choices he thought we might approve of.

"Something simple, nothing ornate," I heard David say.

Where were the child-sized caskets? I thought, turning the pages. There were tiny caskets with teddy bears for babies, and bigger ones with golf clubs for adults, but nothing in between. Then, I thought of holiday catalogs, the way Sam would circle, with his magic marker, the toys or action figures he hoped Santa or Hanukkah Harry would bring him. Maybe it *was* my mind playing tricks, but I felt him there, standing in the empty space between our chairs, circling, pointing to the light-colored one.

Standard size is okay, Mommy, since they don't have my size. Daddy, that one with the Star of David and the blue blanket on top. That's the one.

I felt the slight weight of his hand, or was it his head resting on my shoulder?

David pointed to a casket in the catalog.

"Dark or light wood then?" the director asked.

David looked over at me. "The light-colored one?"

I nodded. Later, David would tell me he felt it, too, Sam's presence. And we would agree that as long as we could stay focused on Sam, we'd be able to keep making these impossible decisions.

The funeral director noted our choice, cleared his desk, and told us he'd need the obituary as soon as possible. "To make the newspaper in time for the funeral. You'll also need to choose an urn," he said, "but there's no rush on that." He handed us another catalog, one filled with urns, to take home.

We thanked him and left with our assignment: to reduce Sam to a column, a newspaper clipping? *No*, I thought, *I'll need to write more than that.*

On the drive home, I found myself stuck in this insane thought loop: *I need to cut his nails . . . I need to cut his nails . . .*

It had been weeks since I'd cut his nails. Remembering how I'd held his hand, his fingertips, and clipped his nails while he looked on. His thumb nails are wide and so I have to clip them *multiple times.* "Mommy, I think that's short enough! What are you doing, digging for gold?" Laughing. "I'm almost done. Just one more clip."

It was like holding a wet match that would never light, yet I continued striking it, confused. My brain was stuck, unable to restart. *I need to cut his nails . . .*

We would end up searching online for an urn, something better than what was in that glossy catalog. Like caskets, urns came in only two sizes: small for baby or large for adult, cuddlesome teddy bears or crisscrossed golf clubs. Nothing in between. The containers were too big, too small, too old, too young. Is there no demand for child-sized caskets and urns? Had nobody noticed this gap in the mourning business?

We had to make do with an adult-sized urn. We chose an urn called *Essence*. It resembled Sam's body—his torso, shoulders, chest, and waist—and its curved sides suggested the shape of a heart. The reflective surface, perhaps, was a two-way mirror. Or, like Harry Potter's Mirror of Erised, it would show us the "deepest, most desperate desire of our hearts." Carrying it requires both arms, and when I hold it now, eyes closed, I can feel his weight, remember his monkey-hug, his legs wrapped around my waist, his arms around my neck, my arms wrapped around his body. In Geraldine Brooks's novel *Year of Wonders*, an incensed and bereaved mother continues to carry her dead child's decaying body, unable to let go of it. *How long is too long?* I needed to keep him, hold him, carry him, and this way—saving his ashes in a body-shaped urn—seemed sound to me.

We also chose two pendants called *Strength*, tiny vessels containing a trace amount of his ashes, a mini-Mirror of Erised. David keeps his amulet in his pocket, and I wear mine on a cord around my neck. Sometimes, when I hold it close to my eyes and look at my distorted reflection, I can see my boy's face—the *deepest, most desperate desire of our hearts.*

Over the coming few weeks, we'd have to return to the funeral home a few more times: before the cremation and then again after the cremation, to pick up Sam's ashes.

First, I'd bring his favorite stuffed animal, Kippy; his favorite action figure, Duke; his favorite Harry Potter book; his soft, colorful blanket; and an outfit for him to wear, SpongeBob underwear, jeans, his favorite Green Day T-shirt, and his sneakers. Carrying Sam's belongings into the funeral home, I tried not to think about the fact that someone would be dressing my little boy and filling his casket with these toys, this book, his blanket, and then . . .

The same woman who'd greeted us before met us at the front entrance. "I'm sorry," she said, eyeing the sneakers on the mound I was holding. "I can't take those. No shoes allowed."

I didn't ask why, and tried not to imagine the reason, but the vision flashed before I could look away. A furnace, rubber soles melting on my baby's toes. *Stop it.* I shook my head to erase the grotesque thought. *No shoes then. Did we bring socks? Yes.*

"I don't want his feet to be cold," I mumbled. "His socks, his blanket . . . he'll need these . . . he'll want this," I said, handing over to the woman my armful of Sam's things, all except his sneakers.

On the next trip back, we brought the *Essence* urn and the *Strength* pendants so the funeral director could fill them with Sam's ashes.

the temple

On Wednesday morning, mustering the strength to walk from here to there, David and I sat in the car in the temple's parking lot, trying to grasp the reality of what had happened and what was going to happen next. I could still see and smell smoke in the air from the forest fires that were burning nearby. Staring out at the sidewalk, I remembered when Sam had come here, to this temple, on his preschool field trip—his *ah-venture*. How he'd said he wanted to come back here again one day. I thought about those mornings, four years ago, when I'd sat here in the empty synagogue, alone, grieving, praying, searching for answers, flipping through that prayer book. How determined—or foolish—I was then, when I still had hope.

"Let's go," David said.

Somehow, we'd survived now for two days on no food and no sleep. We were still walking, talking, moving from one place to the next. David pressed a buzzer and spoke to an intercom, "We have an appointment with Rabbi Matuson." I looked up at the security camera, then down toward the loud, buzzing noise that unlocked the entrance.

Less than a minute after we walked into the reception area, walking at a brisk pace from down a long hallway, Rabbi Matuson greeted us and introduced himself. He had bits of salt for a beard and seawater for eyes, and he wore a thick, dark sweater even though the heat outside was extreme. As he led us to his office, his hands were like cups scooping and shoveling nervously around us as if he were trying to pick up our broken pieces.

The windowless room was lined with books, dark furniture, and one dim lamp. I was grateful for the dusky setting; my eyes couldn't tolerate loud colors or bright lights. In the middle of the room was a round table with three chairs. The rabbi invited us to sit, then placed a fourth chair at the table as if someone else would be joining us.

My hands hurt. I stared down at my lap, at my clenched fists. When I loosened my grip, I saw small, crescent-shaped cuts in my palms.

The rabbi seemed nervous, even more disoriented than we were. "First, let me say . . . how sorry I am . . . for this . . . for your loss. So . . . how do we begin?"

David spoke first. "You may not remember, but we met you a few years back. We attended a few of your Friday night services."

Fear had brought us to this temple before. Not that we *ever* believed that prayer or attending religious services would repair Sam's heart, but listening to stories and music seemed a solid way to spend quality time together. The boys raved about the young, hip acoustic guitarist who played and sang, and after one Friday night, we had a conversation with Sam about how sometimes, being different, or *green*, was good.

"We especially liked your sermon about the green balloon," I said.

The rabbi looked surprised. "Oh! That one, yes . . . the green balloon . . . that *was* a good one, wasn't it?"

"We plan on joining the temple," David said. "Becoming members, paying whatever fee is required for the funeral service."

"That will *not* be necessary," the rabbi said. "You don't have to do that. I think you've already paid enough, don't you?"

We took turns talking, crying, and telling our stories. Now and then, I floated above the conversation and saw our fragile bodies, heard our broken voices, and I swear, I saw Sam, too, in that fourth chair, watching, listening.

"How long have you been married?" the rabbi asked. "How did you find each other?"

"We actually met in high school, but we've been married now for—" David looked at me. "About fourteen years?"

I nodded. "Feels more like forty, doesn't it?" We both smirked.

"Sam was the only one who truly loved me," David said, slumped in his seat.

What a thing to say, I thought. "I love you," I said, shaking my head.

The rabbi cringed. His watery eyes darted from David to me, then back to David, as if he were trying to decide which of us to pull first from the quicksand.

Staring down, I studied the small, diamond pattern in my chair cushion to sort out who we had become: Joey had bonded with Sam, and David and I were bound to Sam's survival. Our marriage had become a twenty-four seven search-and-rescue team. I was *search*— reading, watching, gathering information, contacts, taking Sam to cardiology appointments, carrying my thick binder full of medical research. He was *rescue*—preparing for every contingency, making lists, arranging our lives, weekend trips, or longer vacations, calling ahead to know the availability of emergency services. He'd made a recent call to Cumberland Island, where we would take a ferry, have a picnic, and see wild horses, which is only accessible by boat. I recalled how he'd confirmed beforehand, "They have a rescue helicopter. If anything happens, that'll be the fastest way off the island."

"Sam was five when we found out about the mass in his heart," I said.

The rabbi shook his head. "Was *that* the first time you died?"

The question struck me as odd. But then, I *had* died before, maybe more than once, so . . . "Yes, I guess it was. Then, when he'd made it to eight, we were confident it *wasn't* malignant, the mass. And then nine. He'd just started using hair gel. He just turned nine."

David stared at the empty chair. "He was an extraordinary child. I know every parent says that about their child, but . . . he *was* exceptional."

"We tried to protect him," I said. "Act like everything was fine. But he knew. He *knew* . . . I saw the way he'd look at those crude warning signs at Disney, lightning bolts through hearts. They were everywhere, even the kiddie rides. I saw how he noticed us keeping track of the red emergency phones along the paths at Stone Mountain." *What were we thinking, hiking up a mountain?* "When we ended up carrying both boys on our backs, I was relieved Joey was tired, too, and it wasn't just

Sam. We were all acting brave, but *this* is what we were so afraid of . . . *this*. Every day, everywhere we went, everything we did, it was always a game against dread."

"It was no game, was it?" the rabbi said.

I shook my head. "He complained of chest pain once but assured me it was from tying his shoelaces or from the weight of his book bag. He hid his fear, so I hid mine and dropped him at school." *I let him go to school!*

Pointing to his heart. "Mommy, I just felt a pain, here. But it's gone now—it went away."

Winking, I gave him a thumbs-up. "Nothing else hurts, right? You feel okay, right?"

Nodding, he winked at me, blew a kiss, and waved goodbye.

Sitting in the school parking lot, I called the doctor. "Yes, his breathing is normal. Yes, his color looks good."

"I didn't know what to do. Should I have taken him out of school? Rushed him to the doctor's office, or the hospital, and demanded something be done every time I felt afraid? I thought about it, but what would they do? What would *anyone* do? If he wasn't sick, then . . . I didn't know what to do. He didn't like PE on Mondays. That's when it happened, during PE, on the playground. I should've kept him home. I don't know what to do now. How can he *not* be here?"

The rabbi was a statue with round eyes, not even breathing. David's head was hanging, and his eyes were closed. He had warned me earlier not to say anything to *anyone* that made us seem suicidal, but I didn't care. "I wish I were—I don't want to live."

The rabbi nodded as if he understood and would keep my wish a secret. "I would expect no less. How does one go on after this kind of loss?"

David let down his guard then. "We'd pull a *Thelma and Louise* if we could, drive off a cliff somewhere, but there's Joey, so we'll hold off on that . . ."

The rabbi's eyes ping-ponged from chair to chair. "Do you have someone, a therapist, perhaps, that you can talk to?"

Was this question directed at me? "Yes. Well, Margery Steinem. But . . . she passed away recently."

The rabbi sighed. "Oh, no . . . Yes, I knew her well . . . only two weeks ago . . . I officiated at her service—an amazing woman."

David offered an option. "We can see Randi, Margery's business partner, if we need to at some point. She knows us . . . That's who I've been seeing for four years now."

Nodding, I mentioned someone else. "A while ago, right after we found out about Sam's heart, I met with Reverend Penn. Do you know him?"

"I know Reverend Penn very well," the rabbi said, rocking in his seat. "You made a wise choice. I would've recommended him—even though he *is* on the other team." We all smiled, almost laughed, which felt unnatural, uncomfortable, awkward.

I'm not sure how long our meeting lasted, but it seemed, while the rabbi was nodding his head in belief or shaking it in disbelief, he'd been recording every word, absorbing every tear, studying us, memorizing us to prepare the sermon he would give at Sam's funeral in less than twenty-four hours. So I knew what was coming next, I could feel it, see it in the way David was sitting on the edge of his seat. Any second, he was going to say, "It's time to go."

But I had to ask this question before our time was up: "Where is he? What do *you* believe?"

The rabbi looked stunned; a rabbit caught in headlights. He shook his head and threw up his hands. "I don't know *what* I believe anymore."

David and I shot knowing looks at each other; he liked this answer too. We'd talk about it later and agree that *this* temple, *this* rabbi—for Sam, for us, and who we were—was the right choice. At the end of the day, David's religion was baseball, and mine was TBD, never one to follow any particular path.

"If I could answer your question . . . if I could *tell* you," the rabbi said, "you should question *why* I have an answer. Be wary of those who have answers." With his pointer finger, he pressed an invisible button on the table. "This I *know*: he *is* with you. Watching, listening. He's *not* gone."

I *wanted* to believe what the rabbi said he knew. I *needed* to believe that Sam wasn't gone. That on some frequency, I had picked up his vibration in the air. If I didn't believe my own senses and trust the feeling I had that he was near me, I wouldn't have been able to walk any farther.

Standing outside the temple in the midday heat, David and I were buzzing, alive, euphoric even—from talking? How long was that meeting? Even the pain in my hands had subsided.

"What happened in there?" I asked. "Why do we feel like this? Sam was there—he was *there*. Did you feel something too?"

David was also dumbfounded. "I did. Sam was—he *was* there. I don't know . . ."

whirling

Stupid and smiling, still on a high when we returned home from our meeting with the rabbi, I remember the concerned looks we got. I remember people, sounds, and voices floated in and out of my awareness.

My friend Michele helping Sandy and Doris with food orders, rides; asking how many folding tables and how much flatware we needed. I saw her hands holding a plate of food in front of me, heard her voice. "You've *got* to eat something."

I remember a few neighbors came and went, promising to return tomorrow with coolers, ice, extra chairs. I heard whispers: *What happened?* Questions: *How did he—?* Ignorance: *I know what it's like. My mother died last year, but now, she's in a better place.*

I was screaming inside my head. *Just say you're sorry!* Parents are supposed to leave before their children. They may have lost their mother, their past, but they did *not* know what it was like. I'd lost my future, my heart—my life. And he was *not* in a better place. *He belongs here with us. Just say you're sorry!*

My friends Carolyn and Terri had come from four states away. Had they driven all night?

I heard kitchen noises, cabinets opening, closing, different footsteps, conversations, knocking, the front door opening, closing, Carolyn's voice. "Someone dropped off a sandwich and a can of soup."

Michele's voice. "What? A can of soup?" Then her hands again, taking away a plate of food. A pungent mist, like smelling salts, rained down on the glass coffee table, and a white paper towel moved in circles. While the world around me was bustling, kinetic, I sat, befuddled, my head whirling.

At some point, my father, Don; his wife, Betty; her brother, Kenny; and his wife, Belinda, arrived. I remember my dad's face. For a moment, it felt like he was just visiting for no reason at all. I was just giving him a tour of my home, and he was beating the cancer, and the boys were playing video games in the other room, and we were just so happy to see each other, walking and talking, arm in arm.

"Deanna Lynn, this place is huge! This bathroom is bigger than my bedroom! It's beautiful, honey. Your new home, it's just beautiful."

Their drive across the Panhandle had been long. Hidden beneath his clothes were tubes inserted into each kidney, and bags attached to each leg that were full and needed to be emptied. I noticed a trail of blood on the bathroom floor. He didn't see it. This is when I fell back to earth. The cancer was spreading, he was visiting for a reason—a funeral, and the boys were *not* playing video games in the other room.

"Dad, the toilet's in here." I opened the door to the water closet. "And towels, anything you need, here, in this closet. I'll wait here for you." I gave him his privacy, closed the door, and cleaned up the blood on the tile floor before he came back out.

I remember the searing heat when I opened the front door, squinting, the sun in my eyes. My neighbor Diane was standing there, smiling, handing me an envelope. I still have it, the SpongeBob birthday party invitation.

"I know it's short notice, but I hope the boys can come this weekend. The girls would love to see them. It's nothing big. They can wear bathing suits. We're doing a little backyard pool party."

I stood there blindsided, not knowing what to say. She stopped smiling—like somebody had just died—and I saw my face in her eyes. My first exercise in this life-after-your-child's-death class: telling someone, face-to-face, and processing their reaction while simultaneously managing my own. "Diane, I'm sorry, but . . . Sam . . . he died . . . Monday." *Why am I apologizing?*

She stood there, eyes wide, not blinking, mouth open, then turned and left. She must've run home. I remember closing the door, reading the invitation, and seconds later, she and her husband, Andrew, were standing on our front porch. This time, David opened the door. The four of us stood there, speechless, reflecting each other's horror-stricken expressions.

Now, I realize why I apologized. I was sorry for *her*, for *them*. Because they'd gone into shock and didn't know what to say or do. And now, like us, they'd been rendered powerless too.

I can't explain why, but I needed to talk. I *had* to speak at Sam's funeral. David asked me not to, maybe thinking I would break down or blab on for too long. I know I talk too much. When I was a kid, someone thought it was funny, giving me a T-shirt with the word *blabbermouth* printed over a giant, open-mouthed clam. My grandmother once told me I had the gift of gab, which I liked better than *blabbermouth*. I promised David I would keep my speech short, no more than a page.

It was after midnight. Joey was asleep in his bed. Sandy and Doris were sleeping in the guest room. David was lying down in bed, pretending to sleep. While I wrote my speech, Carolyn and Terri sat with me at the kitchen table for hours, editing and proofreading. From the moment I'd dropped the kitchen phone and started running, driving, speeding, my system had remained flooded with adrenaline, but I knew my friends were exhausted.

"It's good enough," I said, gathering and stacking my pages. "We should get some sleep."

With only a few hours left before morning, we turned the two living room sofas into beds. We opened blankets, stuffed pillowcases, and unfolded the taupe-colored sheets with the raspberry leaves—the ones that matched nothing but felt so soft it didn't matter. I lay down beside Carolyn, closed my eyes, and pretended to sleep, and she wrapped her arms around me.

"Thank you for allowing me to hold you," she said.

Was it me? Were my outer layers so tough, so coarse, that I was untouchable? Was I too stoic, too strong, too hard to hug or hold? Was it that people thought I might break if they touched me? Or was I now, perhaps, a contagion? An alien? Someone who could spread this taboo type of death through close contact? The way others looked at me now, I could almost hear their thoughts. *Don't say anything ... Don't touch her or get too close ... Better to keep a safe distance.*

Carolyn, who'd been my friend since our sophomore year in high school, knew me, my heart, Sam's heart. She wasn't afraid to reach deep inside, to that part of me that was kept so hidden even I couldn't see it.

"Thank you, Carolyn, for being here, for being my friend, for *everything*."

When the girls were breathing deeply and I knew they were asleep, I floated away like a ghost, crept through the house, and sat beside my window under the full moon. Sam's bed was still empty, and I couldn't sleep. While I was still alive, before the adrenaline waned and the deafening silence, like a layer of dust, settled on everything around me, I *needed* to speak.

an obituary

Sam Kassenoff passed away Monday, April 30, with a heart that was full of love and bigger than life. He was a third-grade student in the gifted program at the Bank of America Learning Academy and was also a graduate of the JCA's Gan Yeladim. He lived life with a loving heart and was loved deeply by so many.

Sam was an environmentalist, a musician, poet, writer, comic, storyteller, scientist, with a soul well beyond his years. He loved Harry Potter, the Yankees, the band Green Day, his action figures, and PlayStation. Most of all, he loved his mom, dad, puppy, and his constant companion and brother, Joey.

Surviving family members include his parents, David & Deanna Kassenoff; brother, Joseph Kassenoff; grandparents, Sanford (Doris Roth) Kassenoff, Miriam Klein Kassenoff, Jeanie Wilson, Donald (Betty) Everett; great-grandmother, Sarah Klein; aunt, Debbie (Scott) Sidman; cousins, Shira, and Jack Sidman; best friend, Hannah; and Sam's beloved dog, Reggie.

A service to celebrate Sam's life will be held at 11:00 a.m. today, Thursday, May 3, 2007, at Congregation Ahavath Chesed (The Temple); 8727 San Jose Blvd.

Rabbi Michael Matuson will officiate.

Donations are requested to Sam's favorite charity, Natural Resources Defense Council (NRDC), 40 W. 20th St., New York, NY 10011, www.nrdc.org.

a funeral

By that Thursday morning, the wildfires that had been burning for days converge into the largest recorded forest fire in the history of both Georgia and Florida. A thick layer of holocaustic smoke shrouds the city of Jacksonville, and it rains ashes. The heat is insufferable, yet I'm shivering with adrenaline.

In this nightmare, I remember drifting from one place in time to another, from one scene to the next, along currents of heated smoke or air-conditioned chill, floating through shadows or flashes of light.

Choosing pieces of clothing. What does one wear to their child's funeral? Beneath my black suit, I decide to wear his favorite colors: his glow-in-the-dark Timex, green; his fire pendant, orange; and, because he loved the sea, an ocean-blue shirt.

Arriving at the temple in a line of midnight-blue limos, a pod of blue whales. Nothing makes sense—hot is cold, ashes are snowflakes, cars are whales. I'm sleepwalking, and I can't wake up.

Waiting inside the temple with family in a room that looks like a library. Joining us, the rabbi seems to be revving, too, with adrenaline.

Walking into the sanctuary, down that long aisle, seeing a hand, an arm, a face, Sam's pediatrician, Dr. Katz, reaching out.

Standing at a podium, David and I are facing Sam's closed casket. I take my time, pulling from Sam's book bag a unit of tiny G. I. Joe action figures, including his favorite, Duke, in a ziplock bag; a handful of smooth stones that the boys had drawn faces on with magic markers; and my one-page speech. I arrange it all in front of me, and then I look around. Everyone else seems nervous. I'm not nervous, which is unexpected since I hate public speaking; I'm just not ready yet. I wonder about this, how odd it is that I feel so calm, so unafraid. I have no fear at all. None. I'm indignant. I'm mad-angry. Which is always when my mind is in its calmest, most unfaltering, sharp-witted state. David elbows me and whispers, like a ventriloquist, without moving his lips. "Are you all right? Everyone's waiting. *Say* something."

Now I'm really riled, even calmer than I was a second ago. Holding up my hand, steady, no longer shaking, I hiss at him, "I'm *fine*. Just *wait* . . . just *give* me a *minute*."

Searching the synagogue, gazing out at the sea of faces staring up at me, I want to point to Sam's coffin and keep pointing, punching the air with my fist, my pointer finger. I want to scream at everyone. *Will you believe me now? This is what I was afraid of! THIS! Because—and you should know this if you don't know this already—nothing, NOTHING, is ever what it seems! He was only a boy, but he was an old soul in the body of a child. A magician, a wizard—a genius! He was courageous, magnetic, unpredictable. A dreamer, a soldier, brave but sensitive, and fragile, too fragile . . .*

I want to say all of this, but I don't.

I see paramedics. I see a police officer, Sam's action figure, Duke, standing in the back. In the front, my father is slumped in his chair; my stepmother, I notice, is dressed in pastels, not black, and I'm grateful for this. My mother-in-law is rubbing her eyes. I see Joey in his dark-blue suit, the one we'd just bought for his cousin's bar mitzvah. He looks so small in the crowd. Is he looking at me or staring blankly at nothing? Children believe in magic—as they should. How will he *ever* believe in magic now? How will he sleep now across from the empty twin bed? Who will he brush his teeth with, or talk to about school or video games or girls? Who will he grow up with, play with, fight with, read with, eat with, stand beside in carpool lines, or sit beside at the table or in the back seat? Will he even remember his brother's laugh? How much we all laughed?

Looking down at my speech, the one I'd written the night before, I begin reading.

"Thank you for being with us today. I am humbled and overwhelmed by your love and support. David and I have just had the best nine years of our lives and have been honored to be Sam's parents. And now we've all been brought together because of Sam's heart. The last four years have been filled with fear that this day might happen, but we watched Sam live with such vibrancy, enthusiasm, curiosity, love, and especially courage. His radiant smile will always be our warm, colorful blanket and shine in our hearts forever. Sam was, is, beautiful. Without exaggeration . . . perfect."

I talk about Sam's heart, his action figures, his stories, the things he wrote. "Like this note to a pretty recovery room nurse." I hold up the napkin with Sam's handwriting on it and read it: "'Jenny, call me. Love, Sam K.'" The sea of faces smiles, and a gentle wave of laughter, of exhaling, moves through the synagogue.

I remove my jacket so Sam can see his glow-in-the-dark Timex and his fire pendant, which is lying over my ocean-blue shirt, and I describe how the boys and I would flex our muscles and compare our biceps. I bend my arms, flex my muscles, and speak to Sam as if he is standing right in front of me, not lying in that coffin. "Sammy, you are *so* strong. *We* are strong!" But inside of me, I'm shouting and throwing things.

My mind is racing. Again, I stop myself from pointing to Sam's coffin, punching the air with my fist. *He wasn't finished! I wasn't finished! We needed more time. I need more time. I need to talk about him—about what happened. I don't want to stop talking. If I stop talking, what then? What happens then! I need to keep talking.*

I tell everyone about *Sam's Story*. "I started writing when he was born, but I stopped when we found out about . . . Maybe, one day I'll start writing again . . . about this . . . about Sam's heart."

I end with a poem I'd written when Sam was a baby:

> "I watch him rock to music—his version of dancing
> And we share a laugh
> Knowing by the look in each other's eyes that we feel the music.
> As time goes on, our taste in music will differ
> But we'll share laughter
> Knowing by the look in each other's eyes that we feel the music
> Mother and son sharing the same rhythm
> His smile, her pride
> His laugh, her music
> His rhythm, her heart
> His soul, her son."

I look up again, and someone is handing me my black jacket.

Then David and I sit, and Rabbi Matuson takes our place at the bimah.

I hear the rabbi speaking. His words sound unrehearsed and heartfelt.

"We question *why* this exceptional child, who liked to use hair gel, who loved to live and write stories . . . This magical boy . . . We question *why* his days here ended . . . But *here*, we find no answer."

While he tells a story, I drift in and out.

"Before he died, my beloved grandfather, also a rabbi . . . He meant the world to me . . . Told me this: 'I will always be with you. Touch my face. Your fingers hold memories. I will live in your memory. Always . . .'

"We can only hope. In the end there is right . . . Touch his face . . . Your fingers hold memories . . . Remember his joy . . . He will live in your hearts, *always*."

I drift away, and I see him then, my beautiful boy, standing at the bimah, wearing a sea-colored robe, holding something in his hand—a feather, a pen?—nodding at me. He scribbles something, raising his arms, signing the words with his hands. *I will instruct you and teach you in the way you should go; I will counsel you and watch over you.*

I drift back in, and he is gone, and I hear a man's voice, not Sam's, reciting the twenty-third psalm.

"I shall not want . . . lie down in green pastures . . . beside still waters . . . walk through the valley of the shadow of death . . ."

I see Rabbi Matuson then, lowering his hands, bowing his head, closing his sermon.

No . . . I'm not ready . . . I need more time. Sammy . . . Sammy . . . No! No! No! No!

I'm not ready when my baby, asleep in that standard-sized coffin, the light-colored one with the blue blanket and the Star of David on top, is carried past me. I'm not ready to walk. I'm not ready for the end.

Standing outside on the sidewalk beside Sam's casket, I don't know what to do. I'm holding Joey's hand when my mother pulls him away. Where is she taking him? Bending in half, I lay my head on the grown-up–sized casket, on the blue blanket, and kiss it, weep into it, and bawl or whisper—I'm not sure which; I can't modulate my volume. "Sammy, I love you more than all the sidewalks in the world!"

Searching, circling, I see my father sobbing, the rabbi holding him. Turning back to Sam, I see his coffin sliding into a dark void behind tinted glass, then flashes of sunlight and shadows and distorted reflections of trees moving sideways as the hearse pulls away. Unable to see where it's coming from, eyes closed, mouth open, I hear horrifying, high-pitched, wolflike howling that goes on and on until there is no sound at all. Stumbling, squinting in the blazing heat, reaching for something, someone, I hear soles scraping pavement, a man's voice. "Somebody help her. She's going to pass out." I see somebody's arm, David's? And then, all I see are silent, hot snowflakes landing on my black sleeves.

Drifting again along a current of air-conditioning, I'm standing among a crowd of ghosts inside the temple's vestibule. Mr. Howell, our next-door neighbor from the old neighborhood, is crying. I hug him. The nice man who bought our old house, now Mr. Howell's next-door neighbor, is crying too. He promises to keep the clouds and airplanes on the walls in Sam's old room and tells me he'll never paint over any of it, that I can visit anytime I want. I hug him too. I see my friend Arlene; she's holding me up with her eyes. We blink and nod at each other. I see other friends and strangers, children and adults, teachers and action figures, and for a moment, in a flash, I see Sam among the crowd *and* feel him beside me, a faint touch on my arm.

Mommy, I'm right here . . . I love you more than all the sidewalks in the world.

floaters

I climb out of the dark limo, walk up the driveway, and idle in front of our house as the pod of blue whales circles the cul-de-sac and lumbers away. Outside, in the stifling heat, it's hard to breathe. It's afternoon, though it's hard to tell what time it is; the sun is hidden behind charcoal clouds of smoke.

Inside, my home is filled with people and food, coolers with ice, bottles of soda, platters of meats, cheeses, and fruits arranged on tablecloths I don't recognize. I perform and smile and sigh and pretend to be alive; I act like I care when people speak to me or give their advice.

Stay busy so you won't have time to think about it ...

You realize he's not coming back, don't you?

Be grateful you had him for nine years. Remember, children come through you, but don't belong to you ...

Now, without a podium, interacting one-on-one, I choke. What I want to say is pounding in my chest, trying to get out.

Stay busy? Doing what? What could possibly help me to not think about it? And by it, you mean him? Why wouldn't I want to think about him?

Be grateful for the time we had? I will be, one day, but not now, not yet. I just want him back. He belongs to me!

I know he isn't coming back—I'm not crazy—but then, you don't know, maybe he will return, run all the way home so out of breath that I'll worry about his heart, but he'll assure me, I'm okay, Mommy. I'm here now. Everything's okay ...

What is wrong with me? Why am I carrying on like this, smiling, nodding, acting like I'm fine? What kind of person smiles and acts like they're hosting a party after their child has died? Yes, that's it. This is a surprise party. Any minute now, Sam will walk through that door. Reggie, his "Little Dude" Chihuahua, will run circles around him and nip at his toes. Yes, and we'll all cheer, and he'll be *so* surprised that I'll worry about his heart. But it's not happening. I look around, and everyone is talking or eating, not hushed, crouched and ready to shout, *Surprise!* It seems they knew all along Sam wasn't going to show.

I'm not fine. I'm walking, talking, living, breathing, but inside, I'm dying. I notice Joey and realize he's acting too, interacting with grown-ups, smiling, talking, answering questions. Like me, he doesn't want comfort or pity. Like me, he wants privacy and aloneness. I see it now. It's who we are. It's in our nature. I remember my grandmother being like this: strong, self-reliant, stoic. And now, I've passed this on to Joey. Our outer layers are harder than most, thicker, tougher, more difficult to penetrate. Will he be okay? Before I die, I need to make sure he's okay. For now, though, I need to disappear.

I begin to withdraw into my own world, a mollusk retracting inside its shell. Voices and conversations are becoming muffled and distant. Drifting, I move from room to room, living, dining, kitchen, and then the family room, where I find the life-size portrait of Sam. I pick it up, hold it close, and stare into his eyes. I took the picture last November. The boys were watching the sunset on the ferry ride back from Cumberland Island. I'd submitted the photo with the obituary, knowing it would be cropped to show only Sam's face. I didn't know it would be made into this faux painting. Now, I remember the phone call. A woman's voice asking if she could use the photo. She was going to do something special with it and said it would be "a gift" from the funeral home. This large memorial portrait had been displayed at the funeral, but I hadn't seen it until now. Sam's orange windbreaker had been Photoshopped, inflated, paint added to fill the cropped space where Joey had stood. Right, it makes sense now. Only the deceased are depicted in memorial portraits. But no*w*, Sam's shape looks odd, unnaturally bulky. His eyes, too, look unnatural—peculiar. No, grotesque. They're supposed to be olive-colored with flecks of brownish-orange. But they're not that. They're flat. There's no light in them, no life. It's *all* wrong. None of this is right. Nothing will *ever* be right. I raise up the portrait and place it in the niche over the fireplace and back away from it. No, that's not where it goes. Later, maybe I'll find a place to hang it. Drifting again, I disappear, retracting further inside my shell.

It's not dark yet, but not light either. By early evening, Sam still hasn't returned. The crowd is dispersing. My eyes are burning, aching. When I close them, there's too much light. Bright bursts of color linger like blotches that stay after the eruption of a flashbulb. When I open my eyes, it stays dark. Black floaters block my sight. I'm a bird in a covered cage. Blinding flashes, or dark floaters, either way, I can't see. In some sort of synaptic overload, my brain is shutting down. Maybe Sam *is* back in his bed? Too dark to tell. I'll check again tomorrow. Through the night, I keep my eyes open and stare into the dark and listen for him, and wait, and cry, and listen, and wait, and cry.

6
SEARCHING

lunacy

I remember, after finding out about Sam's heart, how I used to lock myself in the bathroom and cry in the shower. That's where I'd gather myself, my strength. Crouched over the drain, balanced like a circus lion on a stool, I'd watch tears and water pool and drain through my fingers. Then I'd stand, close the faucet, wrap myself in a towel, stay a little longer, shivering, and tell myself: *Everything's okay. He's gonna be okay. Everything's gonna be okay.*

Now, I was too weak, too unsteady to stand or crouch in the shower.

Based on the survival rule of threes, humans can survive about three weeks without food, three days without water, three hours without shelter, and three minutes without oxygen. Three minutes without breath and we begin to die. *How long had he lain on the playground without oxygen?*

It had been four days. Breathing hurt. Everything hurt. My heart, my chest, my arms, my hands, even my breasts ached, as if it were time to nurse?

I lay in the tub, water running, staring up through the bathroom window at the lime-green leaves on an elm tree, until the rising water covered my mouth, my nose, my eyes.

Three minutes without oxygen.

No matter how long I stayed underwater holding my breath, my body—or the soul inside it—refused to die. It would come up yawning for air like a gaping fish. Then, when the water reached the overflow, I'd turn over onto my stomach, on my elbows, gaze into the chrome, and see him there. His face. His eyes. We didn't smile or speak or cry. We just stared into each other's eyes for as long as we could, until the water turned cold and the tub drained.

Day after day, to ease the pain of breathing, I'd bury myself underwater and then come up yawning, turn over, and stare into the overflow, into his eyes.

Mommy, we have the same eyes!

The lunacy had begun, and I'd found a portal.

I liked the word lunacy. It comes from the Latin word *luna*, from the belief that lunacy fluctuated with the phases of the moon.

As crazy or impossible or lunatic as it seemed, if I occasionally saw my deceased son in moments of reflection, or sometimes heard his voice, his encouragement, what harm was there in this? It was *my* way of coping, *my* lunacy. To survive what is an abnormal event, the death of a child, a modicum of insanity—or *lunacy* (see how much better that word sounds?)—is absolutely necessary. No one could pull me back from this place, this dark cave called grief. There's no way around, over, or under it, so I let my lunacy pull me through it.

I don't know how we all kept going, flickering, functioning. After a week or so, Joey returned to school. In the mornings, David took him, and in the afternoons, my friend Akila picked him up along with her daughter Ramya.

Sometimes after school, Ramya and Joey played together, which relieved me. When it was just us two, he would say out loud what I was always thinking: "I don't know what to do."

I tried to fill in for his brother, but I was a miserable substitute. Unable to match his endless energy, it took all the strength I had to deal cards, move a game piece, or roll a die. We played board games like Sorry!, Monopoly Junior, and Scrabble Junior. But I couldn't bring myself to take out The Game of Life—those little pink and blue peg-children Sam had collected were still in the holes of the tiny car he'd used last time we played. I kept a stockpile of absurd games—UNO, Cinq-O, Wig Out!, Slamwich, Would You Rather . . .?—so when we didn't know what to do, we'd find *something* in the hall closet.

After two weeks or so, David returned to work, and for those last days of the school year, I picked up Joey in the afternoons. Though I don't recall driving or pulling up in front of the playground, Akila told me that I did, that she'd seen me waiting in the carpool line with my sunglasses on.

My energy ebbed and flowed. Home alone during the day, I was either sitting or lying on the sofa staring at nothing; or searching for and gathering scraps of information—photos, phone numbers, note cards, letters, books, medical records, school papers, artwork, stories. I remember spreading out all the evidence on the dining room table and examining every piece as if I were trying to solve a puzzle, as if, like Frankenstein, I could stitch the pieces back together until they formed a body.

The latest project Sam had been working on was an interactive poster for a book he was writing about a rescue dog named Blizzard. He'd drawn pictures of the characters, and behind flaps of paper, window shutters with Scotch-taped hinges that opened and closed, he'd hidden tidbits about them or teasers about the story.

When I was a child, I would sleep with a favorite book. I thought if I held the story while I slept, I could enter it in my dreams—feed my fish just so much, and no more; draw my bedroom window around the moon with my purple crayon; or dance where the wild things are. Down deep I was still that child, just an older, sadder version, holding a favorite story, *Blizzard,* and hoping for dreams.

Lying on the sofa holding Sam's penciled pages, his unfinished story about survival, I closed my eyes, hoping I might see him, or at least hear his voice, in a dream. It hurt less to think this way, to *hope* for a glimpse of him—or just a whisper.

Blizzard

Blizzard: Nature's Harsh
by Sam K., age 8

As his first year as a Rescue dog, Blizzard must face his fears and save himself, and the puppies from horrible danger. Can he do it? Can he . . . live?

Chapter 1

Blizzard is a German Shepard with golden fur and a black patch running down his back. His orange eyes shimmer in the moon's light, and his well fed body was healthy and in shape. Blizzard's fast and slender body was good for chasing rabbits or birds. Blizzard worked for a rescue team in Antarctica. He was a great father. Blizzard had 7 puppies, but the rescue team had to help out a lot with that because Blizzard's mate had gone to Canada for training.

"Ever since Miargra left, Blizzard's been a little bit over protective," mentioned the rescue team's co-captain, George. "You think so?" said the team captain, Fred, as he sat down with a cup of coffee and the morning's newspaper. "Kind of," George replied getting up to get some coffee himself.

Two other men trotted down the stairs and into the coffee smelling kitchen. The two men were Dennis, who had an unusually large smile on, and Evan, who also seemed very happy.

"Wha-What is it?" choked Fred, finishing his coffee. "It's Christmas Eve!" Dennis reminded him.

"Oooooooohh," smiled Fred, pulling out a present for George, Dennis, and Evan. Evan got a pair of socks and a mini bucket of hot fudge. Dennis got a candy bar and an I-pod. "Awesome!" Evan said jealously. George had a music CD and a pack of candy corn. "Thanks!" they all said at once, admiring the wonderful gifts.

After everybody ate breakfast, Fred and George walked outside to find Myrtle and Ky setting up a tent for their camp on Tuesday. "Hi, we're almost done," said Ky, looking puzzled at two tent pieces in his hands. Myrtle rolled his eyes and shot Ky a look. Ky shrugged and started working again.

"Ky's a little-er-sidetracked," said Myrtle. "Oh, well, we just came out to see Blizzard," Fred said, but he was interrupted by a horrible sound.

Chapter 2

"CRAAAACKK!!!!" Ky stopped building and murmured, "Uh oh!" Fred gasped, Myrtle's eyes widened, and George's jaw dropped. A crack had shot through a mountain causing an avalanche! Ky jumped up to get Blizzard but when he got to the shed that Blizzard and the puppies lived in, he panicked. The door to the shed was open and the paw prints trailed the opposite way from the shed. He sprinted back to the others and screamed, "THEY'RE GONE!!!!!"

Evan and Dennis came outside in panic too. When they saw the avalanche, they both nearly fainted.

Meanwhile, Blizzard was storming through the bitter cold winds. On his back was a rescue pouch. In the pouch were the 7 puppies, Rage, Lightening, Hope, Tiger, Ron, Duke, and Avalanche. Blizzard was looking for a place to put the puppies but all there was for miles was flat, white, snow. He thought for a minute and then, CRACK! A crack spread in front of him. He turned around, a crack had spread there too. He was surrounded by cracks on an unstable lake.

Blizzard panicked. He didn't know if he should try to attempt jumping over the cracks or swim to the shore, when it parted. Blizzard got ready to jump but stopped to a loud bang. The cracks had parted and Blizzard and the puppies were now stuck in the heart of the lake. He had to think fast. The only choices he had were to sink or swim.

Back at base, Fred, George, Myrtle, Ky, Evan, and Dennis were getting ready to hike out and find Blizzard, but a storm had started raging outside. "We'll wait until morning, see how the weather is then," said Fred looking at the weather on the computer. "What-what will we do?" stuttered Myrtle, pacing back and forth across the kitchen. "Hope Blizzard and the puppies are-are all right," announced Fred, getting up from the computer. "Blizzard, where are you?" whispered Fred, "Where are you?"

Chapter 3

Blizzard was still on a chunk of ice in the heart of a lake with the puppies safely secured on his back. He jumped into the water and struggled to shore. Blizzard and the puppies were fine, but they now had a bigger problem. In front of Blizzard stood a snow leopard, hungry and fierce. Blizzard tore off the rescue pouch and hid it behind a tree before the leopard noticed. SWAK! The claws of the leopard swept across Blizzard's face. Streams of blood trickled down his snout. Blizzard leapt forward and sank his teeth into the leopard's front left leg. The leopard gave an ear piercing roar and stumbled backward. Blizzard jumped on the leopard to knock him down. Blizzard bit the leopard's neck, and it died. Injured and stained in blood, Blizzard stood in pain, horror, and shock all at once.

He limped to the tree that he hid the puppies behind and picked up the pouch. He attached the pouch securely on his back with his teeth and set off again.

The next morning, Fred, George, Ky, Evan, Dennis, and Myrtle got up early to go out and find Blizzard. The weather was fine. At 5:00 am, Fred led the team outside and through the howling winds. At first, they found nothing. Then, they found the trail of Blizzard's paw prints, they were just visible in the white snow.

"This way!" called Fred through the howling winds. Then, Fred stopped dead in his tracks. A low rumbling sound echoed through the air. "Ahhhh!!!" shrieked Fred. Fred had been on loose snow and it had collapsed. One arm dangled to his side while the other held onto the edge. Right when Fred thought he was going to die, Ky, Myrtle, Evan, Dennis, and George pulled him out. "I-I think I b-broke my a-arm," said Fred in pain. "Me and Ky will bring him back to base," said Myrtle, taking out a stretcher. "Got ya," replied George.

Chapter 4

After a few days, Blizzard had recovered from the injuries the snow leopard had given him, and he ventured on through the snow. After walking a mile or two, he lay down.

His short distance between life and death was still losing length.

sleep

Still lying on the sofa, staring at nothing, I couldn't sleep. I couldn't think fast or decide whether *to sink or swim . . . still on a chunk of ice in the heart of a lake . . . in pain, horror, and shock all at once.* I thought about Blizzard. Had he sensed danger, the impending avalanche? Would he survive? Would the puppies live? I thought about the short distance between life and death.

Sammy, where are you?

I couldn't swim, so I sank into a memory.

Sam had just turned two, and Joey would be arriving in a few months. Sam and I were celebrating his passage out of the crib and into his new big-boy bed. We'd just returned from our walk and eaten our cupcakes, and now it was time to rest.

He chose a favorite book, *Sam and the Firefly,* and we climbed into his *A Bug's Life*–themed sheets. A little tentatively, he examined the antennae and bug eyes that were everywhere around us.

I lay beside him, made a parachute with the top sheet, and we sighed as it covered us. He nestled his cheek on my shoulder and focused his eager eyes on the book's cover. I smelled his sweet breath and the lingering scent of outdoors in his hair.

"*Sam and the Firefly*, by P. D. Eastman," I announced, then pointed to the big, red letters. "S-A-M spells Sam. And it is night. And the moon is full and yellow. Hmm, I wonder . . . Is Sam an owl?"

He giggled at the question because the answer was yes *and* no. "Yes," he said, then pointed to the firefly. "Gus." He smiled, already knowing the names and words on all the pages.

I opened the book and on the inside cover, Sam, the owl, was frowning. His eyebrows were raised high in upside-down smiles over his wide, yellow eyes, and he was holding up his left wing, his pointer. "He looks like he's scolding Gus, doesn't he?"

"Um-hum," he agreed, then studied Sam, the owl, and mimicked his expression.

I began reading the story. Sam was up with the moon and looking for fun when a talking light hit him on his head! Then a firefly named Gus showed Sam the tricks he could do with his light. While Gus and Sam spent the night making words out of light, my Sam reached out and touched the pages and traced the lines of light with his finger, then yawned and smiled. His lids were growing heavy, his thick lashes were fluttering, and then his eyes closed.

I closed the book and held it between us in the space warmed by our breath and closed my eyes. Face to face, eyelash to eyelash, we slept. And perhaps together, in a dream, we made words out of light.

How much longer could I survive without sleep? Studies have shown a limit of eight to ten days, but I had exceeded the limit. Even a day without sleep affects one's ability to think or concentrate, make decisions, or memorize details. After two days, brief blackouts, hallucinations, and disordered thinking are common.

I called my doctor, told her about Sam, and asked if she could prescribe something to help me sleep.

"I'll have to see you before I can prescribe anything," she said. "You'll have to make an appointment."

A few days later, at her office, she bounced through the door of the examining room with a big smile. "Hey, lady, how's everything going?"

She had deserted me, forgotten our conversation, or was she acting as if she had? My doctor for seven years now was a complete stranger, an oh so cheerful alien from another planet. And I had to say it again and remind her how everything was going.

"My son, he just passed . . ."

"Oh, right. Sorry to hear that." She seemed unfazed. "What can I do for you?"

"I can't sleep. David's doctor gave him sleeping pills—Ambien, I think." My voice sounded robotic, hollow.

"I *could* give you a few pills, a few nights' worth, but in the long run, I think it'll be better if you get back to the gym, get some exercise. It'll help improve your sleep too."

Her upbeat energy flattened me, and her *get some exercise* solution stung, a slap in the face. I was too stunned—too thick, too impaired—to respond and argue my case for pills over exercise. If she were in my shoes, I wondered, would she return to the gym a week or two after her child's funeral? Would she be able to close her eyes and sleep?

She didn't ask, so I didn't mention what was keeping me awake every night, the things I couldn't stop seeing and hearing when I closed my eyes.

Sleep deprivation was muddling my memory. And my *memories*—my ability to unspool his life and recollect every single one of his 3,346 days—were what I needed most.

Afterward, I called my friend Kim. She was furious. "You've got to be kidding me. I'm making an appointment for you with *my* doctor as soon as we hang up."

A few days later, I met with Kim's doctor and felt less alone when she told me that her sister had trouble sleeping, too, after losing *her* daughter. "I'll do whatever I can to help you," she said. "Of course I'll write you a prescription. You need to sleep. Call me for anything else you need. You've got a long road ahead of you."

Kim had made another appointment for me.

Next, I found myself sitting in a goth-ish hair salon. Everyone was wearing black, the chairs were black, the ceiling was black, the stylist's hair was shiny blue-black, and her dark eyes were lined in black. I appreciated *all* of it.

Beside me, Kim sat on a stool, and behind me, the stylist, though she looked hard, spoke softly. "What are we doing today?"

Dying, I thought, staring at my sunken eyes in the mirror. "Going short," I said.

Almost dead, I wanted less of everything. *Just take it all—our home, all our things, my hair. I just want him back.*

"How short do you want to go?"

I didn't want to feel the added weight of hair. I couldn't care less. I remembered my chemo-cut four years earlier, how I'd been preparing for battle. *If my little boy was going to be an army man, then I was going to be a soldier in his platoon.*

"Just cut . . . all of it."

Kim spoke for me. "Her son died very recently, and this is a very tough time right now."

I held back tears, hearing the truth: *Her son died . . .*

"I'm so sorry," the stylist said. "Let's get you shampooed."

As she combed my sopping hair, water, like huge tears, streamed down the front of my cape. I tilted my head as she gently pushed, and listened as she snipped and sliced, and watched as strands of hair slid down the tear-streaked cape.

"What do you think?" she asked.

I looked up then. "You can cut more."

The stylist, whose name I don't remember, sounded nervous. "This is an emotional time for you. Maybe we can cut more the next time you come in."

I remember David's therapist, Randi, advising him (us) that for at least a year or so, while we were in such a fragile, unstable, and distracted state, we shouldn't make any big decisions, like quitting a job or selling the house, and also to be especially careful when driving. I don't think she mentioned anything about getting haircuts.

I shook my head. "Just cut more, please."

When she finished, I gazed into the mirror. Without my glasses, the blurry image with a boy's haircut might have been Sam, nodding. I thanked the stylist and left a big tip on the counter beside her scissors, then let my lunacy pull me through another day.

a letter

Every day after the funeral, I'd thought about writing to Officer Twisdale (who I *knew* was Sam's action figure, Duke). He knew the same powerlessness we did. He'd heard the same sounds and then the same deafening silence. I wanted to thank him for being there that day, for helping me.

What if he hadn't been there at that precise moment in time, pointing that radar gun in my direction? What if, driving alone, I hadn't made it to the hospital in time to be with my little boy? What if another cop had stopped me, handcuffed me, and not believed me, my temporary insanity? Dave Linden, our police officer friend, knew Tim Twisdale, and told me he was glad it was Tim that day instead of a less experienced officer. "He definitely bent the rules picking you up on the side of the road like that," Dave said.

After two weeks, I summoned the energy to sit up and hold a pen. As I began writing and listening to Sam's voice, I could feel him there with me, alive. I'd found another way of coping, another portal: *writing Sam back to life.*

A letter:

> *May 15, 2007*
>
> *Dear Officer Twisdale:*
>
> *A couple of weeks ago, on April 30, I experienced a parent's worst nightmare: an emergency call that my son, Sam, had collapsed at school from cardiac arrest. Dazed and scared, I raced up Philips Highway to be with him. You saw me, stopped me, and helped me—driving me first to his school and then to the hospital. I am writing to you to speak on behalf of Sam, who, if he were still here, would write something like this:*
>
> *Officer Twisdale, Mr. Tim, thank you for picking my mom up on Philips Highway. She's a safe driver, but she was in a big hurry because she had to be with me. It was really important, and I*

wanted her to be safe. I've seen you guys with your radar guns; we drive on Philips Highway every day from my house to my school. I'm really glad you were there the day I needed you to drive my mom to the hospital. Officer Linden, Mr. Dave, is my best friend's dad. He's shown me all his police stuff. I'm really familiar with what it takes to be a policeman. I was a S.W.A.T. officer a few Halloweens ago. I know you are a special officer. My mom told me how fast you drove and that there was also a motorcycle policeman (which I thought was great too). You had your sirens on and you caught up to our rescue truck. I know you stood behind my mom in the hallway at the hospital. You're a really strong policeman and a really good friend. Thank you.

Your friend,

Sam Kassenoff (age 9)

Officer Twisdale, as Sam's mom, I'm glad you were there Monday, April 30. As a police officer, you never know what you're going to face or whether a person is dangerous, crazy, hurt, angry, or just indifferent. I didn't have time to explain, and you believed me and saw through my temporary insanity. You took control and possibly even bent the rules so that precious time wasn't wasted. The moment you instructed me to wear my seat belt, I knew I was with the right person. The day of Sam's death is a nightmare that my husband and I will have to endure. But your presence of mind and empathy make you deserving of a medal. You are a true example of a public servant. Your colleagues and supervisors should be proud of both you and the officer who provided the motorcycle escort; I know we are.

Through my misery, I've thought of writing to you every day. I hope the delay in my words doesn't diminish their meaning. At my lowest you shined and were at your best. Four years ago when we discovered Sam had a heart condition, I read and put on my refrigerator this quote by Viktor Frankl (a Holocaust survivor and famous author): "For what then matters is to bear witness to the uniquely human potential at its best, which is to transform a

*personal tragedy into a triumph, to turn one's predicament into
a human achievement." Just doing your job you lived the quote.*

Warmest regards,

Deanna Kassenoff

I'd started writing again. Words: 532. And I had walked to the mailbox
and back. Steps: 158. I'd also started counting. Anything that could be
turned into a number, I obsessively counted. Writing (and counting)
was something I could *do*. Whenever I wrote, I felt like I was soldering
damaged wires back together; my dark mind lit up while I searched
through it and typed what came out of it. Counting how many words
I'd typed, or how many steps I'd taken, or how many minutes or days
had passed, felt somewhat productive. Like I was *doing* something
meaningful, purposeful, and I had a sum total to show for it. I rea-
soned that through my writing and counting, I might find a hidden
code, some secret message, the key that would enable me to connect
with Sam, somewhere in my damaged mind. At least this is what I kept
telling myself.

After sending the letter, I felt lighter—a little high, the way a
long-distance runner might feel, I suppose?

To survive . . . a modicum of insanity is necessary.

a feather

Days: 23.

The following week, I was sitting in the left turn lane at the red
light, the same light in front of the school where I had turned three
weeks before, sirens blaring, in a police cruiser, when I heard music
coming from the car in front of me. A teenage boy was bobbing his
head, flapping his arms, playing his air drums, so alive. Green Day's
song "Holiday" was blasting from his windows: "I beg to dream and
differ from the hollow lies. This is the dawning of the rest of our lives."

In a dreamlike trance, I stared at the car in front of me, at my teen-aged son—at his future, the one that would never be—immersed in his music. I was watching him when, from out of nowhere, a white feather floated down and landed on my windshield. It rolled and tumbled down the sloped hood of my minivan, then dropped out of sight. "Sammy?" I leaned forward, my face in the windshield, and looked up at the clouds, then down, peering over the hood, and noticed the boy's license plate. I concentrated on the Picasso-like image, a doodle of red, squiggly lines, and realized what it was—*who* it was: John Lennon, his self-portrait, and above the drawing, in all caps, was the word IMAGINE.

Swimming with the riptide, flowing in the current of my miserable but magical moment, I hadn't noticed that the light had changed. From behind me, in the back seat, maybe it was only my imagination, but I swear I heard Sam's voice.

Go, Mommy. It's green.

As we walked from the parking lot toward the school, I told David about the boy at the light. "He was listening to Green Day ... playing air drums ... he had a John Lennon 'Imagine' tag ... then a white feather landed on my windshield. Remember when Sam used to say *theather* when he was a baby?" Anxious, I chattered on as if I could distract us from what was up ahead. *Keep walking, talking. Look down at the sidewalk. Don't look at the playground. Don't look.*

Standing at the front entrance, we split a Xanax and talked about getting new license plates, something Sam would like.

"I already know which license plate *I* want."

David tried to smile. "I heard a rumor that Green Day might be the surprise guest on *American Idol*—tonight's the finale."

American Idol had been our weekly escape. We'd pick our own favorites, analyze the competition, and debate over whose favorite would win. Sam loved Blake, the beatboxer, and idolized Chris Daughtry, the rocker from last season. He'd sing and impersonate the contestants and keep us in stitches. While we were cheering on those teen idols, we were cheering on ourselves. They kept singing, getting better, so maybe we could keep singing and get better too. As long as those kids had a shot at winning, so did we.

But now, utterly defeated, we were left pining for a glimpse of anything connected to Sam—a TV show, a rock band, a singing contestant, a license plate, a feather. Collecting whatever we could to fill the void.

Like ghosts, David and I floated into Joey's classroom and applauded when he received his awards for citizenship and 'A' honor roll. We floated down another hallway and into another classroom. Sam's teacher handed me Sam's awards: citizenship and 'A' honor roll, a plaque, "Academic Excellence in Math," and a gift basket filled with keepsakes. In it were handwritten notes and sympathy cards from parents and teachers, children's crayoned depictions of heaven, and a stack of colorful *SAMUEL* acrostics—replicas of the acrostic Sam had created:

> S – Smart and talented
> A – Agile mind
> M – Music lover
> U – Unpredictable
> E – Excellent reader
> L – Likable

I thought the other children's drawings might've been a therapeutic activity given to the students by the counselor who, I later learned, had come to talk to the third graders about what had happened to their friend that day on the playground.

That night on the *American Idol* finale, Sam's beatboxer didn't win, but Green Day, his favorite band, *did* make a surprise appearance, and they *did* sing a John Lennon song. Coincidences? No way. The synchrony of it all—the song, the face, the feather, the word *Imagine,*

Green Day singing Lennon's song—had to mean something. I *needed* it to mean something.

In her book, *The Meaning of Feathers*, Nicole Suzanne Brown writes that seeing a feather fall from the sky means you're being asked to pay attention to the world around you. A feather that falls toward you is a reminder that you don't have control over every situation. A feather landing on you means a loved one who has passed is right beside you. If that feather is white, that loved one is guiding you, walking with you. And my favorite tidbit: a feather that lands on your car says stop, sharpen your awareness, and listen to the songs around you; there'll be a message coming.

a mummy

I startled easily. My body, I noticed, overreacted anytime anything, any noise—any reminder of that day—perforated my densely silent world. Sirens were, and still are, the worst, but I also jumped, and still do, whenever the phone rang.

One morning, someone from somewhere called and asked if I would donate Sam's eyes. His eyes? Not his liver or kidneys or lungs— only his eyes? Later, I felt guilty. Because of my snap decision, somebody who'd lost their vision would have to wait and hope for another donor, but grief is selfish, irrational, reactive. I was already up to *my* eyes in nightmarish images I'd never be able to unsee. The taking of my little boy's eyes was too much to even consider.

"No. I'm sorry," I told the caller. It wasn't until after I hung up that I realized why no other organs had survived: *Three minutes without breath and we begin to die.*

Sometime after Sam's cardiac autopsy, I had asked Dr. Angstrom to seek a second opinion, a confirmation, from Dr. Brooke at the Armed Forces Institute of Pathology. A month had passed since Sam's death.

I knew an autopsy report would come, but I didn't expect to receive a phone call from Dr. Brooke himself.

"Was the mass a tumor or HCM?" My heart was pounding, remembering what Sam's pediatrician had said about HCM years ago: *And we don't want it to be that.*

"It was HCM," Dr. Brooke said. "Hypertrophic cardiomyopathy."

HCM can manifest differently in different family members. What if it was hiding, lurking in Joey's heart? That dark cloud overhead wasn't going anywhere. We'd have to stay vigilant, keep seeing cardiologists, checking Joey's heart over the years, since HCM *usually* rears its ugly head during adolescence. I was exhausted. I just wanted to hear better news, something good, some assurance, certainty. "So . . . HCM?"

"Yes," he confirmed. "I'm very sorry for your loss."

I became that desperate, hypervigilant medical researcher again and continued to question him. "What caused it? Is it genetic?"

"Further testing would need to be done," he said.

Later, further genetic testing *would* be done, and we'd learn that Sam was negative for any of the known genetic mutations for HCM.

"It was definitely HCM then? You're certain?" Nervous, I kept repeating myself, pushing, not wanting to hang up because then I'd be alone with the information. In the past, I had seen the phrase "masquerading as" in my research—*a tumor masquerading as HCM.* "Could there be any chance, a one-percent chance, that this was anything *other* than HCM?"

"I don't think so . . . No, one hundred percent sure." He told me he had a daughter—his way, I guess, of saying he couldn't imagine. "Again, I'm so sorry for your loss."

When the call ended, I didn't know what to do. Nothing had changed. Only now, I had a report with the name of the killer printed on it. Lunatic me wrote a melodramatically venomous letter to HCM, the *Heart-stopping Child Murderer.* But lucid me knew I was out of my mind and shredded it. Who would I send it to, anyway?

I searched online and read on Mayo Clinic's website: *Hypertrophic cardiomyopathy (HCM) is a disease in which the heart muscle becomes thickened (hypertrophied). The thickened heart muscle can make it harder for the heart to pump blood. Rarely, hypertrophic cardiomyopathy can cause heart-related sudden death in people of all ages. Because many people with hypertrophic cardiomyopathy don't realize they have it, sudden cardiac death might be the first sign of the condition. It can happen in seemingly healthy young people, including high school athletes and other young, active adults.*

I went to the Hypertrophic Cardiomyopathy Association (HCMA)'s website, https://4hcm.org, and contacted the CEO and founder, Lisa Salberg. She was kind and took the time to review and discuss at length with me Sam's pathology report. But I wasn't prepared for the force of her words, the blunt observations she made about the anatomy of his heart, the extent of his disease.

Using the word *massive* to describe his heart's hypertrophy, its thickness, and heaviness, she explained how *extremely* enlarged his heart was; and in detail, described how it weighed more than the heart of an average-sized man. "He might've been considered for a heart transplant, though that wouldn't have guaranteed long-term survival either," she said. "And without an implantable defibrillator, which—though possible—isn't commonly implanted in young patients, there couldn't have been a different outcome."

It was too soon, I realized too late, for me to be having a conversation about the actual weight of my child's heart. Hearing that there couldn't have been a different outcome was the finishing blow, the last thing I remember hearing before my world went densely silent again.

On the last day of May, the second full moon came, a blue moon, and the lunacy continued.

Feeling lost after those phone calls, I found myself wandering around Sam's room. Unsure what I was looking for, I emptied his backpack, searched his composition books, flipped through assignment reminders, vocabulary lists, journal entries, and then stopped at this title: *The Second World.* The rest of the page was blank, another un-written story. I stood beside his bookcase, staring at his Harry Potter poster, and noticed, for the first time, that there were two feathers, faint like watermarks, floating in the background. I moved to the dry-erase board, where I studied his drawing: *Egyptian Me.* The soldier had square shoulders, chiseled abs, and sharp eyes. Armed with a shield and a spear, he seemed to be standing guard, watching me. Then I spotted Sam's Egyptian mummy kit—the one he'd recently bought with his own money—on the bottom of his bookshelf. I sat on the floor next to it. Opening the mini-tomb, I was relieved it hadn't been sealed with the included curse sticker. Perhaps Sam knew I might one day excavate his mummy, and he didn't want to curse his mommy.

Inside the kit, I found a small booklet and pored over the pages. I learned that Anubis, the ancient Egyptian god of the afterlife and mummification, presided over the dead. In the weighing of the heart, he used the single white feather of truth to measure whether the heart of the deceased was worthy and light before he guided them into the next world. To preserve and keep them safe, the organs were kept in four sacred jars, canopic jars. The heart was the only organ not re-moved from the body during mummification, as it was needed in the afterworld. Often, the ancient Egyptians would create a representa-tion of the body, a replica of the deceased, so that if the human person-ality, the part of the soul called the *ba*, couldn't return to its mummy because it was lost or damaged, the imitation mummy would be there for him.

Next, I examined each amulet sticker, referring back to the book-let to learn about the placement and meaning of each one. Sam had placed the papyrus column of green feldspar on the legs of his mummy to ensure his rebirth and regeneration. He'd placed the Eye of Horus over his mummy's heart to protect his health and bring him blessings of vigor and strength. And below the mummy's heart, he'd placed the scarab of green-blue marble, a symbol of the invisible power of creation.

I wanted to pick up the mummy, turn it over, and look for more, but I was afraid I might unravel it, or worse, affect its journey to *The Second World*. I looked back at the dry-erase board. The sharp-eyed soldier that Sam had drawn nodded at me. *Permission granted.* Gently, I lifted the mummy and found one more charm tucked into the gauze on his back: the amulet of Anubis, protector of the dead. On closer inspection, I thought Anubis, with his wolflike face, looked a lot like Blizzard, Sam's imaginary protective rescue dog. Carefully, I tucked in the plastic mummy exactly how I'd found him.

Then, in a flash, I recalled seeing Sam's art project, his cartouche—images pasted into an oval frame on blue construction paper and colored in with magic markers—among the piles I'd gathered on the dining room table. The ancient Egyptians, I'd learned, believed a person's name embodied their identity, and as long as the deceased's name was remembered, spoken, and written, he would continue to survive and live on in the afterlife. It was the cartouche that marked the mummy's tomb. I studied it then, Sam's cartouche, his name—𓏌𓄿𓅓—in ancient Egyptian hieroglyphics: the folded cloth for S; the sacred vulture for A; the magical owl for M, which made me think of *Sam and the Firefly* and how they made words out of light when the moon was full. And the moon *was* full this day, I thought, which had to mean something. Carefully, I positioned the mummy kit back on the bottom shelf and marked the tomb with Sam's cartouche, propping it up just so beside it.

Sitting there on the floor, I closed my eyes and took a deep breath and inhaled the air in Sam's room. *A feather that lands on your car says stop, sharpen your awareness, and listen to the songs around you; there'll be a message coming.* I thought about the boy at the traffic light in front of me playing his music, flapping his arms, beating his drums, and I felt a drumming in my ears then. I sensed Sam was right there in front of me, waving his arms. "Sammy? Are you there?"

Mommy . . . The Second World . . . Look again.

For some reason, I picked up his composition book again and turned to the blank page, *The Second World*. This time, I held it beside his bedroom window. *Not* blank, I realized. In the sunlight, at just the right angle, I noticed the faint imprint and memorized the message before it faded from my imagination.

> *Anubis, ancient Egyptian god of the afterlife, and distant cousin to Blizzard the rescue dog, presided over the weighing of my heart. And found it to be worthy, and true—and lighter than two feathers!*

whales

Telling silly jokes, waiting for us to smile, performing a two-man act all by himself, Joey tried to make us laugh.

"Was that funny?" he'd ask, and I'd nod. "Then why aren't you laughing?"

Or he'd snap at us if he caught us crying. "Stop it! Just stop it."

He'd tell us *not* to ask him how he was feeling, and if we forgot, he'd remind us. "I told you. I *don't* want to talk about it."

He avoided eye contact, stayed quiet, camouflaged, coiled like a snake ready to strike out if threatened. If he lost in a silly game of cards, he'd storm off to his bedroom and cry. I knew what the waves of sorrow felt like, that out-of-control feeling when the tsunami you tried to outrun pulls you under. This had to be a scary feeling for a little boy. Seeing him lying in bed sobbing, though it was seldom, I understood why he wanted us to just keep going and not cry. Knowing it wasn't about a silly card game, and knowing he didn't want to talk, I would let him cry, release some of the pain, and then say the only thing I could say: "I'm sorry, Joey. I'm so sorry."

Over the summer, I took him to see a grief therapist. After his session, she and I would talk.

"He'll go into Sam's room and play with his toys. He even takes Sam's shirts from his closet and wears them," I said.

The therapist seemed impressed with Joey's way of coping. "He appears to be doing pretty well right now. He's very polite and funny—very mature for his age."

"But he still won't talk with you about what happened?" I asked. "About what's going on or how he's feeling?"

"No. But he's doing well otherwise, right? Socially? In school—his behavior and grades have stayed the same?"

I nodded.

"Then there's no need for him to come back. Maybe one day he'll talk about his brother or ask questions about what happened. But right now, he doesn't want to talk—and that's okay."

In a dream: I flew over a black sea. It was dark, and at first, I didn't realize he was there with me. I was skimming the water, passing over spotted seals, then striped dolphins, close enough to touch, when I sensed another bird flying beside me.

Mommy, did you see them?

Sammy?

Together, we glided and turned, slowed down and sped up. Below us, from out of the black, a pod of beluga whales rose to the surface.

Aren't they amazing?

Sammy?

I wanted to stay there, in my dream, with Sam, but I also wanted to be here with Joey. I wanted both of my boys. I'd have to figure out how to live in two places at once.

In the morning, after David left for work and before it was time to leave for summer camp, Joey pulled out his whale puzzle, the one that had always looked so deceptively easy to solve. Twelve whales, each imperceptibly different, are divided across nine cardboard squares, three across three down. All you have to do is match their heads with their tails. It was easy to match a few whales, but impossible to pair them all. For years, we had tried, but had never solved it. I wondered why, on that particular morning, Joey had chosen *that* puzzle to work on. *Aren't they amazing?* I wanted to tell him about the dream I had, but—

"I did it! I DID IT!"

Joey's shouting startled me. He'd done it, matched and connected all the whales, and he couldn't believe it. *I* couldn't believe it. It felt like a tiny miracle. A moment of levity, a glimmer of hope. Even if was nothing, it was an experience, a connection made in *both* places, and it was mine to do with it whatever I wanted. *That* was something.

"Joey, that's amazing! You did that in, like, two minutes!"

I took a picture of the finished puzzle so that one day if we forgot this, or it seemed impossible again to solve it, I'd have proof that it *could* be done—and that we could feel alive again.

driving

One morning, on the drive to summer camp, "Jessie's Girl," a karaoke favorite the boys would sing together, came on the radio. Joey and I shot knowing looks at each other in the rearview mirror and smiled. Hoping he might talk, I took advantage of the moment and asked, "Do you ever feel like Sam is around you? Like he's with you?"

Before turning away, he caught my eye again in the mirror. "Yeah . . . but then he has to go back to sleep. It's dark in heaven, so you sleep a lot there."

Short and to the point, I thought, wishing I could learn to edit myself the way he did. He'd said a lot in only two sentences, and I wondered what else I could learn from my little boy.

When we pulled into the carpool line, a camp counselor wearing a bright-colored T-shirt and a big smile opened the car door and welcomed us. "Hello! Good morning, Joey Bag-of-Doughnuts!" Then the door closed, muffling the cheerful conversations. I was doing okay until I saw Joey, among the sea of campers, walking alone through those same doors where he and his brother had walked holding hands a hundred times before. Unable to accept this reality, so saturated with grief as I stared at the back of Joey's head, I thought my heart would stop then and there. When a whistle blew, I jumped. A spirited camp counselor, trying to keep the line moving, was waving me forward.

After leaving Joey at camp, though I'd done this drive hundreds of times before, I didn't know which way to turn. This must've been what David's therapist had meant when she'd warned us to be especially careful when driving.

As I drove, passing familiar places, neighborhoods, street signs, that solemn willow tree on the corner, I became disoriented. Not knowing where I was or where I was going, I pulled over and laid my head on the steering wheel and cried. *What if we didn't try long enough to revive him? What if he wasn't gone yet and we left him too soon? What if we'd made him sit, just sit—no bike riding, no running, no phys ed? Sammy, I'm sorry—I'm sorry . . .*

Driving again on San Jose Boulevard. Six lanes of traffic. Right lane. Light poles. I could hit one. Would it work? *How can he be gone? What if I want to go now, join him? Is that so wrong?* I regarded Death, not in my normal voice, but in a more primitive one. I heard myself sniffling, grunting, gurgling, gasping for air. I couldn't breathe; I couldn't feel my arms, my legs, my feet; I couldn't steer the wheel. Cars were speeding by me. A driver was waving a fist, cursing, honking a horn. *How about that raging lunatic over there? You couldn't have taken him instead?* I spat at Death.

My steering wheel locked up and the engine went silent. Coasting, slowing, I could only pull the wheel an inch to the right. I drifted diagonally into a parking lot, came to a stop, and sobbed. I needed help. I needed to talk to someone before I drove myself into a light pole. But who could I call? What would I say? *Help! My son, he's dying again!*

Using the little red flip phone I carried in case of an emergency, I called David.

"You had a panic attack, Deanna."

"No, I didn't. The van stalled."

"Try to start it then. Will it start?"

"It's running," I snapped.

"It didn't stall. You had a panic attack. I've had them, I know. Try driving around the parking lot."

I drove in circles. "It's running okay."

"Are *you* okay?"

"Yes. But it *did* stall."

"Can you drive to the mechanic, get it checked out? Do you need me to come get you?"

"No. I'm fine."

After the mechanic found nothing wrong, I had to consider the possibility that maybe it wasn't the minivan after all; that maybe it *was* me, panicking, stalling, breaking down.

That summer, Joey wanted to celebrate his seventh birthday at Adventure Landing, the same place where we'd celebrated Sam's birthday four months earlier. In the same way he'd wear Sam's shirts, he seemed to want to go back to the same places we'd been before. Though I don't remember being there for Joey's party, I know I was there because I took the photos. When I look at them now, at our sad smiles, I still don't know how we kept going.

Also that summer, a new camp friend invited Joey to a birthday party at Skate Station, another place we'd been to before. Joey knew where to go to get his skates, and I took shelter in a harsh-yellow laminate booth. I wanted to cover my ears, block out the screams and laughter around me. These noises were detonators now. I got up and walked around, ordered a Coke to soothe my stomach, and searched for Joey. Skating around the rink all by himself, I hated seeing him so alone. But I couldn't skate, couldn't move. All I could do was hold on to the railing and watch and smile and wave each time he passed by me. When I started to feel dizzy, I had to look away. I noticed birthday party moms nearby, organizing pizza plates, chatting, socializing. "Be careful!" I jumped when a mother behind me hollered at her kids, speeding by. I headed back to my laminate shelter and kept track of Joey from there. I tried to focus on how well he was doing, the way he was moving, coping, grieving, so determined, headstrong, tenacious. Those qualities that had challenged me during his terrible twos were turning out to be "good qualities later in life," just as the pediatrician had predicted.

Panic attacks, I later learned, are the aftereffects of a tragic event, the tremors after a major earthquake. They were mostly sudden and happened with no warning. Driving was the number one cause—passing by or going anywhere we'd been to before—but social situations like birthday parties; any loud sound, a memory, a song, or a word in a conversation could also set me off course. Learning with each experience, I came to know the signs of an oncoming attack. The racing heart, the need to run, the inability to move or breathe. The vertigo and the dry heaves, though I wasn't eating enough for anything to come up. The grief that was coursing through me felt a lot like fear, only now, the excessive adrenaline was for flight instead of fight.

There was one type of tremor that made my heart race, and took my breath away, but it was the one adrenaline rush I welcomed. It happened whenever I saw another boy who resembled Sam. Once, while grocery shopping, I saw him. I knew it wasn't really Sam walking toward me in the aisle, but a lookalike, walking beside another woman, his mother? On each aisle, each time he passed by me, my heart would start pounding. I followed him, couldn't take my eyes off him, his messy hair, his flip-flops, his mustard-colored cargo shorts, and that cotton tee with the stretched-out collar. I was too sane to be *that* insane, but I allowed myself to go along with the lunacy of it anyway.

lipstick

In a dream, I was walking, and Sam was riding his bike along the edge of the blacktop, concentrating, trying not to slip into the gap between the weeds and the road, an aerialist on a tightrope. Without looking back, he rode ahead of me and left the ground, then flew away. I chased after him, flying, too, but I couldn't keep up. He disappeared in the dark, and I fell to the ground, winded.

Awake then, I heard breathing. *Sam?*

Mommy, I'm here.

Sam? Where are you?

I got out of bed and checked my closet. Maybe he was there? It's my safe room, a walk-in shrine, where I talk to him; where I keep a lifetime of videos and photos and artwork boxed in chronological order. A ruby-red jewelry box, a Mother's Day gift. A large plastic bin full of his things: his baby album; favorite dragon shirt; plastic pet lizard, Lizzy; beloved toy rabbit, Bunny. I stood in the dark listening to breathing sounds, my heart beating. *Sam, are you here?*

Every morning, I return to my closet and perform my daily ritual. I'll dress in his memory in a neutral and safe outfit. Careful, because clothes are reminders of certain days. There are two suits I'll never wear again—one, pale linen, which danced at a bar mitzvah; the other, black linen, which died at a funeral. The shirt and shorts I'd worn on his last day I got rid of; the shoes I don't remember, so it doesn't matter which pair, I guess. I'll begin my routine with the Strength pendant, then slide on the silver ring with the tiny gold heart which cost, with tax, $18.18. Some days, I'll add superficial details to prepare myself as an actor would for a scene: makeup, hair, earrings, and lipstick. It's crazy how lipstick can transform a face so that even the clown wearing it believes she's smiling.

"Why am I even buying lipstick?" I had said to my mother-in-law, Miriam, a Holocaust survivor and educator.

We were standing in the makeup aisle in Target when she taught me a weighty lesson with five matter-of-fact words. "Because wearing lipstick is living."

And so I was *living* ... but in solitary confinement, stuck somewhere between dreams and reality. Grieving, yearning, talking to myself in a closet, my holding cell. Learning, one precarious step at a time, how to get my shattered self out of bed, and dress, don jewelry, his ashes in a pendant, comb my hair, and apply lipstick.

7
REWRITING

remedies

When I pulled into the empty parking lot, I could see waves of filmy heat rippling across the blacktop. It was August, three months after Sam's funeral, when David and I returned to the temple to meet with the rabbi.

Inside the temple's vestibule, vaulting toward us on a cane, Rabbi Matuson greeted David and me. The receptionist, I noticed, didn't look up, confirming what I already knew: we *were* ghosts.

As we followed the rabbi down the hall to his office, we passed by life-size portraits of elderly men in dark suits with spectacled eyes that seemed to follow us. I clung to the child on my hip, my book bag, its thin arms clasped to my shoulder.

"Sit, sit." The rabbi leaned his cane against the table, the same table where we'd sat and talked the day before Sam's funeral. He pulled a tissue from his pocket and wiped his nose. "You'll have to excuse me; I'm feeling a little *flewish* today."

"You should've canceled our appointment," David said.

"No, no, really, I feel fine. I've been waiting for a chance to use that line. A little *flewish*, get it?"

We smirked, almost laughed.

I didn't recall him using a cane. "Did you hurt your leg?"

"Ah, this—" The rabbi flicked his palm. "An old war wound. It acts up now and then."

We three shot looks at each other, each seeming to be waiting for the other to speak. I felt the weight of my tote on my lap and stopped myself from rocking it.

Rabbi Matuson broke the awkward silence then. "How are you both holding up?"

David sat slumped, staring at the table. "Our life was miserable before, but it was great. Now it's just miserable."

The rabbi cringed. "How are you functioning at work?"

"Distraction-survival mode. Every day, I lock myself in my office. I don't see anyone; I don't go anywhere; I stay at my desk, all day. Then I have to drive past the playground again. It feels like I've been jumped by a gang. I'm in a dark alley, and they're kicking the crap out of me. I'm just curled up and can't do anything to fight back."

With both hands cupped over his cane, the rabbi tilted toward David. "Do you remember the Foreman fight—Muhammad Ali's rope-a-dope?"

David sat up then. "Of course. Foreman was the meanest son of a bitch who ever entered the ring. Pounded the crap out of everyone he faced. Ali was the smartest boxer who ever lived."

"Yes." The rabbi leaned in closer. "Ali covered up on the ropes. He just covered up. Kept his hands up in front of his face. Foreman pounded the shit out of him, and Ali made it round to round. Ali came up with his strategy when he was *in* it—the fight—because he *had* to. He was just trying to survive. You're not looking to win this fight. Like Rocky. He didn't win his fight against Apollo Creed. He just went the distance, made it to the last round. You're in the first round. It hurts like hell. You can't do anything except lie against the ropes, block the punches, and try to get to round two. When you get to round two, see if you can make it to round three. Just cover up and wait. The hits will keep coming, but eventually, by round seven, eight, nine, they don't hurt as much as they did in the earlier rounds. You'll learn to take the punches, like Ali. That's all you can do. One round at a time. It's going to hurt all the way to the end. But if you can make it to the end, like Ali, like Rocky, you've accomplished something."

Blinking as if he'd just woken up, David took a deep breath and squared his shoulders.

The rabbi cleared his throat then and regarded me with his runny nose and red eyes. "So, tell me . . . how is Joey doing?"

"He seems to be managing. He's in summer camp right now. This fall, he'll be playing baseball."

We all smiled at this.

"It must be difficult . . . coming back here, to this place."

Clinging to the bundle in my lap, I nodded. My body ached, and I shifted in my chair. "We're so alone now. Everyone moves on, goes back to living. I read somewhere that it takes four to five years to wake up . . . to function again. We won't last that long. I don't know what else to do. I'm just so tired."

The rabbi raised his eyebrows and shrugged. "You can give up. But you're not a giver-upper, are you?"

I stared down at the table. "Most days I can't even move. I'm just waiting here now, dead."

"In grief, you wait, and you *may* remain dead. But *he* is not dead; *this* I know. A tzaddik is alive even in death, crossing the bridge between worlds, changing the destinies of those around him."

I was grateful for his words, what the rabbi said he knew. True or not, hearing that Sam was not dead was still what I needed to hear—and believe.

The rabbi pointed his cane toward me. "Grief is a war zone, the most desolate and loneliest of places. In it, you may remain blocked by the ending you did not choose. Or you may rewrite your story—his story—with a different ending. You're a storyteller, a writer. Yes?"

My seat became quicksand then. "No. Sam was the writer."

"Each of us is a living story. And your story isn't finished yet—*this* I know."

My mind was exhausted and energized at once; thoughts whirling, I felt light-headed. *He is not dead—this I know … crossing the bridge between worlds … the ending you did not choose … rewrite your story—his story—with a different ending … Sam was the writer … Sammy … Sammy … Sammy …* I was cracking like tempered glass under too much pressure, holding my breath, crying without a sound. I reached for a tissue. "I miss him—I miss us, the four of us, who we were, who we were supposed to be. We're all gone now. This is what I was so afraid of—losing him, losing us." I sniffed and stared at the dark wood-grain patterns on the table, which resembled the ripples of black water I had flown over in my dream. "I see him in dreams."

David's head bobbed up and down. "They feel real, the dreams. Like brief visits."

The dreams *do* feel like visits, I thought. "I hate waking up," I said.

The rabbi dabbed at his watery eyes. "A great rabbi once said that sleep was created so that we—our souls—can ascend in dreams to a realm beyond time and space."

While I considered this, ascending in my dreams to another realm, David caught him off guard. "Speaking of great rabbis, what was your grandfather's name? The one you talked about at Sam's funeral?"

The rabbi flinched, his mouth hung open, and he hesitated, the way that lady at the church had before announcing the winner of the Easter basket drawing. "His name was Shmuel."

It was only a name, *Shmuel*, Samuel in Hebrew, six letters, but it felt like a gift, a subtle coincidence. Even if it was nothing, it was something. I reached into my bag and retrieved the gift I'd brought and passed it across the table. "I made this for you."

The rabbi crossed his hands over his heart and leaned forward to examine the cover of the photo book, and its title: *Sam, Sammy, Shmuel, Treasure for 3,346 Days.* "You've written this for me?" He looked overwhelmed as he flipped through the pages.

"It's mostly photos. But it's based on the Tree of Life."

"We want to thank you again for all your help," David said.

The rabbi hugged the book to his chest and stared wide-eyed at both of us. "Thank you. Thank you. You have no idea. Both of you have been a gift, a blessing, to me."

As we hugged and said our goodbyes, I asked for reading recommendations. Any books he thought I might like. While David worked in distraction-survival mode, I survived by reading, searching for ways to break through to that *realm beyond time and space.*

The rabbi jotted down a title. *Sefer Yetzirah, The Book of Creation.* Then suddenly he remembered another, hopped to his bookcase, and returned with a well-worn paperback covered with large gold letters: *The Bahir, Illumination.* On its cover, it was described as "One of the oldest, most important, and carefully preserved of all ancient Kabbalah texts."

"Just something we rabbis read when we can't sleep."

Outside, David and I stood in the parking lot talking, shaking our heads. Rehashing what the rabbi had said, the words he had used, the remedies: *rope-a-doping* for David, *rewriting* for me.

"How crazy was that?" we said, almost in unison. Once again, we felt uplifted somehow by an hour of conversation and the coincidental discovery of a name, *Shmuel*—a small dose of intoxicating serendipity.

I knew the high would last only an hour or so, a day at best, so I squirreled away as many words as I could from our meeting to call up later in case, at that fork in the road, I decided, instead of giving up and remaining blocked, to keep going and rewrite.

David and I pecked each other on the cheek, climbed into our cars, and headed in opposite directions. He drove back to the office, and I flew to the bookstore.

lifesavers

I dove into the books the rabbi recommended. I studied and highlighted lines, penciled notes in the margins, peppered the pages with color-coded tabs, cherry-picking whatever clues my weary brain could hold. I kept at it day after day, searching, fumbling for that magic key that I swore had to be wedged somewhere between those mystical pages. I just needed to find the right words, a spell perhaps, to reverse what had happened.

I read about the magical power of the Hebrew alphabet. It seemed the twenty-two letters of the *alef bet* were the connecting link between essence and form, soul and body. With advanced knowledge and practice, it was believed, the mystic could harness the powers of creation and create a golem, a creature made of clay, or of dust, that could magically be brought to life. In Hebrew, the word *golem* means something incomplete or unfinished, like an embryo's primitive heart tube that, at around day twenty-three, continues to fold and twist into a shape that will become the heart. I envisioned how my plan might go astray. In an attempt at recreating my son, I could end up with a tragic, Pinocchio-like puppet who lacked a heart as well as a soul. I reconsidered my plan. Maybe, with advanced knowledge and practice, I could harness the powers of creation and bring my boy—his heart *and* his soul—back to life using letters and words instead of clay or dust.

Each of us is a living story.

Honestly, though, most of what I read was beyond my understanding.

Just something we rabbis read when we can't sleep.

Maybe that was the point. Maybe all that effort was less about comprehension and more about the process of grief—turning the pages, noting the days, doing, searching, reading, gathering information; filling the void, the silence, with words and ideas.

I see it now, the insanity of it: carrying books everywhere I went, holding on to what was no longer possible, clinging to the unreal, thinking that, somehow, I could still revive my son. But I also see that while I was doing, searching, reading, turning pages, I was also processing, learning, and readjusting to the impossible reality of living without him at my own pace and in my own unique way.

Emily Dickinson wrote:

"Hope" is the thing with feathers –
That perches in the soul –

Imagining that I might one day find a way to save my son, to keep his memory alive, was *the thing with feathers* for me. Maybe I could emulate those sixteenth-century Kabbalists I'd read about who used the term *maggid* to refer to an angelic messenger, teacher, or spirit guide that acted as an advisor and visited human beings through visions or in dreams or through automatic writing. Maybe, through my visions or in my dreams or through my writing, I would find *my* maggid. So every day, for hours, I would sit and focus and meditate on a burning candle or a tree or a photo of Sam's face; from there, I would write whatever came to mind. Perhaps it was the insanity of grief, or perhaps it was my visiting advisor, but when I closed my eyes, I saw him. And when I wrote, I heard him—or maybe I imagined him?—my maggid.

Books were and still are my lifesavers, my companions, my mentors. Sometimes, I even have fanciful conversations with the authors of the books I read.

"If you're going to take part in your destiny, turn your predicament, this tragedy, into something meaningful, you're going to *have* to change your attitude," one of my mentors, Viktor Frankl, told me, or at least this is what I heard while reading his book, *Man's Search for Meaning.* Then he reminded me in a gentle but firm tone: "Even in your hopelessness, you may *still* find meaning in life."

"How?"

"Look for it. In the things you notice or experience, or perhaps, create a work—something that speaks to *you*."

a bottle cap

I spent hours every day writing. Writing about the murmur, that mass, the dreams I was having. I wrote about my grief, and about the things I was noticing or experiencing—the connections I was making.

In a dream, someone, whose face I couldn't see, handed me an old-looking, black telephone receiver with a long, black cord, and told me Sam was on the line. I knew it couldn't be him, but I held the phone to my ear anyway, hoping . . .

Mom?

Sam? It is you.

Yes.

I miss you so much. I love you.

Yes.

I think about you every day.

Yes.

Sam? Sammy? Can you hear me?

I heard crackling, and the connection was lost.

Awake then, though I didn't want to be, I opened my eyes and noticed on my nightstand the glowing numbers on my digital clock: 4:30. Our last day together, 4/30, the number, like a PIN he knew I'd recognize and *know* it was him. *Why* did I go on talking instead of listening, asking him, *Are you all right? Where are you? What is it you're trying to tell me?*

In another dream, I was touching his face, his fleshy cheek, but then it was only his portrait, the photo someone from the funeral home had turned into a faux painting. I realized that by touching it, I had caused it to crack into small, puzzle-shaped pieces that began to fall out of the frame. This made me panic and wake myself before the entire portrait disappeared. I jotted down this dream so I could examine it later.

Even after five months, when I opened my eyes each morning, I had to reset myself to the relentless ticktock of the clock and the silence of every moment in between. Most mornings, and some nights, I'd still check Sam's bed. Maybe he'd be there.

In *The Seven Daughters of Eve,* Bryan Sykes writes about a bereaved mother who sank into a deep lethargy and sat alone on a hilltop, staring into the dark woods, calling after her lost daughter who'd been taken by a cave lion in the night. She took to walking through the woods, searching every bush, behind every tree. One day, with no strength left to struggle, she didn't return from the woods. I wasn't *that* out of touch with reality; reminders of it were everywhere I looked, in everything I did. Sorting half the laundry. Packing one lunch, leaving Sam's lunchbox, with Duke on its lid, crouched, ready for battle, on the shelf in the pantry. Every day after school, pulling through the car-pool line, passing the playground. Cooking dinner recipes for four. Eating out at new places—unable to return to anywhere we'd been before—and saying, "Three," when asked, "How many?" Kissing one boy good night. Finding Sam's bed empty every time I checked. I just couldn't stop looking, calling after him, trying to save him, even in my sleep.

In one nightmare, Sam was asleep in his bed, and I was trying to wake him. I was trying to figure out the defibrillator, fumbling with the buttons—*Which one, which one? Sammy, Sammy!* I pulled him, lifted him, positioned his limp body, animating it as if he'd come to life if I moved him in lifelike ways, but he wouldn't wake up.

I couldn't *stop* searching. I couldn't let go; if I did, our fate would be sealed, unchangeable.

Needing an escape, an alternate reality, David and I immersed our-selves in the TV series *Lost,* about the survivors of a fictional plane crash and their emotional journeys on and off a mysterious island—or was it a parallel dimension, an afterlife?—where they were forced to learn from and make peace with the struggles of their lives. In the end, was it all a dream? Were they all dead? Was my little boy *really* gone?

One Saturday afternoon, outside in the garage, while Joey was riding his bike out on the sidewalk, David and I cleaned out our cars.

Reaching into the back seat, I found Sam's water bottle. I stared at the water left in it as if it were a magic potion. Confused, I stepped back, looked out at the sidewalk to check on the boys, but Joey was alone riding his bike. I crawled back in and looked at the bottle again, at the cap, at his name written in permanent marker: *Sam.* Then at the pieces of him under and around his seat, cookie crumbs, crayon shavings, and a candy wrapper. I argued with myself as I vacuumed. *Keep them. No, they're just crumbs, just garbage.*

When I was done, I found David stooped beside his car, studying a tiny slip of paper. "I found this in Sam's cup holder." He handed it to me. It was Sam's fortune from the last time we ate at our favorite Chinese restaurant.

Courage is not the absence of fear; it is the conquest of it.

Holding back tears, I put Sam's *courage* message in my pocket and turned away. I didn't want to watch as David unbuckled Sam's booster seat and pulled it out of his car.

I checked on Joey again and then watered a plant with the magic potion, put the plastic bottle in the recycle bin, and placed the bottle cap in my cup holder. Sometimes when I'm driving, I hold it and see him in the rearview mirror, taking sips, nibbling cookies.

sanctuary

"Sam Kassenoff!" Joey stood and almost shouted it—without a doubt, loud enough to ensure his brother would live on. We were at Friday night service, and the rabbi had invited congregants to remember those who've passed by standing and saying their loved one's name. David and I sat gripping the armrests of our seats, holding our breath, holding back tears. I wanted to stand with him, and maybe David did too. But we couldn't. We couldn't move.

The rabbi's words had uplifted us before, so I thought returning to the temple would be a good idea. That, somehow, attending the hour-long Friday night family service would uplift us again. We'd dress nice, get out of the house, surround ourselves with nice people, listen to nice words, and then go out to dinner afterward.

Earlier, at home, I had pushed through the inertia, put on a face, and assured Joey, "Absolutely, sneakers are appropriate." On the drive over, we played a word game. For each letter of the alphabet, you had to name an animal, a car, or a baseball team.

"A: armadillo," I said, remembering that first night in our new home, how the boys had been afraid of the monsters that lurked in the dark shadowy woods out back.

"B: badger. Mommy, go. It's your turn."

Coming from the office, David met us out front, on the sidewalk by the lamppost in front of the synagogue. Joey and I passed right through the hearse, or the space where it had been parked. Though it blended in with the night sky, I could still see it; I wondered if Joey saw it too. I hoped he didn't. Together we headed inside, into the lighted vestibule; the murmuring of voices; the smell of furniture oil, old books, and burning candles.

After the service, the rabbi spotted us and asked Joey if he was staying for refreshments.

Joey shook his head. "We're going out for pizza."

The rabbi furrowed his brow. "Oh, I see. I'd sure like to go out for pizza too. It's going to be kosher, right?"

Joey looked confused, so David answered. "Of course, rabbi. We wouldn't eat pizza any other way."

The rabbi smiled and shooed us away, kissed his hand and waved goodbye. A gesture, I noticed later, that Joey began making.

Another Friday night, after Joey called out Sam's name during the part of the service when congregants remember those who've passed, a grandmotherly woman seated in front of us turned and asked Joey if Sam was his grandfather. Though he was sitting, his volume seemed the same as when he was standing. "Sam is my big brother!"

The grandmotherly woman blinked, as if taking snapshots of each one of us with her eyes. "Bless you." She blinked at Joey. Then at David and me, zooming in on our bloodshot eyes, she mouthed the words again. "Bless you."

As the rabbi closed his sermon, raised his hands, and blessed us all, his words morphed into the end of a funeral speech. When the memory of Sam's casket was carried past me, and those wolflike cries that had come out of me echoed inside me, and I couldn't see or feel or breathe, I knew then that returning to *this* sanctuary wasn't such a good idea after all. Six months had passed, but it wasn't about time. I just couldn't keep going back to the place of Sam's funeral. David and I hadn't talked about it, so we didn't know we felt the same way. After we'd gone a handful of times, we agreed we wouldn't be returning. We would have to find a different temple to go to, another sacred place.

After registering Joey for fall baseball, we began dressing in sneakers or cleats and brightly colored T-shirts, getting out of the house, and heading to the ballpark. This is where we found our new temple: outside, surrounded by the evening sky, buzzing lights, the smell of pine and freshly mowed grass; the sound of metallic pings, bats hitting balls, and calls of encouragement. "You got this! Good eye! Keep going!"

Joey was a natural, and being part of a team provided him with instant brotherhood and lasting friendships. For David, whose religion *was* baseball, he'd found a purpose, his calling: coaching. And me? I was content to sit in my folding chair on the sidelines, watching or reading a book.

Baseball would become a long-term solution, a future that we could grow into, one that provided a year-round schedule, daily practices, weekly games, and summer tournaments. That bright green-and-orange diamond would become our sacred place, our sanctuary.

Duke

Days: 213.

It was the end of November when David and I were driving on I-95 toward downtown Jacksonville. Again, I saw too many commuters talking on cell phones. Would they hear the sirens or see the red lights in their mirrors or even move out of the way if they did? As the morning sun glared and rush hour traffic shimmered and snaked along, I couldn't stop the memories of that Monday from flashing across the windshield.

We were on our way to an award ceremony at the Jacksonville Sheriff's Office, where Officer Twisdale would be receiving the Six Pillars of Character Award. I was wearing Sam's glow-in-the-dark Timex, which was working when I wore it at his funeral but had stopped a few months later. Now, its face was dull, and its hands were fixed at 1:38. When I first noticed this, I had to check the death certificate, which was filed away in an envelope that I hadn't planned on opening. *Time of death: 1500.* Exactly 3 p.m.? A doctor had decided this time. *You know he's not here anymore. That's not him. He's gone.*

A dog with a bone, I kept chomping on the time and the word *watch*—a noun, but also a verb. *Watch*: to look at, notice, observe, pay attention, follow, keep an eye out for ... for *what?* For *anything* that might be *something*. For synchronicity, the word Carl Jung used to describe meaningful coincidences, messages or symbols, recurring numbers or keywords that turn up and seem meaningful, at least to the one paying attention to them. My mind kept buzzing, sniffing, tracing an invisible trail, retrieving things it thought might be meaningful.

I was thirty-eight the first time I saw that mass hidden in Sam's heart.

Thirty-eight was the number he used in his drawings on the jerseys of his football players.

Thirty-eight percent (too low) was the ejection fraction on his last echocardiogram.

Thirty-eight was the number of green, orange, and blue stripes on his colorful blanket—that I *had* to count in a desperate insane-with-grief moment.

In an obsessive attempt at connecting invisible dots, particular dates, places, times, I mulled over seemingly pointless pieces of information. I wanted 1:38, the time his watch stopped, to mean something, be some kind of message. I *needed* it to mean something, be some kind of message.

Inside police headquarters, our friend Dave Linden guided David and me past a gym where officers were pumping iron, then up a flight of concrete stairs and down a long hallway where officers nodded and said good morning as they passed. The bulletproof building was a bunker full of rescue heroes and action figures. I could almost hear Sam's excited energy around me.

Mommy! We're inside command central! This is awesome!

The room we entered was full of blue uniforms seated before a podium. I scanned the room, hoping I'd know his face when I saw it. I did. Sam *had* cast the perfect Duke.

Officer Twisdale and I hugged. Then David shook his hand and thanked him again. We three stood there, trying to smile, but our eyes were still sad and powerless.

I didn't know the sheriff would call *us* to the podium. David and I stood beside Twisdale while the sheriff read my letter, the one I had written months earlier. The room was silent. "'I know you are a special officer. My mom told me how fast you drove ...'" My heart was pounding. "'I didn't have time to explain, and you believed me and saw through my temporary insanity ...'" The sheriff kept stopping to clear his throat.

Beside me, Twisdale's dark-blue sleeve was quivering, and he kept whispering, "I'm sorry, I'm sorry, I'm so sorry ..."

I put my arm around him. "I know, I know. It's okay."

Staring at the stark white floor, I started to slip backward into a memory. In a flash, I was standing in that cold, chaotic room, kissing

Sam's toes. *Come back, Sammy! Please come back!* I was spiraling, falling into that silent abyss, when I saw a hand reaching toward me, the sheriff's hand? I watched as we shook hands and then saw more hands. *Applause?* And through it all, beside me, I heard Twisdale continuing to apologize. "I'm sorry, I'm so sorry . . ."

Afterward, Twisdale and I sat alone together and re-collected ourselves. I told him about Sam's action figure.

"His favorite G. I. Joe was Duke. I know it sounds crazy, but I feel like Sam chose you. *You* were his Duke."

Shaking his head, Twisdale was probably trying to push away the images, like I was, but they don't go away. They never go away. He stared at me, or through me, as if he saw Sam standing behind me. "I have no doubt . . . I know that he heard you, and that he was with you," he said.

I tried to smile and not cry. "He was with us," I said, and we both nodded, exhausted.

It seemed pointless, but I needed to ask. "Do you know, or remember, what time it was when I pulled over and got in your car?"

"I'm not sure about the exact time on the report, but I think it was a few minutes before 1:40."

My heart skipped a beat, and the *yes* answers—from that call, that connection, in my dream—floated up like a die in a Magic 8 Ball.

Sammy, it was 1:38 when you . . .?

Yes.

And you were with us then?

Yes.

You saw us touching you, heard us calling you?

Yes.

There were two young girls who had been eyeing us and were now heading in our direction. I remembered Twisdale telling me that day in the police car that he had two daughters.

He handed me an envelope. "Don't read it now but later, okay?"

The girls stood beside their father then, and the younger one, only six, her long, chestnut-gold hair framing her face, looked up at me with innocent eyes. "I hope Sammy is feeling better now."

I smiled and thanked her. "He is . . . He's feeling better now."

I don't recall where I was or what time it was when I opened the envelope and read Twisdale's letter, but I remember reading it over and over again. I liked the way he spoke to Sam. He wasn't afraid to talk to him. But then, why would he be? He was Duke.

To the Kassenoff Family,

Many times I have thought of writing to you to express my deepest sympathy for your loss but had no idea how to even begin. Yesterday I attended a Law Enforcement Appreciation Hunt at D-Dot Timberlands here in Jacksonville. As I sat in the quiet of the woods I began thinking of today's ceremony and what I'd like to say to you. Having two children myself, daughters Madison 11 and Savannah 6, I can't imagine how it would feel to lose one of them.

Ms. Kassenoff, since the day I received your letter, I have shared it with many friends and family who were also overwhelmed with emotion as I was the first time and every time after that I've read it. I still to this day don't know how you found the strength to sit and put those words on paper. A few months ago our Under Sheriff, Frank Mackesy, read your letter at our quarterly roll call while I stood in front of approximately 100 fellow officers from across the city. As I stood there and listened, Mackesy read but had to stop several times to regain his composure. I stood staring at the floor doing my best to control my emotions. Several times I glanced up and noticed numerous officers who were obviously moved by your words. After the roll call, I had officers I had never even met come up and shake my hand telling me good job.

Once your letter was published in our Sheriff's Officer newsletter titled Sam's Story, I again received e-mails and phone calls telling me good job. One of our Assistant Chiefs even took the page out and sent it to me. On it he wrote, "Great job Tim. This is what being a police officer is all about." Over the years I've been asked why I wanted to become a police officer and the answer has always been the same. "To help people." In my 24 years as an officer I've seen and experienced the loss of life on numerous occasions.

None have touched me the way Sam's did. As I listened and watched you and your husband frantically pace around his room touching him to comfort him and telling him you loved him, I have no doubts he could hear and feel your presence.

In your letter you said I was deserving of a medal. Your letter will mean more to me than any medal ever could! I thank you for that.

To Sam I would say … You're very welcome! I'm glad I could be there for you and your mother that day. Little buddy you've touched many people you never even knew and will be missed by many who loved you dearly. You were a best friend, a big brother, and a son. Now it's your turn to watch over your mother and family. We will all be together again one day. Until then, the friend you never knew, Mr. Tim …

My deepest sympathy

Officer Tim Twisdale

a stranger

During the holiday season, while shopping at the outdoor town center, I noticed her in the crowd. The old woman was slumped in her wheelchair holding a baby doll. Its plastic head and naked cloth body lay limp in her arms. Her eyes stared into that other world, fixed on something faraway, while her caregiver window-shopped and steered her along. Dazed by the flickering lights, jingling bells, and fragrances wafting out of every open door, shuffling past hordes of holiday shoppers, I spotted a couple holding hands, a mom corralling her toddlers, a family carrying shopping bags, bumping into each other, laughing. I was dying: my life was flashing before my eyes. My mind had drifted, and I lost sight of the old woman. Disoriented, I looked around, but she was gone. Or not. I *was* her, *am* her, on the inside. Broken, slumped, clinging to my baby, staring, lumbering forward with a cane, my pen, instead of a wheelchair; *that* was the only difference.

A little over eight months had passed, and I was still here, scratching the number of days on the wall in my cave, trying to write, talking to a blank notepad the way Tom Hanks had talked to a macabre-faced volleyball in *Castaway*.

Everything hurt. The mesh beneath my skin holding me together was taut and sensitive to the touch. Sometimes though, I felt nothing at all. Barely alive, losing weight, my body was shutting down. Eating was torture. Sitting across from Sam's empty chair was impossible, so the three of us had found other places to eat. At the bar, the kitchen island, a tray in front of the TV—*anywhere* but in front of that empty chair.

I had tried antidepressants, but they further impaired my ability to function or drive or think or remember what I *needed* to remember. One day at the supermarket, the cashier, about seventeen, had asked if I wanted to donate a dollar to Children's Miracle Network. I think I nodded, wondering if she knew what CMN was. She asked if I was having a bad day? I think I shook my head, wanting to say something snarky. *Well, my son died and I'm still here, so . . .* Pushing my cart then, clanking through the electric exit, I held on as it went over the curb, slammed down, pitched sideways, and almost tipped over, pulling me down with it. On my knees, still holding on, gripping the metal handle, I pulled myself up, one foot and then the other, as if I were done praying, and continued on, unable to remember where I'd parked. So I weaned off the antidepressants and sleeping pills and began listening to that voice inside me again, ignoring outsiders who began their sentences with "You should," or ended them with impatient words like "stuck," as in, "You seem stuck."

As the days continued, I felt more out of sync with the outside world. I craved quiet, stillness, solitude. Most mornings, after David and Joey pulled out of the driveway and waved goodbye, I just sat. In what became a habit of unintended meditation, I'd sit outside on the back patio for hours, staring into the woods, listening to the wind, exhaling, becoming hollower, light as a bird, until I *was* the wind, flying away. Sometimes I'd become so weightless, drift so far away, so high up, it was hard to turn around and come back.

One blustery morning, while sitting outside, I noticed the boys' toy Earth ball rolling in the backyard, forgotten, grimy again. The year before, Sam had been riding up ahead of me when he clambered off his bike, pointing and shouting. "Mommy, look, look!" Joey and I pulled up beside him and saw it then, stuck in the drainage ditch, a teal-blue ball that looked like a large marble. Sam begged to keep it. We brought the muddy thing home, cleaned it up, and enjoyed our Earth ball which sometimes doubled as a lightweight basketball. Now, I watched as it orbited our fenced yard, pushed by the wind. In daydreams, I see him chasing and catching it, holding it over his head, and laughing. *Mommy, look, I've got the whole world in my hands!*

I jumped at a loud noise, a slam—the screen door? "Sammy?" Even though I knew it couldn't be him, when I heard anything that *might* be him, I got up and looked, just in case. The way I used to get up and look, as a child, whenever I heard the tinkling of my lost dog's metal tags. But it was only the wind. A gust had picked up and whirled the Earth ball against the metal kickplate of the screen door.

Standing now, after watching the Earth ball hurry back out to play in the yard, I went inside, found a green legal pad, and lumbered forward with my blue pen to write about the Earth ball, or whatever else came to mind. I didn't know how I was *ever* going to rewrite my story with a different ending. I was just writing along the way until I got there—to the end.

I headed down the hallway to Sam's room. His spy motion detector was positioned on the floor just outside his door to warn him of trespassers. Loud sirens would blare, and in his recorded voice, a warning would play: *Intruder alert! Intruder alert!* I picked up the gray cylinder, wavering about whether or not to touch that button. I wanted so badly to hear his voice. Would it do more harm than good? *Just do it!* I pressed the red button and waited. Nothing. *No!* Brain-dead, I had pressed the record button on the device instead of the black play button. *No!* Just like that, I had erased his voice. I folded on the floor, then realized I'd been recording my crying. Carrying his spy toy, I curled up on the sea-green carpeting in his room, pressed the red button again, and recorded over my moaning with silence.

Maybe I *was* there—at the end.

Lying on the floor, with what little strength I had left, I pulled off the cap of my pen and jotted these words:

> I wrote myself to death.

Maybe this was the end of my story, a suicide note? Below that line, I wrote another word:

> Grief.

I drifted up and saw my body lying on the floor and imagined the crime scene then. The chalky outline. Badges milling about, dusting for prints, for clues, rummaging in Sam's room where my body lay, pen in hand. The investigator concluding: "No foul play here. She died of grief—real shame. Take that note for evidence. Let's go."

I hovered for a while, a soul between worlds, studying my aching hands. Time seemed to be standing still, yet I was declining, aging at warp speed. Pieces of my mind were disappearing. We think we'll never forget, but we do. We lose the most insignificant memories—and *these* are the ones that might be the *most* significant.

I wrote more:

> Bones hurt brittle too weak to move. Head aches.
> Eyesight? Losing it. Insane. How can I live with the
> unthinkable unsayable unimaginable without being
> grievously insane?

Was it insanity or grief? Or both? I wondered. Insanity *is* needed to grieve. So both—whatever.

I scanned the horizon of sea and sky in his wallpaper border, then the lime-green frogs surfing in his curtains. I remembered how alive we'd been, plucking handfuls of paint cards together, comparing shades of green with our swatch of material, those frogs, picking out *this* pale-green color on his walls. I looked up at the yield sign above his door—*Surfer Crossing*—with the silhouette of a boy holding a surfboard, then over at his microscope. He had examined insect wings, wisps of hair, his own spittle. A glass slide was still under the lens. *What did he examine last?* I surveyed his desk, a small, grown-up world of sticky notes, homework reminders, colored pencils, and photos of friends; a close-up of Reggie, his dog, stood front and center. Then I stopped at Duke; he was still standing guard, saluting, leaning against the lamp on the nightstand.

The room smelled stale, unused. I knew the dust was there, on things, toys, furniture, his bedding, his shoes. My Sam wasn't here, yet all of him was *everywhere*. And I couldn't wipe him away. So I let the dust stay.

It was almost time to pick up Joey from school. Feeling dizzy, I pushed my weight up onto Sam's bed and sat. I ran my hand over his tiki-style comforter, over his pillows, his sheets, their sand-colored palm leaves. I hadn't washed his sheets. It took me six months to empty his hamper and wash his clothes, smelling each folded piece before putting it away. I needed his unwashed sheets for any scent or trace of him that might be lingering there. How many yesterdays ago was it? I'd just made his bed and stuffed his pillowcase and fluffed his surfboard-shaped pillow, folding over his comforter so a triangle of top sheet was showing. He noticed everything, and everything mattered to him. Every experience, every detail, new sheets, even the triangle.

"I've never seen *these* before. Mommy, you got me new sheets?" He dove into his bed. "They're so soft! I *love* them. Thank you, Mommy."

Propped up on his pillow, Sam's stuffed animals, Robbie, in the red dog sweater (the one Reggie had worn as a puppy), and Rover, with the felt-pink tongue and puka beads for a collar, sat staring at me, with shiny, unsuspecting eyes.

Sitting on the edge of the bed, I filled the rest of the page:

> Too miserable too quiet too empty too permanent.
>
> I look at his brother he's not laughing
>
> his chair he's not sitting
>
> his bed he's not sleeping
>
> his toothbrush he's not brushing
>
> his bike he's not riding
>
> his toys he's not playing
>
> his computer he's not working
>
> his books he's not reading
>
> his dried blueberries he's not eating.
>
> Too much of him here for him to be there.
>
> I should be there.

Holding my notes, I stood and walked to the boys' bathroom and gazed at my reflection, at the stranger in the mirror. With one hand, she was pressing her chest, as if to keep a wound from bleeding. Her other hand was curled and close to her hip, holding something, though nothing was there in the mirror. She appeared to be in the dark, squinting, searching, adjusting to the harsh vanity lights before her eyes settled on mine.

You know he's afraid of the dark, I told her.

She looked away and lowered her hand, and I saw the gash in her heart then. My chest hurt and my head throbbed. I noticed both her hands now were clasped at her hip.

You're there with him, aren't you?

After a long minute, she lifted her head and nodded.

So he won't be afraid ... Will you stay there with him? I asked.

Her eyes were watery, round, staring at me as if she were trying to tell me something. But I could only see and not hear her. We both seemed to be struggling for air, trying to breathe, crying. She looked down at the pad and pen in my hand.

I'm trying to write ... find a way ... to save him—bring him back, I told her. *Will you tell him that? Tell him that I'm trying.*

She nodded again, and I wiped my eyes.

Carpool—I have to go.

With an inexplicable energy, a smoldering ember still glowing inside me, it would happen. I'd come to life, put on a mask, and become a different person. My robot batteries fully charged, I'd walk onstage and perform. After school, once Joey was in the back seat, I would talk and smile and make conversation. "Tell me about your day." Capable again, I would play yet another game. "A: aardvark. Your turn." I would make dinner, oversee homework, and head back out, with Joey in the back seat again, to baseball practice. "B: beluga whale. Your turn."

One night at the ballpark, a new friend, who had told me her husband had committed suicide, explained what she had learned about grief. "You fake it till you make it."

Unwittingly, I guess that's what I was doing. But this paradox of living and dying at the same time—driving, smiling, faking it, then seeing *her*, the stranger in the rearview mirror—was grueling, disconcerting.

I had questions: For how long am I supposed to fake it? What will making it even look like? When will I know if I've made it?

8
GRIEVING

dust

It had been eight months since Sam's funeral. Days: 254.

My dad wasn't supposed to die this day: January 9, 2008. He'd been out shopping. He went to bed unusually early, feeling a little under the weather, and passed away that night. My stepmother, Betty, called the next morning, to tell me about my father's last moments, how he had smiled before closing his eyes. "It was the most beautiful death I've ever seen, Deanna."

My warrior-like father had been living with cancer, fighting it every day, for twenty-three years. There were those days when it seemed like the end, and I'd drive across the state to be with him and say goodbye. "Dad, if it's possible, if you see him, will you make sure Sammy is okay? I love you." Whenever he hugged me, he'd squeeze so hard it hurt. I miss that pain, those bone-crushing bear hugs.

At my father's funeral, I felt numb, dehydrated. Nothing but dry bones. This loss went right through me, leaving a gaping hole—no jagged edges, no bleeding, no tears. I had known this day would come, but I hadn't known I'd be unable to cry *or* feel anything at all.

I kept replaying the phone call we'd had a few weeks before he died. He was worried about me.

"Sweetheart, you *will* experience joy again. You'll see."

"No, Dad, sorry, I *won't*." Why didn't I just fake it? Lie, assure him, so he'd die believing that I'd be okay?

I'll always remember what he used to tell me: "Sweetheart, you've got to keep living. Eat good food, have meaningful conversations, and delight in an occasional vodka and tonic. And remember to *always* keep learning. Never stop learning. I'm so damned proud of you, Deanna Lynn."

The following month, in February, on the five-hour drive home from yet another funeral (David's ninety-nine-year-old grandmother Sara had passed away), Joey caught us off guard.

"Where is Sam's body? Is he in a cemetery?"

I looked over at David. He was tight-lipped, concentrating on the road. This conversation was *all* mine.

"No . . . He's not in a cemetery."

"Where is he then?"

I was hesitant about having the cremation talk, but glad Joey was talking, asking questions.

"Sam is at home . . . I didn't want him to be scared, all alone in a cemetery, so I kept him with us."

"What?" He looked shocked, a little scared. "What do you mean? In our house?"

I imagined what he must've imagined: his brother's body, hidden somewhere in our house.

"He's in an urn . . . that shiny, metal container on the bookshelf in the family room . . . Have you seen it?"

He shrugged and shook his head.

For the past nine months, though I hadn't been hiding it from him, I hadn't pointed it out either, uncertain how much to show or tell him. What was or wasn't age-appropriate?

"In an urn? His bones and all? How does he fit?"

I searched for the right words, an answer that would be *mostly* true. "Well . . . we're all made up of energy *and* matter. And . . . after we die, our energy leaves. And our body—our *matter*—stays. It turns into dust."

He didn't miss a beat. "How long does it take? Dinosaur bones are still around."

Right, fossils. "Well, in some situations—"

"In a cartoon, I saw a guy burn up and turn into a pile of black ashes. Is that what happened?"

I knew the cartoon, and I knew he was fishing for the whole truth, and growing impatient, but the whole truth was still unspeakable. So I skirted around the words *burn* and *ashes* and instead stayed with words I felt more comfortable saying: *urn* and *dust*.

"Not exactly," I said. "It's not exactly like that. It does happen quickly, though. What we have in the urn, it's only Sam's matter, his dust . . . Maybe, one day, we can take him somewhere special, and scatter his dust . . . Maybe in the ocean?"

"No! I want him to stay with us."

I exhaled. What a relief, the cremation talk had come to an end. And, unexpectedly, a decision had been made.

"Okay then. Sam stays with us."

a messenger

Spring came. I hardly remembered the last few months, the holidays. Surely, we had celebrated Hanukkah and Christmas? I had proof: pictures of wrapped presents, Joey in pajamas reading his letter from Santa, and a drum set I don't remember buying. But there it is in the photo, Joey sitting behind it, smiling, holding up drumsticks.

Before, on Easter morning, in their bathrobes and bare feet, the boys would forage together around the house and outside on the patio for plastic eggs filled with treats.

Now, constantly forgetting things, sometimes not knowing what day of the week it was, I had waited until the last minute to buy an Easter basket for Joey. I couldn't care less about the holiday, but then, how sad would it be if the Easter Bunny stayed away from our house or just plain forgot? The holiday, another one without Sam, another first, was only two days away.

On the way to Target, my fuel gauge, I noticed, was on E. I pulled into a filling station I'd never been to before. Unlike the newer, galactic gas stations with umpteen pumps, car washes, and mini marts, this one was old, small, with only three pumps, and quiet except for the occasional whoosh of a passing car. Set back into a thicket of trees, it was almost hidden from view, unless, like me, you were below empty, desperate, and looking. While filling my tank, inhaling the sweet mixture of pine forest, earthy dampness, fuel, and some sort of weed or wildflower blooming out by the road, I noticed Sam's birthday, March second, and age, nine, on the metal flip sign: *Unleaded $3.29.*

Not paying attention to what I was doing, as I pulled out the nozzle and carried it back to the pump, I dripped gasoline across my sandals, my toes. I looked down and there, almost touching my wet toes, was a butterfly as big as my hand. It had spots like eyes on its pale-green wings; orange, feathery feelers; and a sheer, white body. One wing was fluttering, the other was damaged, slightly torn. Gently, I picked up the papery creature and put it on the carpeted floor in my minivan.

After grabbing the last Easter basket on the shelf, I returned home with the butterfly and surprised Joey. Together, we placed it in a large box filled with sticks and leaves and a small shallow bowl with a teaspoon of orange juice in it—sugar for energy.

The next day, when Joey checked the butterfly, he wasn't moving.

"Is he dead? I don't want him to die."

Why did I bring home more grief?

"Mommy, look! It's flapping a wing. It's still alive!"

But the butterfly hadn't touched the orange juice, and it couldn't fly, so it *was* going to die. If we weren't able to save it, I thought, at least we should know its name. I searched online and scrolled through hundreds of photos of butterfly species, but none matched. It was unbelievable that something so impressive could be so hard to find.

On Easter Sunday, I emailed the University of Florida's entomology department with an attached photo of the butterfly.

The next morning, I got a reply from Lyle at the university's Insect Identification Laboratory. I couldn't help but notice the email's time-stamp: 8:30. Reversing it, reading from right to left, I couldn't help but see 38, that recurring number again.

Lyle explained that our butterfly was a moth, a luna moth, and "a rarity to see." The luna moth, or moon moth, only lives for seven days. And he didn't drink the orange juice because he doesn't have a mouth (he'd already eaten his fill as a caterpillar). "Based on this one's feathery antennae, it's a boy." In Lyle's attached photos, I noticed the luna moth caterpillar looked a lot like the very hungry caterpillar in the book, one of our favorites, by Eric Carle. I remembered how, at the end of the story, the boys would squint and smile at the puffs of air when the cardboard pages—the butterfly's wings—flapped over our faces, and the butterfly flew away.

Days: 329.

That Monday afternoon, our moon moth died. I framed him in a shadow box and placed it beside Sam's urn.

In searching and reading more about our visitor, I learned that luna moths are associated with change, inner transformation, endings and beginnings, death and rebirth. In some cultures, the luna moth symbolizes the soul. My mind lit up when I happened upon another possibility, a phenomenon described by Lurianic Kabbalah as *ibbur*, the temporary transmigration of a departed soul who wishes to complete a task or perform a mitzvah, a good deed. Sometimes this benevolent form of possession is brought about for the benefit of the living person, the "host" soul, who may not even know the tzaddik is there filling their emptiness, repairing their brokenness. This coincided with what the rabbi said he knew: *A tzaddik is alive even in death, crossing the bridge between worlds, changing the destinies of those around him.*

Encountering the luna moth—*and* on the full moon—fueled me with encouragement and the energy to keep going, to keep paying attention. To keep gathering what seemed to be plausible evidence that Sam *was* alive even in death. Even if it *was* just an insect and nothing more, even if I *hadn't* temporarily "hosted" my son's soul—though if I had, would I even know?—I was learning how to *be* in this world. I was readjusting to life, recalibrating my senses, reconstructing my story. I was repairing myself—or maybe, possibly, could it be *me* who was being repaired? *That* was something.

less alone

"You should come down and meet Carla McClafferty," my mother-in-law said, urging me to drive to Miami to attend the lecture she was hosting. "She'll be speaking about her latest book, *In Defiance of Hitler: The Secret Mission of Varian Fry*. But the first book she wrote was about the loss of *her* son. I really think you should meet her."

"Thanks, Mi Mi, for thinking of me, but . . . I don't know." Sam had been gone only a year; I could barely move.

"She's flying in from Arkansas. I've already spoken with her and told her you might be there. You'll *really* like her. She's fabulous, and the three of us will have lunch on Saturday, my treat."

Let the fabulous world out there bustle about, I thought. I just couldn't. I didn't want to go anywhere, do anything, meet anyone. Plus, the drive was too long, five to six hours depending on traffic. Then again, a hotel room all to myself, a weekend away, was tempting. At least *there*, alone, I wouldn't have to censor myself. At home, when I slipped, said what I was thinking out loud or mentioned Sam's name, both David and Joey would shut down.

Once, wanting to remind David of something funny, I brought up the time Sam had come to Joey's defense. "Remember that time Sam yelled at you? 'He's *just* a little boy! He *doesn't* know any better! Why don't you pick on someone your *own* size?' and you were trying not to laugh?" But by mid-sentence, he had already turned away from me.

Another time, hoping to get Joey talking, I brought up a memory. "When you were a toddler, Sam used to translate your words for us when we couldn't understand what you were saying. You remember that?" At his brother's name, Joey gave me the side-eye and turned to stone.

Burying the pain—silencing it—only makes it worse. But if I'd said that, it would've created more distance between us. I resented it, having to muzzle myself. How long would we go on *not* talking about Sam? How long could we pretend to ignore the Sam-shaped void that was in every room, every closet, every doorway? I wanted to talk about him, say his name to someone who wouldn't shut down, turn away, or turn to stone. I was miserable and wanted company. Maybe I *should* make the trip to Miami to meet Carla. She had experienced this kind of loss and had survived it—written about it, even. I wanted to know how she was walking, talking, writing, speaking. I wanted to ask how she was doing it, rewriting her life, her misery. So I booked a hotel room and packed my suitcase.

Did we eat dinner? I don't remember.

After the lecture, back at the hotel, Carla and I sat outside by the pool at a table with an umbrella that was wrapped up for the night. The sky was black, a salty breeze was blowing, and though it was too dark to see the ocean, I could hear waves rolling in and slapping the shore in the near distance.

"It was Thanksgiving Day," Carla said. "Corey fell off the swing in our backyard. He was fourteen months old. I couldn't wake him up. I rode in the ambulance with him to the ER."

Both Carla and I had screamed, pleaded, begged, bartered, and prayed for our little boys to wake up.

"Sam was nine. We discovered a mass in his heart when he was five. He was running on the playground at school when he collapsed. The mass turned out to be hypertrophic cardiomyopathy."

We'd both been to those same places, alongside those same people, police, paramedics, ER doctors, heard those same noises, voices shouting and crying, and screaming over that same nightmarish silence.

"Having Ryan and Brittney forced me out of bed in the mornings. But while they were in school, for the first five years, I just lay on the sofa. I could barely move."

I nodded. "I don't think I'd be sitting here if it weren't for Joey."

"You're doing amazingly well," Carla said. "You've made this trip *and* you've started writing."

Like long-lost friends, we talked for hours, until after midnight. Bonding with another bereaved parent, connecting with someone who got it, gave me an energy that felt like hope. Though nothing had changed, I felt different, less alone. I remember the last thing she told me as we pushed our chairs in and headed back inside: "After you finish writing a book, just know this: nothing changes. It doesn't change anything."

As the more experienced senior member of this unimaginable club, Carla only wanted to warn me, a fledgling freshman, about the harsh reality of my future. I knew what she meant. Writing a book wasn't going to bring Sam back, but maybe, in time, the writing would change me. Because I couldn't keep living feeling the way I did.

The next morning, even though I'd only slept a few hours, I woke up feeling a little less dead, a little less desolate, a little less miserable.

one year

The Arctic Tern
Sam Kassenoff, age 6

The Arctic Tern weighs about 2/3 of a pound, and measures 12 to 15 inches long. It has a white, forked tail, a black cap on its white head, and a red bill, an accent color, and tool for fishing.

Tern colonies breed in the Arctic Circle. They lay eggs in grassy areas and both parents care for them. The colony flies to the edge of the Antarctic ice pack. Its days are long and sunlit from one hemisphere to the other. The Tern spends each of its 20 years of life flying the earth's circumference.

Dread is the sudden silence that follows the noise of a socializing Tern colony right before they take to the air and fly away to begin their migration, the longest migration of any bird.

We'd come to the end of our yearlong migration, the last day of April, the one-year anniversary.

My habit of sitting outside on the back patio, staring into the woods, had become more intentional now. The practice of being not in the past or the future but in the present had positive aftereffects. When I drifted too far away, or found myself panicking, stiffening, gripping the steering wheel too tightly, I could bring myself back to my breath, back *in* the moment. I was learning to pay attention to my breathing. It sounds ridiculous, but sometimes I'd realize I *wasn't* breathing.

I'd started practicing yoga. Every morning, I'd salute the sun, move into down dog, become a warrior, a tree, a child, then finish in corpse pose. The stretching and breathing helped ease the physical pain. If I skipped a day, the throbbing in my back, where grief seems to live, would remind me to unroll my mat, bend, stretch, lie dead, and breathe.

I'd taken to walking, venturing outside. Alone, I'd wander alongside the wooded areas, bird-watching or looking for the luna moth, searching every bush, behind every tree. I was a modern-day version of the bereaved Cro-Magnon mother Bryan Sykes had written about.

The day before the one-year mark, while I was out walking, two shadows skimmed across my path. Above me, two terns, white with forked tails and black accents, were circling. I craned my neck, held out my arms, and pretended to fly with them. Gliding up and over the treetops, observing myself from a distance, I realized how small I was, a tiny ant scouring the sidewalk for a crumb. Drifting too high up, I brought my attention back to my breath, back to *now*. On the sidewalk, skipping in front of me were two feathers, white with black tops, as if they'd been dipped in ink. I picked them up and folded them, one and then the other, into the shape of a heart, then tucked these pieces of treasure into my pocket and continued on.

That night, the night before we were to begin our next yearlong migration, I sat beside Joey's bed, watching him sleep wrapped in his cocoon of blankets. I examined the tufts of hair, the freckled nose, the full cheeks, and thick, dark lashes, and then his uncovered toes. I shook my head and looked away, trying to loosen the grip of that memory, standing at Sam's feet, touching his toes with my face.

You know he's not here anymore. That's not him. He's gone.

No. No. No. I shook my head again.

People often mistook them for twins, which irked Sam, who was two years older. Sometimes, seeing the resemblance between the boys threw me off-balance. I'd see Sam in the shape of Joey's shoulders or the way he walked, or I'd see it in a sideways glance, a gesture, a shrug, or an eye roll, and I'd have to shake my head. Then I'd torture myself: How can he *not* be here anymore? How will Joey, the little brother, one day be older, taller, deeper voiced, than his *older* brother? I had considered looking into getting some sort of age-progression software (if one were available) to generate images of Sam and age him along with Joey. Talk about torture! I knew this was way too far.

Breathe. I guided myself back to now, where I had two sons, one in *this* world and one in *that* world, two boys folded into one heart, two feathers in my pocket.

April 30, 2008. Days: 366.

In the morning, I lit a candle, one we kept in a silver holder that matches the Essence urn. I woke Joey, who slept like a rock and never seemed to remember his dreams.

But this morning, he said, "I had a dream about a pirate ship. And I was on it. I think Sam was with me. And we found a briefcase." He seemed excited.

I was excited that he'd said his brother's name. "What did the brief-case look like?"

"It was old; it had buckles."

"Was there anything in it?"

"It was full of papers—some envelopes too."

I wanted to know more, but he'd already bounced onto the sofa with the remote control to check in with SpongeBob.

While I packed one lunch and made one breakfast, I wondered if he remembered the day cruise we'd taken with my father in Panama City Beach. It was just after we'd returned from Boston for all of Sam's tests and were trying to live normally. Joey was only three, and Sam, five. They'd never been on a real pirate ship before and held hands the whole time. That summer day on *The Sea Dragon*, sailing out in the Gulf of Mexico, parents and grandparents—"hostages"—were told to sit and relax while the mini-pirates ran amok, ate hot dogs, scrubbed the deck, played games, hunted treasure, and even shot off a cannon. When friendly boaters passed by and waved, the child-marauders yelled, "Arr!" and waved back with their swords. I remembered how my dad's face mirrored mine, contemplative, concerned, vulnerable, vigilant, forcing a smile whenever Sam looked in our direction.

I returned to my breath, back *in* the moment. Though I'd been doing this for a year now, every morning, standing in the kitchen across from the empty recliner where Sam had been sitting, reading quietly that morning, not a day goes by without *Monday* as the backdrop. But this day, the ding of the toaster oven, the buzzing of David's electric razor in the background, and the volume of the TV were louder, more jarring.

David had taken the day off, so after we drove Joey to school, we went to IHOP for breakfast. He didn't want to be at the office, and I didn't want to be at home. So we ate pancakes. It all seemed ridiculously wrong. *How can we be sitting here eating pancakes?* I thought. But then again, I guess eating pancakes, like wearing lipstick, is *living*.

At one thirty that afternoon, on the school playground, Sam's classmates, his teachers, Principal Alder, the paramedics, Officer Twisdale, Joey, David, and I circled the tree that had been planted where Sam had lain one year ago. A group of David's colleagues had purchased the beautiful oak tree in Sam's memory.

We played a song, "Good Riddance (The Time of Your Life)," from Sam's Green Day CD, and tried to sing along.

"Another turning point, a fork stuck in the road. Time grabs you by the wrist, directs you where to go."

But as the song played, our voices trailed off.

"So make the best of this test, and don't ask why. It's not a question, but a lesson learned in time."

And children began crying.

"It's something unpredictable. But in the end, it's right."

And the circle broke apart.

"I hope you had the time of your life."

After everyone left, and David and I were alone on the playground, he broke down beside the tree, crying on his hands and knees over our Sammy, still lying there in the mulch.

The sun in the sky was the same as it had been the year before, too bright. All I could do in that moment was close my eyes and breathe, stand there as still as the tree, alive but motionless, and provide shade.

That night, at All-Star Baseball tryouts, David and I sat in the bleachers wringing our hands, nervous, hoping Joey would make the team. We started clapping when he stepped up to the plate.

"You've got this, Joey!"

In came the first pitch. He swung and missed.

"Next one's yours, Joe-D!"

In came the second pitch. He swung and hit the ball in a high arc over the field and over the fence. The coach had instructed him to run after any hit, so he could time him running the bases. But Joey stood there holding his bat, looking over at us with his mouth open. He'd never hit a home run before.

We were standing, cheering, laughing. "Go, Joey! Run . . . RUN!"

Maybe *that* was the moment I realized it. I'd have to make the best of this test, and not ask why. Life was going to be like this: one moment, one way, collapsing, broken; another moment, another way, rising, euphoric; and sometimes, it would be both ways at once: laughing *and* crying at the same time. Joy *and* grief would live *and* breathe together, side by side.

a sign

Almost every day, on my way to pick up Joey, I drove past an animal hospital, one with the yellow wood siding and the lifelike alligator statue on the grass out front. Weekly, they updated their large-lettered sign with pet-related reminders or quotes.

It was Thursday, one year after Sam's funeral, when I saw "SAM" in big block letters on the sign. There was an 'E' missing, and I smiled reading the quote: *"EVERYONE SMILES IN THE SAM LANGUAGE."*

When I pulled into the carpool line, I spotted Joey and squinted at the letter in his hands. *Are you kidding?* He was holding a huge, papier-mâché E.

On the drive home, I asked him about his art project that also, on closer inspection, had small, yellow smiles painted on it. "Why an E and not—oh, I don't know—a J or a K?"

He shrugged. "I like the letter E."

It was as simple as that. It was pure magic.

bereaved

Sunken in my folding chair, holding my knees to my chest (though it was hard to sit any other way in those canvas chairs that collapse and fit into a carrying bag), I was here but somewhere else. It was this way each time we went to the ballpark, whether at baseball practices or games. For the first few years after Sam's death, small talk with those who didn't know led to questions and made me anxious, anticipating the *one* question that was kindling for every conversation: "Is Joey your only child?"

I wanted to answer, say Sam's name, talk about what happened. Most bereaved parents do—want to talk, that is.

Our shadow child is always with us, *here* or *over there*. Though most people think the last thing a bereaved parent wishes to talk about is him or her, the child that died, but we're already broken. Remembering our deceased children, talking about them, keeping their memory alive, *this* is what pieces us back together, makes us stronger. Each word that comes out, each memory we share, helps loosen grief's grip a little more so that one day, being sociable—making small talk about the weather, the food at the concession stand, or how well our team is doing this season—will cause less anxiety, and rejoining others in lighter conversations will become easier.

I just wasn't ready yet. I needed more time to create an elevator speech, to edit and prepare and rehearse my lines. So when someone pitched the question, I wouldn't choke, panic, say too much or not enough, or worse, fumble and lie: "No—I'm sorry, what? Yes . . . Joey's my only child."

For the first few months after Sam's death, I suffered stabbing headaches in and around my eyes.

"Narrow-angle glaucoma," the ophthalmologist said. "Yours is the worst I've seen."

I wondered if the pain was from *not* crying. I didn't ask. The question sounded ridiculous in my head: *My son, he's gone, and it hurts when I cry, so I wonder, did this happen, this buildup—of tears?—because I've been stopping myself from crying?* Suppressing grief, like pruning branches, I've learned, only causes it to mushroom.

After the surgeon used a laser to puncture a tiny hole in the iris of each eye to relieve the pressure and drain the built-up fluid, the headaches receded, and my vision improved. But despair seemed to be seeping from my pores.

During the first few years, every few months, another spidery, reddish speck, skin cancer, would bloom on my face—on my eyebrow, my temple, my scalp, my left cheek, right cheek, then another on the left.

Each time, while the surgeon cut, cauterized, and stitched, he didn't talk or smile or make eye contact. So I'd lie there, numb, staring at that pattern of specks in the ceiling tiles that I swear coalesced into the likeness of Sam's face. I didn't ask: "Might there be a connection between my son's death, my grief, and this recurring skin cancer?" What was the point? With each throbbing, black caterpillar of sutures, I could feel my body giving up, my immune system weakening.

People stared at me in the grocery store, at my battered face, probably thinking I'd been in a car accident. I wanted to scream at the world: "My son died! That's what happened! This is what grief looks like!"

To an outsider it may seem counterproductive to write about grief while sinking in the quicksand of it, but the cerebral process of writing and editing, the fastidious attention to every letter, every comma, every word, is the ultimate distraction. When I'm hyperfocused, fully absorbed in the task at hand, hunched over my keyboard, a rat's nest for hair, nibbling almonds, alone with my thoughts, slowly but surely pecking away at my story, the left and right hemispheres of my brain, logic *and* imagination, fuse to form new pathways through grief. Ways that didn't seem to exist before, or that I was unable to see until the words, like puzzle pieces, were set just so. I'm able to examine and process and come to understand *not* my child's death, but my reaction to it, my grief. Instead of floating somewhere in the gray middle, I'm standing at the control center, taking charge of my mind, my*selves*. Even though I stop at every line and second-guess myself, obsess over every word, every decision—because every time there are dozens (oodles or reams) of word choices—there is always *only* one right word, and I know it when I hear it. Editing paragraphs line by line, combing out knots, rearranging sentences, rewriting them, carving each into a shorter, sharper point with exactly the right handpicked words, *this* is what lights up both sides.

Right: Is that last paragraph too long, too many words?

Left: Yes! Delete, delete. And change your opening word, sunken, back to submerged.

Right: Nope! Sunken is the one.

Sam's voice: Yes, Mommy, sunken, I hear it too—that's the one!

Left: Fine, we'll go with sunken then. Next, same paragraph, closing sentence: kindling?

Right: Yes, kindling. It feels right. I'm leaving it.

"What happened?" someone asked, one night at one of Joey's baseball games.

What happened? The question triggered me. The thoughts welled up inside me: *My little boy ... he was running on the playground at school when ...*

Pointing to my face, I made a joke. "Got into a fight. You should see the other guy." I paused for a laugh and shrugged. "Skin cancer. I grew up in Miami, so . . . I'm going by Scarface now."

Left: What is wrong with you?

Right: What? You know that's what I do—make jokes, hide behind my sense of humor. Hey, that gives me an idea for the title of a book I might write one day: When Bad Things Happen to Fun People.

Left: No comment.

My world was—and always will be—divided into those who knew and those who didn't. On the sidelines, sitting there among the moms and dads; little brothers pushing matchbox cars; big sisters giggling, braiding ponytails; babies sleeping in strollers, I blended in, but I didn't *fit* in. Nobody knew. Nobody could see him, or how broken I was, or hear the lunacy going on inside me.

Right: I can feel it. He's here—over there, in the shade.

Left: He's not here, or over there.

Right: So you say. But what if he is here, or over there beneath that tree? What if he is and you don't bother to look? You don't bother to listen? Or make any connection at all? Imagine his face, how sad you'd make him, ignoring him, not paying attention.

Left: I don't see anything beneath that tree. I don't hear anything.

Right: Because you can't see him, or hear him, you think he doesn't exist anymore? Even if he is gone, as you say, what harm is there in these visions? I bring a smile to his face because I still see him. He knows I love him, still, and that I will never forget him. Even if you are right—and maybe you are—and I'm only imagining what I see or hear, it doesn't matter. I won't stop looking, listening. You suffer your way, angry, blind to the possibility of him. And I'll suffer my way.

Left: Fine. Can we focus now on the ballgame—try and act normal, be sociable, and fit in? Can we at least do that together?

Right: Fine.

Joey played baseball year-round. Our colors changed with the seasons. In the fall, we wore gray with red accents. In winter, bright yellow. In spring, orange, and in the summer, a cool white with red lettering. Migrating from season to season, we mingled with different families and made seasonal friends.

Sometimes, the conversation went well.

A mom who didn't know asked. "Is Joey your only child?"

"No. Joey's older brother, Sam, died two years ago."

"I'm so sorry for your loss. If you don't mind me asking, how did he die?"

"He had hypertrophic cardiomyopathy, HCM. Maybe you've heard about the high school athlete who collapses during a game? Sudden cardiac arrest. Sam was running on the playground at school when it happened."

"How old was he?"

"Sam was only nine."

"You never do heal from something like that, do you?"

We shook our heads and sighed in unison, then focused on the game, cheered for our team, and had other lighter conversations until the season ended and we migrated our separate ways.

Sometimes, the conversation went wrong.

One season, a mom I hadn't met before unfolded her chair beside mine and we started chatting. We had a lot in common, and I felt pretty balanced in my chair, slathering on sunscreen, being sociable.

"Is Joey your only child?"

What I almost said: *No, he has a brother. Sam's twelve now. The boys played together all the time—they were always laughing. There was always something funny. Though sometimes, when Sam laughed too hard, I worried about his heart. He's not here—well, he's here, but . . .*

But I stuck to the line I'd rehearsed: "No. Joey's older brother, Sam, died three years ago."

As if she'd seen a ghost, her eyes widened, she stiffened, turned away, and stared straight ahead for the rest of the game.

When I was a kid, I played a game called Don't Spill The Beans. Each turn, you placed a kidney bean, one at a time, onto the plastic kettle, which teetered as the beans piled up; you lost when the kettle tipped, and you spilled the beans. I had spilled the beans. And though I'd lost my son, I felt sorry for this woman. She had no lines prepared for this, no words.

I was stunned by her abrupt reaction, but after a few seconds, I shrugged it off. I'd given my best performance, and regardless of what others thought or said, I wasn't going to apologize anymore for *my* loss or the way I delivered my lines. It was one of those defining moments. Sitting there, after spilling my beans, looking at the back of her head after she'd repositioned her chair, I knew I had crossed some invisible finish line in my grieving. I was beginning to feel more comfortable in my cut, cauterized, and stitched skin, more confident in myself and who I was now in my grief.

It became more awkward when she avoided me for the rest of the season as if what I had—a dead child—was contagious. *It's not contagious; it's random—a cancer cell, a drunk driver, a tumor masquerading as HCM!* But, in all fairness, I remember reacting the same way once. I had stiffened and turned away too.

One evening, the year before Sam died, the boys were outside playing, I was making dinner, and the six o'clock news was on in the background. It had happened less than a mile away. "A branch from the pine tree fell," the anchor announced, "killing the five-year-old girl while she was playing in her backyard. The branch missed her younger brother who was playing only a few feet away." Terrified by the unpredictable randomness of death, I turned off the TV, hurried outside, scanned the spindly pine trees out back for suspicious-looking branches, and called in the boys. What I had feared most was that lethal mass in Sam's heart, but I had *not* considered a tree branch.

Like that mom at the ballpark who had turned away, I had also been afraid to look at the news of another child's death, at the bereaved mother; I was afraid that if I did, it might happen to my child, to me.

9
MIGRATING

waiting

In her book, *The Worst Loss*, Barbara Rosof wrote, "The same loss that forces the need for change also renders you, for some time, unable to do much about it."

More than three years had passed, and I was still longing for things to be the way they were; to use the plural, *boys*, again. To hear Joey laugh and talk and say his brother's name: "Sammy, I caught a lizard! Sammy, want to play secret spies? Sammy, want to go to the pool now? Sammy . . ." I was waiting for *something* to change. Vacillating between logic and imagination. Waiting for my left and right brain to come to an agreement, or a compromise, on how to rewrite our story with a different ending.

Left: He's gone.

Right: He's not gone. I still see him, and hear him, in dreams.

In a dream (or *was* he there at midnight, standing beside my bed?), his face was glowing. Was he holding a candle? No, I saw his hands; he was holding them out. *I love you*, he said.

In another dream, we just stared at each other, blinking back tears. He looked worried. *Rest, Mommy. You need rest.*

Joey was a fourth grader now at the new neighborhood school, a short bike ride away. Every morning, we rode past the lake, alongside the woods, and up to the corner, where I waved goodbye and he went on and joined his friends. I'd just gotten home and put my bike away when I heard the thud on the window above the front door.

Outside on the porch, lying near the welcome mat, I found a small, olive-gray and yellow bird. Its ice-blue eyes, the color of a husky dog's, were open, seeing. It wasn't moving, but it was still breathing; I could feel its tiny heart racing. While Reggie skimmed the concrete with his nose, I sat on the patio floor holding the stunned bird in a shoebox, waiting for it to recover and come to. Sitting there, I remembered that day a handful of years ago when I had to teach the lesson I feared most.

The boys had been six and eight at the time. We were riding our bikes past the lake when I pointed at a raft of little black ducks. "Those are called coots." Heading south on the shaded path alongside the woods, we saw a black racer, then a marsh rabbit twitching its nose, eyeing us. I was telling the boys about the pet rabbit I'd had when I was their age. "Her name was Trixy."

"That's a funny name," Sam said. "What color was Trick-see?"

"She was all black except for a white spot over her mouth, like a milk mustache."

The boys laughed at this, and a nearby mockingbird laughed too. All of a sudden, we came upon a family of birds with black racing stripes on their breasts, killdeers. Instead of flying away, the two adults and two babies, miniature versions of their parents, ran, shrieking and scattering as we approached. We stopped, dumbfounded. The mother bird was screaming on one side of the path, and the babies were running and peeping frantically on the other side.

It all happened so fast. One chick was running toward the road.

"Mommy! Stop him! He's gonna get run over!"

But the tiny bird kept running and the mother bird kept screeching and the boys kept screaming, pleading. The truck didn't hit him, but the truck's wake did. The turbulence dragged and tossed his body over and over in somersaults. He couldn't have seen what hit him; it was only wind. Behind us, frantic and circling, peeping and screeching, the killdeer family, minus one, scurried into the brush to hide.

As traffic continued to swoosh by, the tiny bird lay on its side, limp, expressionless, a broken toy.

"Mommy . . . is he dead?"

"Stay here." I left the sidewalk and went to the roadside. The tiny bird was beyond saving, and I had to give the lesson I feared most: "Sometimes, horrible things happen. And some things we have no control over. It's okay to cry, but we've got to keep going. Come on. Let's go. Get back on your bikes. And one more thing. Never, *ever*, run or play near traffic—you hear me?"

Both boys nodded, and we continued on, slower than before, quieter. "I'll be really careful around traffic, Mommy. I promise," Sam vowed.

We'd gone about a mile farther to an apartment complex, our turn-around point, to stop for a water break when Sam stumbled off his bike and said he felt dizzy.

Speeding with adrenaline, I assembled every detail at once: Sam's bike rolling, falling over, wheels spinning, slowing; Joey picking it up, putting down the kickstand; Sam's eyes swimming, his face pale despite the heat. With killdeers still screeching in my head, I acted calm and helped him pull off his helmet.

"You're okay, you're okay." I guided him and Joey into the air-conditioned front office of the complex. The receptionist looked up and asked if everything was all right. "Just a little overheated." I sat Sam down on a sofa and went to refill our water bottles. My hands were shaking; my heart was pounding. *Breathe.* In my head, I ran through CPR steps: *Call 911, pulse, compressions, breaths . . .*

After a few minutes, Sam assured me he felt better. "I'm okay, Mommy. We can go now."

We studied a large map on the wall which showed the apartment buildings and the surrounding area. I pointed out where we were and explained the compass rose, the four directions. "We'll head west and then north to get back home."

The receptionist was watching us. "Do you homeschool them?"

I laughed. "No, no. Just doing camp-mom this summer."

"You're a stay-at-home mom?"

I nodded.

"It shows. Your boys are so polite, so well-behaved."

I thanked her. I felt lucky. But then luck is random; it changes with the wind.

We took our time pedaling home and tried not to look at the tiny body still lying in the road.

Sitting there, holding the stunned bird, I brought myself back *in* the moment, back to the small bird's breathing, its tiny heart racing. I held one hand over the shoebox, just in case, and massaged the dog's ear as he sniffed around the edges, a little too excited. "Reggie, no. Good boy. Friend, not food."

After waiting twenty minutes or so, the small, husky-eyed bird, which turned out to be a white-eyed vireo, regained its senses. It seemed confused but calm, curious even, looking up at the dog, then at me. I imagined its shrill, whistly voice: *Thank you for waiting. I feel better now.* It stood and stretched. Using its wings for balance, the vireo leapt out of the box, stumbled, hopped, and tried to take off. After a few attempts, it remembered how and flew away. *Goodbye!*

"The two most powerful warriors are Patience and Time," said Tolstoy.

Some days, unable to do much else, all I could *do* was sit and wait. At the same time, I remembered what it was I already knew: *Sometimes, horrible things happen. And some things we have no control over. It's okay to cry, but we've got to keep going.* One day, I would find a way to bring Sam back to life. Patience was my superpower now.

desire

Years ago, I found a small book of Buddhist scriptures on a sale table at the bookstore. On its red-and-gold jacket is a mandala with a tiny

Buddha in the center and tinier Buddhas around him. From time to time, when I need reminding, I rediscover it on my shelf, the way I find that outdated bottle of vitamins in my cabinet. I always mean to take both daily, but then I forget to get them out, open them up, shake out a pill or consume a line or two:

"Life is full of dukkha (suffering)."
"Desire brings grief."

Once, in a desperate moment, needing to see and hear him, his voice, I watched a video of Sam that he'd recorded himself. In an imaginary concert, he was performing "Boulevard of Broken Dreams" with Green Day. On the large TV screen, he was almost life-size, *there* in the room. After he began to sing, the microphone flopped down and fell from its cradle, which was a little funny. Without missing a beat, he bent, picked it up, and with his free hand, swept the hands of imaginary fans on his way back to the imaginary stage. He kept singing and held out his arms, but his microphone flopped down and fell again. I started to laugh, but then stopped when he pointed to the audience, at me; pressed two fingers to his throat; and lip-synched the lyrics.

Check my vital signs, to know I'm still alive, and I walk alone . . .

He's still alive. How can he not be? Some mornings, I still woke up confounded. *How is this possible? This is how it is now, how it's going to be?* But then I'd get out of bed and wade through the day, something inside me, an indescribable force, urging me on.

Mommy, it's okay to cry, but we've got to keep going. Come on. Let's go. Get back on your bike.

April 30, 2011. Days: 1,461.

I opened the small, red-and-gold book with the mandala and tiny Buddhas on it and consumed another line:

"The world is impermanent."

I lit the candle beside Sam's urn for the fourth time, then went for a walk.

The weather had turned from warm to hot. Trees were lush with new leaves. Raspberry-colored flowers had burst from the azaleas. Star jasmine filled the air with its fragrance. Hummingbirds zipped in and out of the bottlebrush tree. Green bean lizards—like the ones the boys used to catch and tag and dot with a permanent blue marker before setting them free again—were bolting from the new foliage up the gray-painted stucco. As I was leaving, just outside the front door, I made eye contact with one. "I see you, Green Bean." Then I zoomed in close enough to marvel at the iridescent, aquamarine eye shadow it was wearing and snapped a picture.

I kept going, living *for* him, never, not for a second, living *without* him. I took the paths we used to take, to the places we used to go—up past "the swamp" to that heart that someone had carved in the side-walk. Maybe I was imagining things. The way my shadow was shaped, the way it moved and leaned toward me on the sidewalk and whispered in my ear. How does one describe a color or a sound or a scent? I just knew it, felt it, sensed it. He was *here,* or *over there*—still alive.

The month before, while out walking up by the lake, I found another luna moth, already dead, lying in the grass next to the sidewalk. The color of the moth's wings reminded me of Sam's eyes, pale green. I scooped up the papery corpse, cupped my hands around it, and carried it home. This one I keep in a baseball display cube near my desk as a reminder: *The world is impermanent.*

As the arctic terns continued their migration—*the longest migration of any bird*—from one hemisphere to the other, I followed them, their shadows on the sidewalk, as they passed over me. Occasionally, I saw the rabbit, or his twin, hiding at the edge of the woods, nibbling greens under the only tree there was with orange flowers. I gardened, planted lemon balm (Sam loved lemons), pinched off the leaves, inhaled their scent, and added them to my tea or my lemonade.

A birdwatcher now, I kept track of the killdeers. Their new home was beside the lake, on the grass between the water and the hedges—away from the busy road. Around the ground nest was a miniature fence made of sticks and bright orange tape, thanks to the lawn service crew. Four birdies were running in all directions on the green, chips off the old killdeer block with their black racing stripes and high-pitched cheeps. I checked on them daily. Funny little things, to prefer their feet on the ground, while I would prefer wings to fly away with.

One morning, I noticed the fence and nest were gone and the lawn had been freshly mowed. I missed those quirky little runners by the lake, their voices, and the sounds they made. "Keet. Keet. Kedear. Keedear." I had to readjust to the quiet again and remind myself: *The world is impermanent.*

I recalled thinking I wouldn't last four years. But as it turned out, every month, every day, every hour, every minute was impermanent too.

It had happened so slowly it was hardly noticeable—how I had changed. All those black caterpillars, sutures from skin cancer removal, had turned into thin, well-crafted scars that blended with "the lines" on my face. I was moving through the days and functioning and remembering where I'd parked the car. I'd made peace with the silence and solitude of grief. I still hoped for dreams of him, then went on living in or in between those dreams. It was a balancing act between inertia and forward motion. Walking that tightrope between the past and the present. Finding that path where logic and imagination compromised and collaborated.

Left: All right, I'll try and help you rewrite this story with a different ending. Together, we'll find the words. But we're not using that title you mentioned.

Right: Which one? When Bad Things Happen to Fun People?

Left: That's the one.

Right: Deal. All right? You'll help me find the words then?

Left: Who do you think has been helping you remember where you parked your car?

Right: Oh, yeah, right, that makes sense.

treasure

Another fall came; another school year began. Sam would be fourteen and starting high school, a freshman now. For five years and five months I had let the dust in his room stay, unable to erase even the smallest atom of him. But the room smelled stale. Even his comforter, pillows, and stuffed animals were covered in a gauzy blanket of dust. It was time to bring his bedroom alive again. Decide what to keep or give away and dust off the things that mattered most to him: his Green Day CDs; his magic kit; his guitar; his camera; his books; his mummy; his desk; his awards; his action figures; his hero, Duke, still standing at attention, on the nightstand.

I picked up his camouflage backpack, which was still filled with subject folders, composition books, neon highlighters, and a third-grade day planner, then sat for a while, holding its weight on my lap. I remembered one summer afternoon, sitting in a movie theater, at a matinee, holding him, *his* weight, on my lap, rocking him in my seat. During the opening scene, there was lightning, thunder, an intense drumbeat, and Sam, fifteen months old, covered his ears and hid his face while the gorilla rescued a human infant from a big cat. When the music played and Phil Collins sang, Sam looked up again, awestruck. The gorilla, a grieving mother who'd lost her own child, adopted the baby and named him Tarzan. Sam was sleeping, his head heavy on my chest, when Tarzan was leaving for another world, a human world beyond the sea. My eyes teared up when the gorilla mother told her son he would *always* be in her heart. Carrying my baby boy out of the theater, his sleeping face on my shoulder, I knew the time would come, though I didn't like thinking about it, when I would have to let him go.

Where to begin?

I got up and put an audiobook into Sam's CD player: *This Is How: Surviving What You Think You Can't* by Augusten Burroughs. I chose the "How To Remain Unhealed" chapter and pressed play, and Burroughs talked to me while I filled boxes with things to donate, sell, or trash.

"Parents who have lost a child should be told that they will never heal from their loss. They will always have a terrible, wide hole within them. And other holes, smaller ones . . ."

I pressed the back button and replayed the chapter. There were holes in my mind; I was slow to grasp concepts. No matter how hard I concentrated, new words, thoughts, and ideas went right through me. To retain things, I had to read them again and again. I listened to the chapter a third time to absorb the words.

"So, no, if your child dies, you will not heal . . ."

Blown away by this unexpected windfall, I had to sit. The weight I'd been carrying for so long had shifted. The words were like fast-acting medicine. Now I could move forward in the direction of just *doing*, just *living*, just *being*—nothing more, sometimes less—and away from that impossible goal of *healing*.

It took two full days to revive Sam's room and sort through his things, sit with each piece, each memory, and decide what to do with it.

"Sam, I'm sorry for invading your privacy . . . for picking through your things . . . for getting rid of anything you might want to keep. But you're older now—you don't play with these toys anymore. And you've outgrown these shirts . . . these shoes."

I donated the dress shoes he wore only once. Threw away the broken Happy Meal toys, but kept his pastel toothbrush in the cup beside his sink. I cleaned and organized the remaining toys and books, and finally washed his bedding. Then I polished the furniture with a heavy coat of Pledge. The scent of lemons filled the air, and for a few minutes his room, a shrine now, came back to life.

"Sammy . . . I miss you."

Don't cry, Mommy.

After several trips to and from the garage, I was exhausted. There was one bag of trash left to tie up and take out. For some reason, I checked it again, just in case I'd thrown out something I shouldn't have. There, mixed in with the garbage, a fluorescent green rubber band, buried treasure, caught my eye. I took back what I decided was *not* trash and put it around my wrist. Then, erasing my footprints as I went, I vacuumed my way out of the room.

As I was putting my newfound treasure into my ruby-red jewelry box, the one that had been a Mother's Day gift, I found something else. On the inside of the fluorescent green rubber band, there was an inscription—Sam's handwriting in faded blue ink: *I love you more than all the sidewalks in the world.*

Not because I couldn't retain it, but because I wanted to hear his voice, I read it again and again before putting it away.

"I love you, Sammy."

I love you, too, Mommy—more than all the sidewalks in the world.

On the morning of the garage sale, vultures circled the cul-de-sac. Throngs of shoppers swooped in and picked over my son's worldly remains. Without any remorse, they grabbed things—toys, games, books, matchbox cars, plastic animals, marbles, clothes.

An eagle-eyed woman told me she was a dealer looking for resale value. She picked through Sam's bucket of Lego bricks, removed the generic pieces, then paid and made off with a trove of Lego blocks to resell on eBay.

A man walked away with Sam's bike, which was rusted and missing a few spokes. I'd thrown in the helmet for free and handed it to his little boy who looked excited, which made me smile, so I let the bicycle go.

Pushing a stroller, a mother—who looked nothing like a vulture— seemed to be wavering over what turned out to be a serendipitous find, the *SAMUEL* step stool that had helped toddler Sam reach the sink and brush his teeth. Each letter was a puzzle piece that fit into the face of the step.

"Do you have a Samuel too?" I asked. She nodded. "Then you should take it. The letters are glued together so you won't lose the pieces." She smiled, handed me a few bills, and carried away what would now become her treasure.

The emptiness inside me felt even larger. That *terrible, wide hole within* had expanded. But then, of course it had. How could it not? I was letting go of him or at least relaxing my grip. The process of letting go was going to take a lifetime. I knew this now. But I also knew—I had seen it with my own eyes—that it was *in* the letting go that I might find buried treasure.

growth

In *The Diagnostic and Statistical Manual of Mental Disorders*, the bible of psychiatry, the death of a child is called a "catastrophic stressor."

Living with a catastrophic stressor means working at accepting other collateral damage—an impaired body; a failing memory; an inability to focus, think, or concentrate. The inability to concentrate, I learned, is one of the most common of all responses to loss. How was it even possible to live in such an altered state?

For a long time, I wondered if I'd ever be able to see or hear the world in a sharper, less muddled way, or be able to think or read or write, much less rewrite my story with a different ending. A new tremor: *What if I'm unsuccessful, and something else extremely unfortunate happens, and I don't live long enough to finish this? I need to save him. I need to finish this!* And, if I'm only able to focus on and draft one or two sentences a day, how long will it take then to write an entire book, one that'll bring my boy back to life, before it's too late? *How much time do I have left?*

I was spinning off course, forgetting to breathe. *Stop. Come back to your breath.* I pulled myself away from the lunacy and back to the present and reminded myself: *Follow your breath. Count. In . . . and out. One. In . . . and out. Two . . . Be here, only here, and breathe . . . Three. One breath at a time. Four. One moment at a time. Five. Right now, in this moment, you're thinking, reading, typing, and focusing—writing this. Only this.*

In November, seven months after Sam's death, our dear friend, Miss Eva (which is what the boys called her), had surprised us with news that she'd arranged for an orange tree to be planted where she first met Sam, at the JCA.

It was a bright and balmy fall day, the kind of day a young citrus tree would love, when we gathered on the playground at the JCA's Gan Ye-ladim, or Garden of Children, the school where Sam had grown from busy bee to kindergartner, to plant a tree. Our tight circle of friends, Eva, her daughter, Angelica, and her son, Christopher; Kim and Dave, and their daughter, Hannah; and David, Joey, and I hugged and talked while waiting for Sam's tree to arrive.

When Mike the tree guy from the Flying Dragon Nursery showed up, I noticed he was dressed in green and orange. The company's logo reminded me of *Eragon*, the book Sam had been reading—the movie we had watched together—about a boy chosen to fight evil with, what else, a flying dragon!

As Mike the tree guy dug the hole, I tried to ignore what looked like a small grave. After he placed the tree in the earth, he created a moat around it. "To ensure proper watering," he said. Then he explained to us how uncommon this green-orange tree was, that he'd felt compelled to choose it and didn't know why. "It'll actually produce green oranges!"

Oh, come on! Green oranges? I thought. Sam would flip if he knew that an orange could be green! I didn't tell the tree guy these were Sam's favorite colors, or maybe I did; I don't remember. While someone fetched a watering can, Mike showed us how to cover the roots, pat down the soil, and pile on the pine straw. Once the moat was filled with water, Mike disappeared into the periphery, and our close-knit circle grew quiet.

Earlier that morning, I'd written a poem, *To Sammy*, and rolled copies into scrolls tied with orange and green string. As we passed them around, I realized, regrettably, that they looked like party favors. I was going to read it aloud but couldn't. I'd spoken in a synagogue to a crowd, but here, where there were only nine of us, I choked. So David read *To Sammy* as we stood around the uncommon green-orange tree. Then everyone took turns talking, sniffling, laughing, and remembering Sam. Which is what I needed most—for others to talk about him, or *to* him, to keep him alive, and not be afraid to say his name.

Just before leaving, I kneeled beside the small tree and draped a memorial plaque, which looked like a necklace, over and around its small branches. I knotted the colorful cord I'd embellished with Egyptian beads and touched the small, brass pendant that was shining through the leaves. "Grow, okay? Don't die; grow."

Did I say this to the young tree? To Sammy? To myself? I'm not sure. I heard myself say it, but the whispering had come from that black hole.

Looking back, if I were to label each year, each annual migration, with its own theme, the list would look like this:

Year one: A black hole.

Year two: Routines and rituals.

Year three: Patience.

Year four: Coming to my senses.

Year five: Readapting to my reality.

Year six: Growth from that black hole.

Year two. I remember, over the Christmas break, pushing my cart up to the checkout line at Target, walking right into the trap that had been set for us impulse buyers, and picking out that tiny, ten-inch, potted and already decorated tree for $9.99. I didn't have the desire or the energy anymore for holiday decorating and put out only what Joey requested. Standing there in line, he was thrilled with the big box in our shopping cart, *his* find, a new, shiny, fiber-optic tabletop Christmas tree, which lit up in a dazzling series of different colors, so it seemed like a win-win. This year, a menorah, a light-up tree, and a tiny Norfolk Island pine would get us through the holidays.

Year three. That tiny, already-decorated Christmas tree, now about fifteen inches tall, had been dwelling, still decorated, on the coffee table in the living room. It seemed to be longing for some fresh air, so I carried it outside to the patio, dusted off the silver glitter, removed the tiny silver ornaments, and repotted it in a large, lime-green pot.

Year six. The unadorned Christmas tree that had been living outside on the patio looked sad, neglected, more brown than green. Though slumped, it stood now at about thirty inches tall. I'd never had a green thumb, so I didn't have much hope. In a last-ditch attempt to save its life, I decided to replant it again. Maybe this time, I thought, it would be healthier and happier out in the backyard. There, at least, it wouldn't be root-bound, and it would get watered regularly from rain or sprinklers.

I chose a spot between the house and the woods, where the other tall pines could watch over him. After I dug the hole, I lowered the sad-looking Norfolk Island pine into the center of it, and then, the way Mike the tree guy had taught us, I shoveled the black earth around it, covered the roots, patted down the soil, created a moat around it, and filled the moat with water.

Today, sitting here writing *this*, when I look out my window at that evergreen now, years after replanting it, I marvel at its color, a deep green; at its height, taller than the roofline; at how its branches have multiplied and spread, wide enough that I can sit under them now; and at the way it looks, with its two trunks, like two brothers, or mother and son, side by side, growing, rising together, from that black hole.

willower

I *was* changing. Dying *and* living. Though we may not realize it, what literally makes us *us*—our bodies, tissues, and cells—is changing daily. Old cells die; new cells are born. Some live for only a day, some for months, and some for years, but the cells in our brain, eyes, and heart last a lifetime. The minister's prediction, "In time you'll be a different person, whatever the outcome," had come to pass. I *was* a different person now, except for those parts of me that would never be replenished with new, stronger, more energetic cells: my impaired brain, trauma etched into its neurons; my sad eyes, images burned onto their inner lenses; my broken heart, a terrible, wide hole within it. For as long as I live, these organs will remain the same.

Days: 2,557. Seven years had passed, and again April 30 proved to be the most beautiful, blue-skied day of the year. New life was buzzing and blooming, and everything around me was shimmering and green. The sun was shining, so overly bright and optimistic it didn't seem plausible that anything catastrophic had happened. Though I'd wished for black clouds and rain—Non-stop. All day, all night. Thunder too. Angry, roaring thunder—instead, there were gentle breezes coaxing music from the wind chimes, rustling the new leaves on the trees. Just outside the front door, I spied another green bean lizard not so camouflaged in the jasmine and marveled again, close-up, at the iridescent rings around its eyes. "I see you." I leaned in and examined him, and he cocked his head sideways and studied me with one eye. I noticed then, as I was leaving for my walk, beginning again after yet another yearlong migration, how my ability to focus, think, concentrate, and see the world in a sharper, less muddled way sometimes ebbed and sometimes flowed.

This was the year I created a blog, a website where I could share stories and photos. I knew from past experience, after meeting Carla years ago, how talking with another bereaved parent had helped me to feel less alone and less miserable. Maybe now, I thought, if I shared my experience, showed how I was surviving, walking, talking, living, and rewriting my life, my misery, I could help another bereaved parent to feel less alone, and less miserable too. First, I bought a how-to book and learned how to use WordPress. Then, for months, I brainstormed before coming up with an identity for my site: a logo, a title, and a tagline. I decided to make the luna moth my logo, and "Rewriting life after loss" my tagline.

But my thoughts kept circling back to this: There wasn't a word—I couldn't find one—in our vocabulary that identified the bereaved parent. A glaring problem that needed solving. In an aha moment, I combined the idea of a willow tree, symbolizing deep mourning, with the word willpower, for the sheer force it takes to carry on despite the worst loss. From this, I coined (and later trademarked) the term *willower*. And *that* became my site's identity, its title. Finally, I got up the nerve to click the "Publish" button and started posting.

A post:

May 1, 2014

My old refrigerator had been making a sick, whining sound for a few months. On this morning it shook and sighed and stopped running, lights out. As I poured my coffee and made new plans for the day, I noticed Reggie then staring up at me with big, apologetic eyes. Not for the death of our fridge, I'm pretty sure, although he was able to sense when I was sad or stressed. No, he was apologizing for the slimy, grassy puddle of puke on the carpet. "Oh, Reggie. It's okay." I kissed his little coconut head. And as I sprayed and dabbed and wiped and cleaned up the mess, he watched me with absolute devotion. Back in the kitchen, I chucked a few things, milk, cold cuts, cheese, into a cooler and filled it with ice, and then left to hunt for a new refrigerator.

After spending a few hours at home improvement stores walking up and down the aisles, I was hating the fact that choosing a basic thing like a refrigerator was turning into a complicated thing. I didn't need a four-door fridge, an iPad in the door, or the latest German innovation.

I headed to the Avenues Mall where I'd grab lunch at the food court and then check out the appliance department at Sears.

While eating my taco salad, I people-watched. Pairs of new moms with babies in strollers were poking at salads, chatting. Retired couples were eating without talking. Fashionistas were strutting, designer bags on their arms, cell phones to their ears. Cleaning women in maroon-and-black uniforms were maneuvering between tables and chairs with their carts and brooms, silently sweeping, picking up trash, spraying and wiping. One, an older woman with graying hair, was focused on what she was doing, head down, pushing her broom toward her dust-pan. Another, a middle-aged woman with dark hair, was wiping tables. And another, a younger woman with a ponytail, maybe in her late twenties, appeared from out of nowhere. Seeming eager, she hurried up to the older woman, who stopped sweeping then and looked up. The ponytail held up an open wallet. "Wanna see a picture of my baby that died?"

Being only a few tables away, I couldn't help but overhear the conversation.

"Your baby?" the older woman sounded shocked.

"Yes, she was born April twenty-first," the ponytail said.

"When? Last year?"

"No, nine years ago. She had a heart condition. She died May twelfth. She was twenty-one days old."

The older woman shook her head at the photo for at least five seconds (a polite amount of time), then continued sweeping and moved away from the young mother holding a dead baby in her hand.

Finishing my taco salad, I replayed the young mother's words in my head. *Wanna see a picture of my baby that died … April … nine years ago … heart condition … May … twenty-one days old.* Then pulled from my purse a small, private investigator–sized notepad (the one with the faux leather cover that I carried around in case I thought of something I didn't want to forget), and jotted down the details.

Scooping salsa with my chips, I kept watching. The other cleaning woman with the dark hair had begun wiping a table nearby when the ponytail, who seemed to be on a mission, approached her. With her chin up, she said it again. "Wanna see a picture of my baby that died?"

The dark-haired woman's eyes became huge. "What . . .?"

"She was born April twenty-first. She died May twelfth. She was twenty-one days old," the ponytail said again.

The other woman looked stunned. Like she wanted to run but couldn't.

Oh boy, I thought. Who to feel sorrier for? I gathered my trash and left. Processing what I had just seen, and overheard, walking through the mall toward Sears to shop for a fridge, questions (the answers came later) and thoughts ran through my mind.

Why do we bereaved parents need so badly to talk about our dead children? Why do we need to show their pictures to co-workers, strangers even?

Because we do; we are never detached from our deceased children.

Why do we recount the days they lived? Why is it so important that we state the dates of their births and deaths?

Because it is. Their time mattered; matters. They matter, still.

Should I go back and find her, introduce myself, and ask to see that picture of her baby? No. Just keep walking.

Though I didn't go back, I did learn from that young mother whose baby lived for twenty-one days what it looks like to be unafraid to speak about the unspeakable, to share your story and show a picture of your baby that died. Which is why I decided to continue her mission, and with my chin up, share this story on my blog, *Willower.org*, and now here.

When I walked into the Sears appliance department, a cheerful salesman greeted me.

"Hello! How are you doing today?"

In a millisecond, I thought this: *My son died ... His heart ... He was 3,346 days old. Wanna see a picture of him?* But instead, I said this: "I'm doing fine, thanks. How 'bout you?"

"I'm great! What can I help you with today?"

"Well. My refrigerator died. So . . ."

Centuries ago, the incantation *abracadabra* was believed to have healing powers. The eleven-letter word was worn as an amulet to ward off lethal diseases. Rabbi and scholar Lawrence Kushner said, in *The Book of Words*, that "God just spoke and the world became reality. (The Aramaic for "I create as I speak" is avara *k'davara*, or, in magician's language, abracadabra.)"

Abracadabra. While I was talking (writing, sharing, posting), I was creating my new reality. I didn't realize this at the time; I was just doing it—writing a blog, a book? Learning as I went, migrating, circling back, starting over, trying again, one word at a time, making it, lasting another day. Early on after Sam's death, when I was just beginning to write, what I was trying to do, what I wanted most, was to connect with him, somehow, in *that* world. But as I began sharing my story and receiving positive feedback from other *willowers* who were living with the same unspeakable story, I discovered that it was important for me to connect with others in this world too. In the process of crafting and building these sentences, typing the word *abracadabra*, which itself is a tricky passage over the keys, requiring my left hand to dance alone over the letters in a fun but clumsy way, I was gathering my strength, repairing some of the damage, and crawling out of that black hole. It was *in* the rewriting and rereading of each tricky word, forgetting myself, as if in prayer, practicing year after year, whispering and then speaking each line as if it were a reviving spell, that I was turning my miserable reality into a meaningful one.

In grief, all we can do is take notes and learn as we go, keep walking through the damage—talk and share and create as we speak—and stay at it, try to make something of it, our loss, and find new meaning in that. It's *in* the act of creating where we find our therapy, our purpose, our reason to live.

Reggie

Days: 3,288. The number reminded me of long ago, when I found Psalm 32 and chose verse 8: *I will instruct you and teach you in the way you should go; I will counsel you and watch over you.* A '3' for the month of Sam's birth, a '2' for the day, and an '8' because . . . if he lived to be eight, then . . .

Sam would have been eighteen now. On my 2016 wall calendar, I'd circled March 2, his birthday, and I'd drawn a heart around April 30. It's not like I could forget the dates and needed reminding; these were just the small private ceremonial gestures, circling, drawing, that I did to acknowledge the days of his birth and death. Otherwise, still, David and Joey and I didn't bring it up, or talk about Sam, or how we were feeling. We kept our memories, and whatever thoughts we had, to ourselves. Though we didn't mention them, we knew the dates as they came and went. But to keep this three-legged stool from tipping over, to stay balanced and sturdy, we just kept going. Is there a wrong or right way? I don't think so. We each have to get to where we're going on our own schedule, and sometimes we have to take separate paths.

It had been a long nine years—a lifetime! If you've come this far in the book, thank you for staying with me. You've got to be worn out; I know I am. Why don't we take a break and rest here, in this chapter, before continuing on? I'm going to head outside, watch and learn from the dog how to be mindful (or mindless), to *sit and stay* in the moment, to rise above the thoughts, the clouds, and *be* the blue sky— *sunlit from one hemisphere to the other.*

Always underfoot, Reggie follows me out to the patio. I sit, and he stands at my feet. Starting behind his ears, I knead him from head to tail. "How're you feeling today, Reggie? You remember Sammy, don't you?" He knows that I'm talking to him and revels in the attention.

He blinks and licks his lips. When I stop stroking him, he nudges my hand. *More, please.* So I continue, and he seems to smile. I smile too. And just like that, he leaves and trots over to his doggie door. He does a down-dog stretch, then pushes the corner of the rubber flap and slips through the Chihuahua-sized opening.

Outside, he sniffs a path that leads to a patch of sun and flops onto his side. Then on his back, he wriggles in a way that can only be described as bliss. He loves a freshly cut lawn. Rolling onto his stomach then, front legs out, chest high, ears alert, sphinxlike, he squints at the sun and soaks up its warmth. Watching him, I am present, just here, *now*, enjoying this moment too. When a dragonfly skips by him, he jumps, and I laugh, which startles him again. But then he sees me and wags his tail. *There you are.* A breeze blows, and he stays for a moment, nose quivering, searching, reading the air. And just like that, he leaves his patch of sun and prances back to his doggie door and returns to my hand for another back rub.

I remember Sam sitting on that floor in that nice lady's kitchen surrounded by eight puppies, and on the periphery, sitting politely, watching, waiting, hoping to be chosen, sat number nine. He is still the same, the back of the pack, submissive, cautious, and fearful, particularly of adults. He still prefers children to grown-ups—after all, his master *was* a little boy. He was a working dog. Maybe not the type that finds drugs or bombs, but he could stand on his hind legs and dance with his partner, Sammy. "You're king of the mountain, Reggie Jackson Little Dude!"

Reggie is thirteen now. His golden-brown fur has grayed, and he looks like a wise old man. He's quiet, catlike, curious, independent, and, at times, aloof. Though he's still playful, he spends most of his time lazing by the front window in his daybed (there is also a *night* bed) watching the world go by. I wonder about his heart—if it's broken too. For all his doggie years, this hypersensitive little character, it seems, has absorbed his share of our fear, our sorrow, and grief, and yet he's a faithful and constant friend. If he's not beside me, he's watching me from across the room, or, if he loses track of me, he's checking every room to see where I am—*how* I am—throughout the day and night. He's *my* living, breathing, snoring, tail-wagging connection to Sam. A part of my little boy that I can still touch and hold, play with and take care of, talk to, soothe, and smooth his furrowed brow. He is *my* heart therapy now.

Sam

Mom, wake up. Wake up. Come look! The moon is full.

I opened my eyes. The beams of moonlight shining through the blinds matched the bluish glow of the clock on my nightstand: 5:51, 3/2. The time and the day that Sam was born, eleven years ago. He would be twenty today.

He would be taller than me now. His voice would be deeper. But what would it sound like? How would he wear his hair? I wondered. Would it be short? Or would it be long, curly and shaggy like Joey's? His hair now, as it was then, would be the same color as mine. So without my glasses on, whenever I gaze into the mirror, the blurry image I see could be him. Would his sense of humor be intact? Yes, he would be *even* funnier. We would laugh about the "Joke List! And more!" that was still taped to his bedroom door, though his spy motion detector, which had been positioned outside his door to warn him of intruders, was gone now, put away somewhere. His laugh—I've tried to imagine it—would be louder and lower in pitch. I would hear him and his brother, their boisterous laughs, through the walls.

It made no sense. I had him for nine years, nine birthdays, nine photos on the wall. How could this be, that I'd lived *without* him longer than *with* him?

In the distance, an owl was calling. I hurried outside to sit with him until the sun rose and he had to go back to sleep.

Happy twentieth birthday, my sweet boy.

On this day, March 2, four years ago, I had just arrived at the ballpark when a nice dad whose son played on Joey's team, and who didn't know us well, said hello and asked how things were going.

"Good," I said. "You know, busy. Baseball. School. Baseball. Joey's playing on two teams, so . . . baseball seven days a week."

He chuckled and nodded. "Oh yeah. Same here. School. Baseball. *And* my daughter plays soccer. I'm always running from one place to another. And the two kids are always fighting—constantly at each other. Good thing, only having one, you don't have to deal with *that*."

It was a benign thing to say, but the innocent punch to my gut knocked the wind out of me. Holding my breath, I slipped out of my body and hovered above us and watched as baseball-mom me acted normal, like nothing had happened. She shrugged, nodded, and smiled. "Yeah . . . right."

No, wrong, I thought. *I have two sons! I'm always running, too, from one place to another! My other son, Sam, Joey's brother, died seven years ago . . . Today is his birthday. He would be sixteen, a junior in high school, driving, dating . . . To hear my boys fighting—constantly at each other . . . I would give anything to have to deal with that.*

It's okay, Mom, I heard Sam's voice. *It's okay. Don't get upset. I'm right here.*

"Well . . . have a good game," the nice dad said, unaware of Sam's shadow standing beside me.

"You too," I said, maintaining my smile. Slipping back into myself, I took a breath, and with my folding chair in one hand, cooler tote in the other, went on my way in search of a shady spot where the two of us, my invisible son and I, could sit and watch the ballgame together.

Before the game started, I noticed Joey, almost fourteen now, standing alone by the fence. He seemed a thousand miles away, deep in thought. I zoomed in and captured this in a photo, wondering where he was in that moment. We were passing over Sam's birthday, no party, no cake, no mention of it. That's how it was now. Each season, though, on his uniform, Joey wore the number 32—his brother's birth date, March 2, and also, if anyone asked, Sandy Koufax's number. Whenever I look at that picture of him in his gray-and-blue uniform standing alone, or at *any* of the pictures I've taken of him since Sam's death—the loudest and the quietest moments, his grand slams, and his silent courage—I shake my head and give each photo the same invisible caption: *There's no word in our vocabulary for the bereft sibling.*

A note:

> Joey, I'm so sorry. This wasn't the plan. We were supposed to be four.
> I love you,
> Mom

Joey

Some believe the number 18 represents new beginnings, opportunities, and success. In the Chinese culture, eighteen is considered to be very auspicious. In Hebrew, the letters that symbolize hope and good luck and spell the word life (*chai*) have a numerical value of 18.

Joey's graduation ceremony, as part of Atlantic Coast High School's class of 2018, was held May 25 on a sunny Friday afternoon. Inside Jacksonville's Veterans Memorial Arena, the air crackled with electricity. Families sat in clusters, fidgeting with cameras and cell phones, chattering, pointing, laughing. I felt off-balance, the way I did when Joey used to hit home runs, euphoric and empty, present and distant. We weren't sitting in the nosebleed section—David, his mother, Miriam, his sister, Debbie, and I—but still not close enough to the arena floor to make out who was who among the sea of black caps and gowns. As the procession flowed down the middle aisle that divided the rows—twenty-two, I had counted, and chairs, fourteen on each side—I estimated a little over 600 graduates. Finally, spotting Joey by the shape of his bushy, shoulder-length hair, a replica of my own, a sponge that puffs out with humidity, I zoomed in, focused, and clicked a picture.

I remembered long ago, when Sam had told me about the apartment he would have one day, and how he and Joey would live together in this future apartment.

Mommy, I'm gonna go away to college and have my own apartment one day. But if you miss me too much, then I'll come back home and stay with you.

I will miss you, Sammy. But . . . I still have plenty of time to get used to the idea.

After he graduates from high school, Joey can come live with me. Okay, Joey? After you graduate, and it's your turn to go to college, you can come live with me in my apartment. Don't worry, Mommy; I'll look after him.

The *would-bes*: They would be looking after each other. Sam would be here for the ceremony, home from college. We would be cracking jokes, hooting, hollering, and cheering for his little brother. So proud, holding up our cameras, smartphones, and snapping pictures, snorting, giggling, and nudging each other.

Sam, did you know your brother was voted Best All Around! I saw it in his yearbook. He never even told me. Did he tell you?

Yep, that's my little bro—Best All Around and a 4.56 GPA! Mom, I lost him again. Where's Joey's hair now? Do you see it?

There it is! Grinning, I pointed, zoomed in, and clicked another picture.

Joey had inherited my hair, along with my widow's peak. His baby hair, like mine, was light, so I knew it would turn a darker shade of brown later, but I never dreamt his smooth little boy hair, which was easy, cooperative, with only a subtle wave, would turn into a mane of unruly ringlets. (Sorry, Joey.)

What *do* we inherit? What features, quirks, variants, anomalies, and marvels do we carry inside us? And what do we pass on?

His frame he got from David, broad-shouldered, thin, and tall, as well as his milky skin tone. His eyes are mysterious hybrids. A marbled, brownish meld of green and yellow that reminds me of the painting he made when he was three, mashing and mixing his colors into swirls of mud.

He's headstrong, determined, and fiercely independent. As a baby or toddler, he never liked being held or holding anyone's hand, except Sam's. At one, he refused help brushing his teeth. At two, he couldn't wait to go to school like his big brother. While other teddy bears cried and clung to their mothers, Joey broke free from my grip, strode into his preschool classroom, and never looked back. He didn't even want a kiss goodbye, which his teacher assured me was a good thing.

He's quiet, reserved, tight-lipped. If I ask him a question, he'll give me the shortest answer possible every time. Once, when I posed my usual after-school query, "Tell me something you learned today," five-year-old Joey replied: "I just forgot what I remembered I learned." After Sam and I finished laughing, I jotted that zinger on a slip of paper, wanting to remember this moment, that line. I see now that those unexpected one-liners were Joey's dry sense of humor in the making.

But what damage is hidden inside *his* heart?

His brother's funeral was eleven years ago, yet if I slip and mention Sam, or a memory, he avoids eye contact and remains quiet, keeping whatever sorrow or anger he has inside tightly sealed. And I have to remind myself what that grief therapist said years ago: *He just doesn't want to talk—and that's okay.*

Loss and grief change the way our genes function, leaving marks, like pits and bruises, I suppose, in our DNA, our bodies, our brains. What obscure sources of gloom, pits and bruises, exist deep inside *his* body, *his* brain? I worry. What letters in *his* story have been altered, crossed out, or erased? What memories, vestigial remnants, does he have of Sam? Does he remember the laughter? He still doesn't want to talk about his brother, so I don't know.

For a long time now, I've wanted to tell him about this dream I had almost a decade ago: I was standing behind him in the bathroom doorway, fuming, scowling at him in the mirror, supervising, holding out a washcloth, *choosing* this battle. "Why, Joey, every night, is it *so* hard to just wash up and brush teeth?" Sam used to manage this *wash up and brush teeth before bed* ritual. And Joey used to follow his brother's lead. As dreams often go, it happened in the blink of an eye. Sam appeared in the mirror, standing beside Joey with his arm around him. In alliance with his little brother, he glared at me and spoke with his eyes. *He's doing it! He's brushing, Mommy. Be more patient with him.* Then he kissed Joey on the temple, and when I blinked again, Sam was gone, and I opened my eyes, awake then.

Back in the present, I zoomed in on the big screen that hung from the ceiling in the center of the arena, timed it just right, and recorded video of Joey walking across the stage, shaking a hand, graduating with honors, as his name was announced: "Joseph Kassenoff."

Hearing his name, I smiled, remembering how he *hated* being called Joseph. We'd never really called him that; it had always been Joey. When he was a toddler, if anyone called him Joseph, he would insist his name was "Doey, not Jofess." On the first day of kindergarten, when I introduced Joey to his teacher, she frowned. "In my class, we use our proper names. It is *Joseph*, isn't it?" We stood there, stupefied. I knew Joey didn't like her rule, but he would follow it until first grade, when he could go back to being Joey again.

Choosing a name the second time around had been easier. We already had a short list.

"I like Joe D.—like Joe DiMaggio," David said.

"Joseph it is—and we can call him Joey." Then, after searching for a middle name, wanting something clean and simple between his first and last names, I found there weren't many one-syllable options that started with D. "How about Dean?"

"I like it," David said. He was happy, I knew, as long as the result was Joe D.

It felt kind of sneaky, choosing the male variant of *my* name, but why not? I liked the result too: Joe D. And now, with those four letters, I get to pass on a small piece of me that Joey will carry with him forever.

A note:

> Joey, you'll be leaving for college soon. (And because I'm writing this in the future, I already know you'll study economics and graduate with honors, and that you'll head off to Cornell where you'll continue your studies. Cornell University! Can you believe that?)
>
> I'm SO proud of you! Who you are, and who you're becoming.
>
> I've left you this note to remind you — in case you "just forgot what you remembered you learned" (smiley-face) to take care of yourself, your body, your brain, your heart. Take walks. Laugh as often as possible. And remember—especially remember this— to laugh at yourself. "A merry heart does good like a medicine."
>
> I love you,
>
> Mom

eleven years

Even now, in private, when I'm meditating in the dark before sunrise; or if I'm in public, sitting inside an arena; when I'm outside in a shady spot, or driving, or out walking; I still sense his presence *here* and *there*, or hear him in my thoughts, or see my shadow son in my daydreams. Some days he's grown, and some days he's still a boy. "Perhaps this is the true meaning of continuing the bond with the deceased child," Henya Shanun-Klein, a professor of psychology and a thanatologist, wrote in *Gili's Book: A Journey into Bereavement for Parents and*

Counselors. We see and relate to the "real-image," the one that's frozen in time, conjured in our memory, and we see the "shadow-image," the one we fantasize about, our *would-be* child who grows and ages over time. Though fully aware of the reality of our loss, we never really say goodbye.

"The truth must dazzle gradually," said Emily Dickinson in her poem, *Tell all the truth but tell it slant* —

Grieving, like writing, is hard work, done mostly in solitude. It's painful; it's insane; it's miserable. It hurts your eyes, your head, your back, and every bone in your body. It's unpredictable and feels like fear or panic, especially when the truth intrudes just as you thought you were doing okay. It requires patience and time and endurance, as well as lunacy and logic and creativity and endless self-editing, adding in the right words and memories and erasing or rewriting the wrong ones.

Gradually, the ache and the yearning lessen. We learn to live *without* our departed children—and all the future events that have died with them—but we are never detached from them. We carry them with us—in our pockets, in a pendant, a ring wrapped around our finger, or hidden in our hearts. We survive, and continue moving from *here* to *there*, migrating through time—through milestones, birthdays, and anniversaries—and eventually, the days and nights turn into years. The progress happens so slowly that we can only see it, how far we have come, when we look at the distance in our rearview mirror.

It takes time—perhaps eleven years—to gradually absorb the truth.

So I guess you could say I've graduated. I've come to what feels like the completion of a cycle. I've learned to live again, and laugh, to enjoy good food and meaningful conversations. Occasionally I pick out a new shade of lipstick, though mostly, these days, I wear tinted ChapStick.

Rewriting life after the worst, most blinding loss is a never-ending process, a lifelong migration.

. . . the longest migration of any bird.

10
SEEING

crazy math

May 29, 2018.

Like slivers of moonlit water, 4,057 days have disappeared into a black sea.

Should I rewrite that? Rereading that first line, I wondered if *slivers of moonlit water* was too theatrical. But this is what I see when I look out at time, at the growing gap between my little boy and me: a dark sky; an endless, black sea; an occasional swell, a distant wave; a sliver of moonlight; enough to catch my eye, enough to keep searching, hoping . . .

I'm looking over at the papery luna moth in the plastic baseball display cube on the windowsill beside my desk, the one I'd found years ago, already dead, lying in the grass next to the sidewalk. It *was* the color of Sam's eyes, pale green, with flecks of brownish orange, but over the years, the sun has bleached it to an almost white with light sepia eyes.

I turn back to my computer screen and continue typing.

While counting the days, I noticed *this* year was the same as *that* year eleven years ago. Different, of course, but the same; the calendar days are the same. The past, like a sheer fabric, has superimposed itself precisely over the present. A parallel universe in which every minute is the same.

April 30, the day Sam died, again fell on Monday. May 3, the day of his funeral, when I spoke and mentioned I might write about this one day, on Thursday. Followed by the days of lunacy: lying in the tub, waiting for the rising water to cover my mouth, my nose, my eyes. *Three minutes without breath and we begin to die.*

But this year, the full moon came twice in March; the first on Sam's birthday, March 2, and the second, the blue moon, twenty-nine days later. The next full moon rose on April 30, the anniversary of his death. And on this day, May 29, the full moon, the Dragon Moon, turned out to be the 138th moon I'd counted since I'd started counting, keeping track of time, waiting.

The ancient Chinese considered the Dragon Moon to be magical. It was believed, when people bathed themselves in its brightness, the old became younger; the infirm found new health; the weary grew energized; and despair turned to joy. According to legend, a story told under the Dragon Moon would never be forgotten.

I want to stop here and linger for just a while longer, stay with the idea of the *Dragon Moon,* bathe in it, feel younger, less weary. I want to *believe* in its magic. I want to tell you this story under *this* moon, so it will never be forgotten—so *he* will never be forgotten.

In a detached kind of way, for years now, my soul, who takes up little space, and stays mostly hidden in a tree like a bird, has been observing me, listening and watching while I work inside my head, analyzing dates, numbers, my word count.

How many letters are in this word? How many words are in this sentence, this paragraph, this chapter?

Tracking and tunneling and digging, like a low-to-the-ground dachshund, I try to flush out anything that insinuates a pattern, a significance, something meaningful to me. I know it when I come to it, the way the dachshund knows when he roots out the rabbit.

138 moons!

I don't need to speak out loud for her to hear me. Though sometimes, I do need to *hear* the words, say them out loud, before typing them.

"April 30, 2007. If you multiply this—4 times 30 times 2007, it equals 240,840," I said, punching the numbers again into the green plastic calculator, the one I'd bought Sam for a dollar. I repeat each sequence, punch in the numbers at least twice, sometimes three or four times to confirm, because I'm not sure about this one-dollar calculator's computing ability.

"And then, if you divide 240,840 by 18, because Monday, April 30, begins the eighteenth week of the year, it equals 13,380—which is the time, 13:38 or 1:38 p.m., when his watched stopped. Do you see it?" I asked, turning the silver ring on my finger (the one that cost, with tax, $18.18) so that the tiny heart, a raised droplet of gold, is facing me. "It's something, right? Even if it's nothing, it's something."

My soul gave a slight nod, just enough to help me feel less alone, less insane. Though we're different, she resembles me, like a reflection in a window, the way she moves and sounds, though she's still older, wiser, quieter—and *way* more patient than I am.

3,346 days!

"Look at this: when you take the number of days Sam lived, 3,346, and multiply 3 times 3 times 4 times 6, it equals 216. Which, as it turns out, according to gematria, the numerological system used by Kabbalists, mystics, and now me, is the numerical value for the word *Gevurah*, the Hebrew word for inner strength, bravery, and courage of the heart! This *has* to mean something," I said, while continuing to add in my head, *2 plus 1 plus 6 . . .*

9 years!

Balanced on her branch high up in a tree, sitting lotus-style, unaffected, quiet, composed, my soul listened to me ramble on. She could close her eyes, leave for days, and open them to find me still in the same place, doing the same thing.

"I've spent more years without him than with him. Counting the days, weeks, moons, the stripes on his colorful blanket, occupies my mind. It feels productive. Or maybe it *is* a compulsion; an itch I have to scratch. I wonder, if I dropped a mess of toothpicks on the floor, would I count them too? I don't know, maybe? Probably. Searching and finding, then counting these pieces feels like I'm solving a puzzle. Fitting and snapping odd-shaped things into the empty spaces, the holes, in my mind, gives me a sense of validation, of possibility. That maybe our lives and our deaths aren't so random and meaningless after all. That there *is* a reason, an answer, or some kind of mathematical solution. Nothing may turn out to be something, right?"

She looked down at me and tilted her head just so, the way one does when offering their condolences.

"What? Why the look?" I said. "You know this is what I do, my crazy math. How else am I supposed to make sense out of what makes *no* sense at all? One day, I'll solve this. Someday it'll all mean *something*, won't it?"

My soul isn't one for small talk, especially about the weather. I admire this about her and try my hardest to be quiet, but . . .

I rubbed my temples and groaned. "This past April 30, the weather was cooler than it was eleven years ago. Otherwise, it was the same. Why does April 30 have to be the brightest, greenest, most beautiful day of the year? In eleven years, it has rained only once on this day! Again, the sky was clear. The day was alive and bright and blooming with new colors. The birds were singing as if nothing was wrong—when everything was, is, and *always will be* wrong! I keep telling myself to just keep going, keep counting those toothpicks! But what am I even trying to say? Where am I even going with this? I keep getting lost, ending up back at the beginning again, starting over, never finishing. I keep *not* finishing. Why? Am I afraid to finish? Afraid the result will be flawed? Not perfect? Or worse, that I'll bring him, the essence of him, back wrong? Maybe this *is* crazy, trying to *rewrite* my story with a different ending." I exhaled. "I know, I know, you're going to say: *rewriting*, like *grieving,* is *all* part of the process. And that *the process* involves starting over again and again."

My soul shrugged and pinched off the tip of a small shoot growing from her branch.

I raked through my tangled hair and moaned. "I'm losing my mind! Outlining, rearranging lines, moving paragraphs around. Does this go up here, down there? What do *you* think?" Caught in a knot, I moaned louder. "Ugh! What is this chapter even about? Do *you* know? Can you *please* help me?"

It was almost undetectable, but I knew she was shaking her head at me. I heard a sigh. I know her face—I knew it from the first time I saw it, when I'd gazed at my reflection, at that stranger in the mirror, over a decade ago.

"Already, too much time has passed since his heart stopped," I said. "*You* can sit and wait lifetimes. I can't. This is *still* a rescue mission. I need to bring him back. Time is of the essence." My heart started beating faster. My mind was a frantic mouse running inside a wheel, trying to beat the clock, change the unchangeable, and keep him alive. Somewhere deep inside of me, I still believed I could keep him alive.

My soul shifted her position. Pulled up her legs, wrapped her arms around them, and rested her chin on her knees. "You won't accomplish or solve *anything* in such a harried state. Why don't you stop and take a break? Clear your head," she said. "How does the song go? *Free your mind* ..." She started humming and swaying, and I pretended to ignore her and kept at it, reading, typing, highlighting, counting words, deleting, retyping.

"I'm afraid if I stop, I might forget the little things that happened on the most insignificant days—and it's those little, seemingly insignificant things that are the *most* significant."

She stopped swaying and motioned with her chin to the books on my desk. "Why don't you read something else? Or go outside, get some air, take a walk? I know your mind won't stop running, but you can change your pace or at least run in a different direction. You may find something significant by searching somewhere else."

I stopped working and took a deep breath and stretched my aching back. I knew she was right. So I grabbed a few books and left my desk.

the rabbit

Sitting outside on the patio, closer to nature, I did feel better. That is, until I heard children screaming and shouting on the playground at the nearby elementary school. Changing directions, I tried instead to focus on the pinging of a nearby cardinal, the chortling of a chickadee. Then I opened the *Webster's New World Dictionary*, the one Sam used. The spine must've been pressed open to this page before, the way the paperback separated at the letter R. The index words, *quintuplet* and *rabbit*, were in the upper corners; and *rabbit: a swift, burrowing mammal with soft fur, long ears, and a stubby tail* sat right below *rabbi: an ordained teacher of the Jewish law* at the bottom of the page.

"This is something," I said, staring at the page.

My soul nodded. "Yes, it is."

When I looked up, I noticed him then, the rabbit, facing me, planted only a few yards away. "I see you." I smiled, wondering if Sam could see *me* through the rabbit's eyes.

For months, the little brown rabbit would pop out of the woods and sit at the edge of the yard and watch me. Curious, he didn't seem to mind the dog either, and Reggie seemed calm and only a little curious about him, as if he sensed this bunny was a pal and not prey, which was a relief.

Years ago, for Easter, our dear friend Eva had given each of the boys a plush toy rabbit, which happened to look exactly like the real rabbit that popped out of the woods now and then. The boys' bunnies were twins, and both were named Bunny. For some reason, the dog was obsessed with these rabbits. Any chance he got, Reggie would snatch one and run off with it in his jaws. I remember having to pry the plush toys from Reggie's mouth; both Bunny 1 and Bunny 2 had puncture wounds and patches of missing fur.

I stared into the rabbit's eyes and spoke to him. "To see . . . maybe souls need the eyes of living creatures." I held up the dictionary. "Did you know that 'rabbit' is right below 'rabbi' in the dictionary?" He hopped forward and looked at me sidewise, his nose twitching. "Maybe it is so. A rabbi, a teacher—*my* teacher, above, and his rabbit, with seeing eyes, below."

I like that, Mommy! Write that down.

I looked up at my soul and noticed that she was smiling too.

"I need your help," I said. "I need to find him, but I'm exhausted. I'm so tired. I feel like I've hit a wall, a dead end."

"Perhaps, you have *come* to the end. Endings are always beginnings."

I looked back toward the edge of the yard. The rabbit was gone. I scanned the entire border between his hiding place and the grassy open space, but he was nowhere in sight.

"You'll see him again," my soul said. She knew my mind, every bough, every branch, every shoot, every injury, every thought. She'd seen it all through my eyes. Then it dawned on me: might I be able to see through her eyes? She was already nodding. "Yes, you *are* able to see what I see."

"I need to see my boy. I need to know . . . Can *you* see him?"

She turned away from me and looked at something off in the distance. Whatever it was, I couldn't see it—or wasn't ready yet to see it. So I picked up *The Oracle of Kabbalah* by Richard Seidman and went back to my reading.

I opened to the chapter about the eighth letter of the Hebrew alphabet, *Chet*, the symbol for life and fear, and read this quote by Rabbi Nachman of Breslov: "All of this world is a very narrow bridge. And above all, have no fear at all." I thought about Sam's painting: the thin, orange boy crossing that narrow, red bridge, the thick, horizontal line supported by two curved pillars (like the Hebrew letter *Chet*), and the words he had brushed above his swirls of finger-made clouds: "good day."

"Sam taught me that *every* day is a good day," I said. "He embodied this."

My soul, I realized, was concentrating, reading the same page. "Rabbit Nachman also mourned his beloved son," she said, raising an eyebrow.

"Did you say *rabbit*?" I asked. And then I noticed it, the typo: a 't' had been added to the word *Rabbi*, which made it "Rabbit Nachman" instead. Like a magic trick, the rabbit had disappeared from the edge of the yard and reappeared on the page I was reading. "This *is* something significant!"

My soul, still smiling, brought her palms together in prayer position, closed her eyes, and bowed her head.

It might've been the sounds coming from the nearby playground, or it was nothing at all. The images are always there in the back of my mind, loaded and ready to fire. In a split second, the flashback mushroomed, and I saw it all happen again: *Sam running. Tumbling. Collapsing. His Timex, still ticking, lying on the ground. The cloudless sky, the heat of the day. Sirens, horns, revving engines, electronic beeps, radio voices, doors slamming, footsteps running, voices shouting. Someone hollering through the chaos, "WHAT MEDS DOES HE TAKE?" Then my voice, still hopeful and strong, answering back, "TOPROL!"* I clenched my fists and pressed them into my eyes. "I wasn't there in time. I should've *known* when he didn't wave goodbye. I was *supposed* to protect him. It was *my* job to keep him alive!"

"Enough of that!" My soul jumped to her feet, curled her toes around the branch, held out her arms, and steadied herself as if she were on a balance beam. "It's not easy walking this narrow bridge between life and death. Even for the bravest warrior, the wisest wizard, or the most agile magician, it's *never* easy." Flapping her fingers, she motioned for me to climb up onto the branch.

From our perch, I could see a parking lot in the distance, empty except for my old minivan, and Sam's toy, but now life-size, penny-colored PT Cruiser parked under an old oak tree.

She pointed to a sidewalk leading to what appeared to be . . . a temple? "Let's go now." She held out her hand. "You need to talk to him. Stop asking all those books, stop reading and counting and searching, and start listening to *me*. It's time. Come!"

Meditating.

We stood at the temple's entrance, before a large set of doors. Up high, resting above them, was a bright-green luna moth the size of a dessert plate. When my soul pushed open the doors, a vacuum of air pulled the luna moth inside, and I followed it with my eyes as it fluttered down a long, dark hallway.

"Follow him."

"I was *going* to," I said. "I know what to do now."

Touching my shoulder, my soul cocked her head and looked at me the way a bird would, with one eye. "I only wanted to be sure. Sometimes you see the way but forget to breathe and focus and stay."

time

Clutching my book bag, which felt like a child over my hip, its thin arms clinging to my shoulder, I followed the moth down the dark passageway. I could hear and feel my heart beating as if I were inside it. When I came to a narrow but open doorway, I remembered to breathe and focus and stay, and slipped through it, into complete darkness.

I couldn't see, but smelled something lemony . . . furniture polish? I was staring into the pitch-dark, waiting for my eyes to adjust, when someone struck a match. In the flare, face-to-face, I saw my boy standing in front of me, holding the flame.

"Sammy? Sam? Is that you?"

He looked older, no longer nine, but not a teenager either. His hair was wavy, a little messy, not long, not short. And he was wearing a gray hoodie jacket, similar to one he used to wear when he was little.

A small table that resembled an ocean, its veneer rippling with dark waves, separated us. On it, there was a black-and-white candleholder that looked like a dolphin—no, a killer whale, an orca. Like the whale menorah we'd set out every year for Hanukkah, this one, too, was made of wood, carved in a way so that it balanced on its belly. Nine slender, white candles stood on its scooped back. The first taper, the helping candle, went where a breathing hole might be, and the others rode along the curve of the whale's back to the tip of its tail. *A menorah-orca: a menorca.* I tested the word in my head, and Sam smiled, reading my thoughts.

As he lit the candles, the past and the future disappeared, and we were enveloped in black as if a cape had been draped over us. I concentrated on his eyes, which grew wider and shined brighter with each flame. Staring at each other over the flickering candles, now a single curve of light, neither of us moved. Wanting to speak, I opened my mouth, but nothing came out. *Breathe. Focus. Stay.*

My eyes burned with tears. "I'm sorry, Sammy. I'm so sorry ... I should've done something. I should've known when you didn't wave goodbye. I wasn't there—I drove as fast as I could—I didn't know what to do."

"Mommy, I know. I know. It's okay. Do you remember our rides home from school, when you'd look in the rearview mirror, and I'd blow you a kiss? I'm okay."

"Sammy, I just want you back. I miss you so much. Isn't there a way to—?"

The candlelight fluttered, and his face faded for a second. I closed my eyes and focused on my breath, on letting go of desire. I knew it would only bring more grief, and when I looked again, his face was bright and back in focus.

"Mommy, you and I, we're in this place between *here* and *there*, between *this* world and *that* one." His hands became iridescent fish shimmying, swimming apart, and I watched as one of the fish went on swimming toward the door. "For now, you live *there,* in *that* one."

"But I want to stay *here*, with you. I'm not afraid of—"

"I know, brave Mommy. You're not afraid of anything. But you have to stay *there*, in *that* world. And I'll be right *here*." He tapped his chest.

"I'm sorry, Shmu. I'm sorry it's taken me this long, this many years to face you, talk to you. I just couldn't before now. I couldn't see you or even say your name without crying. Sweet boy, I have so much to tell you, show you. How long, how much time do we have together?"

"As long as it takes, Mommy. As long as it takes."

In the dim light, scanning the room, I was able to make out familiar shapes, his bed, his desk, his bookshelf, but I noticed something unfamiliar on a small table in the corner, a wooden chess set. The chunky dark and light pieces didn't look like conventional chessmen. Unlike any I'd ever seen, the oddly shaped soldiers appeared to be handmade. Maybe it was the flickering light, but I thought I saw them moving, the chess pieces. Or maybe it was the board, the way it was glowing—moving, breathing? *Breathe. Focus. Stay.*

From my bag, I pulled out a large envelope, opened it, and set the glossy booklet onto the table. "Sammy, this is the police department's newsletter." I opened to the page titled *Sam's Story* and pointed. "That's him, Officer Twisdale, the policeman who helped me. Daddy and I attended the ceremony where he received an award. He looks like Duke, doesn't he?"

Sam gaped at the glossy page, studying the way he had been Photoshopped in to appear just over Duke's shoulder. "Are those wings? Over his pocket?"

He noticed *every* detail. "Yes. Those *are* wings. The silver wheel is for motion, and the wings are for speed. He had to pass the most dangerous and difficult law enforcement tests to receive that pin."

Rubbing his chin, Sam nodded. "Did he get a medal that day, at the ceremony?"

I shook my head. "Not exactly a medal, but an award like a medal—*better* than a medal."

He sat up taller. "If I were to meet this Duke, I would say, 'Mission accomplished, soldier.'"

I pulled out a piece of paper. "He wrote us a letter. Do you want to read it?"

He leaned in. "I do—yes! But … would you read it to me, Mommy?"

"'… I'm glad I could be there for you and your mother that day. Little buddy, you've touched many people you never even knew and will be missed by many who loved you dearly. You were a best friend, a big brother, and a son. Now it's your turn to watch over your mother and family. We will all be together again one day. Until then, the friend you never knew, Mr. Tim …'

"Sammy, he was a *true* soldier, an action figure just like Duke."

Clinging to the bundle on my lap, I watched a tendril of smoke rising. "Sam? How long now? How much time do we have left?"

He was watching the same tendril, then brought his gaze back down to the menorca, checking it as if it were a clock. "As long as it takes, Mommy."

I pulled out another picture. "This is the luna moth that I framed in a shadow box."

Sam beamed. "I *knew* you would find him—and on the full moon too. We do have the same eyes, don't we, Mommy?"

We blinked and looked into each other's eyes, and I smiled and nodded. *He already knows the story*, I thought. "All this time, you were there, weren't you? Reading over my shoulder, whispering in my ear, helping me write this?"

He grinned, but then his eyes, like mine, went back to the flames. When a trickle of wax dripped from a candle and slid from the whale's back into the dark waves of the table, I felt a sense of urgency. "Sammy,

I need you to know, I would've given you *my* heart. I know you know this, but I need to be sure you know how *much* I love you—more than *all* the sidewalks in the world."

For a moment, my vision blurred. *Breathe. Focus. Stay.* "Sammy, your heart—I was so afraid . . . to lose you. You knew, didn't you, how afraid Daddy and I were? How could you not? I didn't know what to do, how much to tell you. I should've told you more, but I didn't want *you* to be afraid. You weren't finished—you're *not* finished! Sammy, I'm trying to write this, but *you're* the storyteller. *You're* the writer. How is our story supposed to end? How are *we* supposed to end? I don't know what to do."

The tapers, which seemed like timekeepers, trickling wax instead of sand, had melted halfway down. I heard the ticking of a clock but didn't see one in the room. Stalling, trying to prolong whatever time we had left together, I kept talking.

"Sam, the owl, was it you? Did you call us outside that morning before sunrise? Joey, Daddy, and I woke when we heard it—you—calling. *Who-Who-Who-Who-Whoo.* Did you see *us?* Was that you perched on a branch in the tree just beyond the fence? The owl—you—was much bigger than we expected. Did you see us tracing you, your silhouette, with our pointers? You called once more—*Who-Who-Who-Who-Whoo*—before you lifted off. Your wings sounded like whispers, and you disappeared into the woods. We chattered on about that owl, wide awake then, guessing it flew off somewhere to sleep for the day. Was it you? Sammy?"

He smiled but didn't answer me.

Not wanting our time to end, I zeroed in on the glowing chess set and motioned to it. "What can you tell me about those pieces?"

"Right, yes!" He clapped his hands. "Mommy, I want to show you all the soldiers."

Somehow, in the blink of an eye, between us, on the table that resembled an ocean, the board game had been set up, and the flickering menorca, like a chess clock, sat beside it.

"Hem, hem." He pretending to clear his throat, then tickled the air with his fingers. "These sixty-four squares, and thirty-two figurines, half dark, half light, have captured the human imagination for fifteen hundred years. Mommy, can you imagine?"

An empty sponge ready to absorb every detail, I *imagined*, and the magician cast his spell, grinned, and circled the chessmen with his hands.

With a deliberate pace, he pointed and announced, "Pawn. Castle. Knight. Bishop. King. Queen. Carved by hand, *this* set is one of a kind. Each piece is engraved with a composition of Hebrew letters, and each letter has a personality *and* a magic power." With his finger, lightly, he kissed the tallest pieces on the board. "Two *Lameds* form the king's crown, and the letter *Shin* is the queen's crown."

I leaned over the table. "How many letters are there *here*?"

He fluttered his fingers over the figurines. "Here, there are twenty-two letters. The twenty-third letter is missing."

I scanned the board. "Where is it? Why isn't it here?"

He held out his palms, as if he were presenting a scroll or a sword. "We can only see this mysterious letter in our dreams—waving, signaling us to walk toward it, toward the future, the unknown." He lowered his hands and laid down the make-believe scroll, or sword, then tapped his temple with his finger. "When we play the game of chess, we become smarter. And when we combine letters with magic, we become wiser." Sweeping his hand over the front line of troops, he plucked a stocky piece from a square, held it between our eyes, and lowered his voice. "Mommy, look closely. Listen carefully."

Sitting on the edge of my seat, mesmerized and wanting to learn more, I leaned in, and the lesson began.

11
A DIFFERENT ENDING

abracadabra

"Mommy, this is the pawn. He acts as a shield and moves *only* forward—no drawing back."

The pawn had knots for fists and two dot-sized holes for eyes, but no mouth. The shape of a tiny mallet, or keyhole, had been chiseled out of its square breastplate.

Sam touched the top of the pawn's head, and it appeared to bow. "This faithful soldier performs deeds that are of key importance in the game."

For a minute, I was standing outside on the patio on a bright, cloudless, short-sleeved January day, just after the New Year, taking a picture of Sam and his friend Dominick playing a game of chess on the patio. Then I realized, when I saw this photo years later, that Sam had been wearing the same outfit he would wear to school in 117 days, on that Monday when he was up early and ready for school, dressed in his favorite jeans and powder-blue polo shirt, his Indiglo Timex. How long has it been now? How many minutes have passed, how many days, more than a decade? *Breathe. Focus. Stay.*

My mind returned then, and I was sitting *here* in the dark, staring at a glowing chessboard, learning about soldiers, and magic letters.

Sam picked up a pair of chessmen and handed one to me. "This is my favorite piece: the professional army man, the knight."

At first, I saw a miniature gondola, but then a horse, its head held high, tail curled over its backside. Then, nestled between head and tail, cloaked in scales of armor, a chiseled soldier holding a sword.

"The stamping steed takes the brave knight across the board, to the other side and back again." Sam juggled his horse from one pretend cliff to the other. "The knight's more important than the pawn, but less important than the king or queen; *his* purpose is to protect them. He can jump over others and moves two squares, then left or right one square, in the shape of an L." The horse and rider leapt again, and Sam raised the knight in a ceremonial way, then lowered and set him down on the board, nudging the horse into the center of its square. "Mommy, a soldier's virtue is hidden in his heart."

"Then the knight is my favorite piece too." I nudged my knight into the center of his box, repeating Sam's gesture, copying the particular way he'd moved his knight, so I wouldn't forget.

He picked up another piece and handed its look-alike to me. "The bishop represents religion. Historically a priest, but this one's a rabbi." He rotated the piece, admiring it, then drew an X in the air. "The bishop follows the same color path throughout the game and moves only diagonally."

The bishop's face, I noticed, had no eyes, only a beveled slice in the wood for a mouth. His neck was long, and his frame square, yet somehow the lines that shaped the piece seemed to be connected and entwined. A sword was whittled at his side and a prayer shawl folded over his shoulders, with scratches for fringe that brushed his boot. "Sam, are those boots and a sword?"

"Yes, Mommy! This swashbuckling bishop who sees without eyes is armed with insight *and* courage." Sam slid the chessman back into position, then lifted the next piece along with its twin, and handed it over to me.

"The castle, or rook, is a shelter, a home."

"It looks like a houseboat—or a dahabeah?"

Sam gasped and the board grew brighter. "Mommy! Where did you learn that word?"

"*You* studied Egypt; *I* picked up a thing or two."

Beaming, he held up his castle and drew a cross over the chessboard with his finger. "This piece moves only in straight lines."

Examining my castle more closely, I saw the moat encircling it like a Hula-Hoop, the drawbridge, and then, the crosshatching carved from bottom to top. I pointed to it. "Sam, is that a—"

"A ladder, Mommy; yes, it's there for us to climb."

Climb? I gazed down at the castle in my hand, then followed the ladder to the top. "There's even a teeny tiny flag," I marveled.

"That's for sending secret messages," he said, matter of fact, returning his castle to the board.

He lifted the dark king and motioned for me to pick up the light one. While I cradled mine like a bird, he held his with his fingers splayed, the way a zookeeper would display a rare lizard, I thought. My mind wandered to another memory. We were in a classroom at the zoo, on a field trip, staring at a chameleon, its toes gripping, tail winding around the zookeeper's splayed fingers. "Don't be loud. Touch gently," said the zookeeper. "Note his scales. His eyes, how they move independently. He *never* misses a fly." Sam's eyebrows were raised high in upside-down smiles. Next, we touched a snake, then a chinchilla, then a skink—but *definitely not* the wolf spider. Then we picnicked in the mulch before leaving on the bus, a big, yellow bird. *Breathe. Focus. Stay.* My mind returned, back in the dark again, sitting, trying to look, listen, learn, understand, become *wiser*.

"Mommy, are you here?"

"Yes, Shmu, I'm here. Mommy's here. I see you. Go on."

"The king is the tallest piece—the most important piece, but *not* the most powerful. He's wise but not a warrior. He can only move one square at a time, so he must be well defended. Without him the kingdom collapses, and the game is lost."

Sam tipped his king and looked inside it, so I checked inside my piece too. The hollowness was the shape of a heart. Extending up from the emptiness were two antennas, or stems, with leaflike finials for the crown's points. The king's hands were empty cups, and he was broad and blockish down to his square foot, which peeked out from beneath his robe.

Sam set down his king and spoke more slowly than before. "The king's foot faces forward, toward the future, toward *living*—because there *is* more, Mommy." His voice sounded weaker. The chessmen were dimming, their energy fading.

"Sammy? Sam? Don't go. Come back. Please, come back."

"I'm here, Mommy." Picking up the last piece, holding it to his face, he brightened again. "The queen is the *most* powerful piece in the game—more powerful even than the king. She is made of air and water and fire so she can move in *any* direction on the board."

The queen resembled a perfume bottle: delicate, with a rounded torso; an egg-shaped head with a crown of flames; a smooth, polished face; crescent eyes, closed or looking down; and a gaping mouth, in mid-sentence. Her cloak was carved to flow diagonally across her body, and she appeared to dance and move, hands and feet in all directions, which made her arms seem more like wings. It was an illusion though. As I stared longer, her dance became letters. *Aleph. Shin. Mem.* "Sam! I see them now, the letters."

He nodded. "Mommy, did I mention? The queen is *also* a storyteller."

I smiled then, making the connection—a storyteller, of course, with a gaping mouth—when another candle burned out and the room grew darker. "Sammy, I'm afraid I'm going to forget *everything* you've told me."

"Mommy, you already know all these things."

"What things? What things do I know?"

"You see these letters, right?"

I nodded, concentrating, trying to memorize each letter, every detail of this dream, afraid I might wake up at any moment.

"And you see these soldiers, right?" He touched each piece, then picked up the queen and closed his hands around the delicate piece. "Abracadabra!" he whispered. Then, he opened his hands and a tiny bird—a white-eyed vireo?—leapt out and onto the game board. It stretched its wings, looked up at Sam, then at me, hopped a few squares, then flew off and disappeared in the dark.

"Sammy! How . . .?"

He smiled and, as if casting a spell, waved his hands in circles over the chessmen. "Imagine the rest, Mommy. And remember, the letters are magic."

Holding my breath, I looked around the room, at the bookshelf, the desk, the bed, then down at the chunky dark and light pieces, then rubbed my eyes and adjusted my glasses. Refocusing, breathing again, I stared at his face from across the ocean—over what was now a smaller, dwindling curve of light, hovering above a saddle of wax on the whale's back. I was trying desperately to memorize the details of his face—the outline of his cheeks, pinkish remnant of that V on his forehead, pale-green eyes with brownish-orange flecks, heart-shaped mouth, the imprint above it where he pressed in thoughts. I heard the clock ticking again. "Sammy, what time is it?"

He pushed up his sleeve and looked down at his Indiglo Timex. "Mommy, I don't know. My watch stopped—it *was* 1:38."

Feeling a surge of adrenaline, remembering what had happened, grasping the fact that I would never touch or see his beautiful face or hear his hearty laugh or hold his warm hand again, I panicked. Reaching across the table over the dark, rippling waves, I took his hand, turned it over, and stared at it, at his perfect fingers, soft and pink, with traces of green ink on them . . . finger paint? "Did you have art in school that day, sweet boy?" I whispered, then brought his hand to my cheek and closed my eyes.

Inside my broken mind, I was lying beside my little boy again, my hand on his chest, my face to his face, eyelash to eyelash, staying, and lingering, and waiting. "Sam, when you wake up, I'll be right here."

Wandering back in time, I was holding him again in a baby blanket, white, pink, and blue stripes, and carrying home that keepsake for his baby book, those tiny footprints stamped in black ink.

Then, falling in a nightmare, unable to wake up before hitting the ground, holding a child-sized blanket, brown, covered in stupid, smiling monkeys, and carrying a pocket folder containing a larger hand and footprint stamped in green ink. *What is this? No, no, no, no!* "Sammy, come back. They made a mistake. Sweet boy, open your eyes. Wake up, breathe, come back!"

Breathe. Focus. Stay. Remembering where we were now, in this place between *here* and *there*, I opened my eyes. "Sammy, you didn't have art that day. No . . . you had phys ed."

my mission

I wanted to hold him, tell him how much I loved him, but I was afraid if I moved, he'd vanish. So I didn't move. Seeing each other's thoughts, we both tried to smile, put on our brave faces.

"Sam, I *see* you. You *are* still alive. You're here. How?" I fidgeted with the square ring on my finger, twisting it in circles until I felt the raised edge of the tiny heart.

"You see me in your own reflection, in your memory, your imagination. I live on in you and Daddy and Joey, but I *did* die, Mommy."

I shook my head. "What about this place? These pieces? You turned the queen into a bird!"

"Mommy, *you* created these soldiers. *You* wrote this. *You* carved these letters, polished these sentences."

I stared at him, confounded. "What do you mean?"

"Just look. You counted the number of days I lived and engraved it on the base of each piece."

I picked up a pawn and turned it over: *3,346.* "I don't understand."

"You're a writer, a storyteller, too, Mommy."

I stared at the queen's gaping mouth, at the letters she was made of—air, fire, and water. Every time I looked at her, she seemed to change. Peaceful and still one moment, smoldering and kinetic the next. When I spoke, I thought I saw her mouth moving. "Am I losing my mind? My beautiful boy . . . Am I only imagining you? Are you *not* real?"

"Imagined or real, Mommy, what you *see* makes the story."

I pressed my aching forehead. Playing *imaginary* was exhausting. "Sammy, I'm losing my words—my memory, my ability to think." I thought I heard him say it. *Patience.* Or maybe I did? I suddenly felt the weight of my body, its heaviness. In my muddled mind, I didn't know which one to do, *weight* or *wait.* And then *patience* popped in again, and I thought about it—always having to be *patient.* What choice did I have? What choice *do* I have? I felt dizzy.

"Sammy, I'm sorry, I'm so tired . . . I'm running out of words. I can't *find* the words—I'm just so tired."

He cupped his hands and leaned in and whispered, "They will come back, Mommy, the words. They *will* come back. And like fireflies that create light from their bodies, your words, too, will create light."

I stared at his hands, waiting for fireflies—or another bird—to fly out of them, but none did. "Sammy, I don't know what to do."

"Mommy, each of us has a unique mission."

"Then what is mine? What is *my* mission? Sammy, what do I do now?"

He opened his hands like a book, and a luna moth's wings were the pages. All of a sudden, the moth lifted and flapped its wings and fluttered toward the door, then disappeared through the narrow opening. "Mommy. You're almost *there.*"

Another candle had gone out, and the light of his face, like the moon, was waning.

Breathe. Focus. Stay. "Sam . . . Shmu? Are you a rabbi?"

He grinned and shook his head. "No, Mommy, but perhaps a visiting rabbit, watching; or an owl calling, whispering; or the luna moths you find, the ones with feathery antennae. Or, for a day, a guide, a messenger, teaching you in the way you should go, counseling you and watching over you."

I nodded and tried to smile. "And what is yours, Sammy? *Your* unique mission?"

He swept his hands over the glowing game board. "To show you . . ."

"What, Sammy? . . . Sam? . . . Show me what?"

"Letters and magic, Mommy. You're almost there. Don't give up. But you need rest. Rest now, Mommy."

"You need rest, too, Sammy. Rest now, my sweet boy."

His lids were heavy, and he closed his eyes. I didn't know what to do. I stood and went to him and knelt and put my face to his. To check his breathing? To smell him? To kiss him? He didn't move when my cheek grazed his. He didn't open his eyes. Touching yet not touching, we were eyelash to eyelash. I wanted to stay with him. I wanted to wake him but knew I couldn't.

Time kept pulling me away, pushing us further apart. Now there was only one candle, one flame, burning. I picked up my bag and checked on him again. Still asleep. "I love you, Sammy," I whispered, then went to the door and turned back to look at him once more. "Good night, sweet prince. I'll see you in the morning."

Just before the last candle went out, he opened his eyes, kissed his hand, held it up and waved, a tiny flag sending a secret message: *I love you more than all the sidewalks in the world.*

"Sammy, I love *you* more than all the sidewalks in the world."

my beautiful boy

Walking back up the dark passageway, I passed like a spirit through my temple walls—muscle, scar tissue, and skin—out into the sunlight.

On the sidewalk, that large, bright-green luna moth lay broken, one wing fluttering against the breeze, its pale moon eyes watching me. Using a piece of paper, I lifted and carried him to the shade under an old oak tree, where I knelt and lowered him to the ground and let him slide from my page. When he was safely camouflaged among the fallen leaves, I stood, and my book bag tipped over. Its contents spilled out and scattered about the roots of the tree—pages, letters, pencils, pens; stories of survival, soldiers, and rescue dogs; drawings of hearts, stitched and patched; photos of laughing, of costumes, of brothers holding hands and running to the sea; a water bottle cap with Sam's name in permanent marker, a straw still in its wrapper. I dropped to my knees, raking up papers and pictures; I was gathering and stuffing them into my bag, before the wind took them away, when a page caught my eye, a drawing. Our *favorite piece*. The knight was standing on the right side of a bridge, facing left, toward a lemon sun on the other side, and scrawled below the bridge, was a note that I didn't recall writing:

> *Their end is imbedded in their beginning, and their beginning in their end ... like a flame in a burning coal ... let him look at the flame rising from a burning coal or from a kindled lamp. The flame cannot rise unless it is unified with something physical, The Zohar states.*
>
> *(from Sefer Yetzirah, The Book of Creation 1:7)*

I sat back on my heels, my knees wet with earth, and read the words over and over again, then closed my eyes and touched the script lightly as if I were reading braille, fumbling for dots of understanding. *Sam ... I miss you. Your eyes. Your face. Your voice. Your fingers. Your toes. Your laugh. Your curiosity. Your magic. Your endless imagination. Your stories. I miss all of you.* I opened my eyes and studied the bold soldier in my hands, ready to ride across the page, and thought of my teacher, my guide, my messenger instructing me and teaching me in the way I should go, counseling me and watching over me. *Sammy ...*

Kneeling there in the shade, holding that page, the letters that I didn't recall writing began to light up, like fireflies, and my words came back to me then. I remembered what my soul had said, *endings are always beginnings*, and for the first time in a long time, I knew what to do.

I looked around, but no one was there. Sam's penny-colored PT Cruiser was nowhere to be seen. Or it was at home on a shelf, covered with dust. How long had I been here? I stood up and looked down at the stains on my knees and didn't care. Securing my book bag, perching it on my hip, its thin arms gripping my shoulder, I returned to the sidewalk where I felt the words, like a warm breeze, kissing my ear: *Imagined or real, Mommy, what you see makes the story.*

Another day or so, after another year or so, I rewrote my story with a different ending. One in which Sam lives—if only in my imagination.

"After all, words do create worlds. And sometimes, in *this* world, words are what we *need* to believe in."

"And magic. You *do* believe in magic, don't you, Mommy?"

"Of course, my beautiful boy. Because of you, I *do* believe in magic." I closed the book and touched his warm cheek. "That's enough for tonight. Go to sleep now."

"I love you, Mommy."

"And I love you. I'll see you in the morning, brave boy."

"I'll see you in the morning, brave Mommy."

author's note

Over the years, learning how to write, practicing, reading, taking classes, writing, and rewriting this book gave me a reason to not give up but to keep going. In sharing what I've learned, I hope I've inspired you to find your reason to not give up but to keep going too. Because Sam loved writing stories, I'll keep going, and writing, for him.

To get a behind-the-scenes look at my rewriting process, see chapter photos, and listen to audio recordings of chapter excerpts, visit https://willower.org. Don't forget to subscribe. While you're there, drop me a note and say hello at https://willower.org/connect. I'd love to hear from you.

Thank you for reading. It would mean so much to me and future readers if you would leave a thoughtful and detailed review wherever you bought this book.

Sincerely,
Deanna Kassenoff

www.ingramcontent.com/pod-product-compliance
Lightning Source LLC
Chambersburg PA
CBHW030412130626
46549CB00004B/1740